Student Teaching and Field Experiences Handbook

SIXTH EDITION

W9-BSM-133

Betty D. Roe
Professor Emerita, Tennessee Technological University

Elinor P. Ross
Professor Emerita, Tennessee Technological University

Sandra H. Smith
Director of Teacher Education, Tennessee Technological University

PEARSON

Merrill
Prentice Hall

Upper Saddle River, New Jersey
Columbus, Ohio

D. Roe, Elinor P. Ross, Sandra

ces and index.

885-8

tudent teaching—Handbooks, manuals, etc. I. Ross, Elinor P. (Elinor Parry)
II. Smith, Sandy H. III. Title.
LB2157.A3R59 2006
370'.71'1—dc   222005047947

Vice President and Executive Publisher: Jeffery W. Johnston
Executive Editor: Debra A. Stollenwerk
Editorial Assistant: Mary Morrill
Production Editor: Alexandrina Benedicto Wolf
Production Coordination: Amy Gehl, Carlisle Publishers Services
Design Coordinator: Diane C. Lorenzo
Photo Coordinator: Lori Whitley
Cover Designer: Thomas Borah
Cover Image: Super Stock
Production Manager: Pamela D. Bennett
Senior Marketing Manager: Darcy Betts Prybella
Marketing Coordinator: Brian Mounts

This book was set in New Caledonia by Carlisle Communications, Ltd. It was printed and bound by Command Web.
The cover was printed by Phoenix Color Corp.

Photo Credits: Courtesy of AVerMedia Technologies, Inc., p. 142; Scott Cunningham/Merrill, pp. 72, 94, 150, 176, 206,
223; Laima E. Druskis/PH College, pp. 9, 224; Larry Hamill/Merrill, p. 168; Anthony Magnacca/ Merrill, pp. 30, 104, 111,
162, 216; Mike Peters/ Silver Burdett Ginn, p. 40; Barbara Schwartz/Merrill, p. 2; Blair Seitz/Photo Researchers, Inc.,
p. 213; Anne Vega/Merrill, pp. 64, 118, 120, 154, 195, 204.

The Interstate New Teacher Assessment and Support Consortium (INTASC) standards were developed by the Council
of Chief State School Officers and member states. Copies may be downloaded from the Council's website at
http://www.ccsso.org.

Council of Chief State School Officers. (1992). Model standards for beginning teacher licensing, assessment, and
development: A resource for state dialogue. Washington, DC: Author. **http://www.ccsso.org/content/pdfs/corestrd.pdf.**

Pearson Education Ltd.   Pearson Education Australia Pty. Limited
Pearson Education Singapore Pte. Ltd.   Pearson Education North Asia Ltd.
Pearson Education Canada, Ltd.   Pearson Educación de Mexico, S.A. de C.V.
Pearson Education—Japan   Pearson Education Malaysia Pte. Ltd.

10 9 8 7 6 5 4 3 2 1
ISBN 0-13-119885-8

Dedicated to Michael H. Roe
and
David, Dusty, Mandy, and Tyler Smith

Preface

Student Teaching and Field Experiences Handbook is designed for students who are in pre-student-teaching field experiences or actual student teaching. This practical guide offers theoretical background for particular strategies and provides examples for implementation for those who are directly involved with preschool, elementary, and secondary students.

The book provides practical suggestions needed by busy student teachers. Rather than supply all the information students require in their methods courses, this book serves as a refresher of past lessons, fills in some gaps omitted in some methods courses, offers practical teaching suggestions, and provides a framework for critical analysis of teaching activities. We hope that this will not only give prospective teachers greater confidence as they prepare for their profession, but also make the preparation more enjoyable.

TEXT FEATURES

Each chapter opens with an introductory case study, followed by questions to initiate discussion. These questions, along with the end-of-chapter discussion questions, encourage reflection about the chapter content and suggest ways to apply the information.

Throughout the text, case studies focus on situations that student teachers may encounter. Analyzing these case studies and considering the other discussion questions in the chapter are good seminar activities for student teachers and practicum students.

Activities related to topics in each chapter enable students to apply information from the text to actual teaching situations. A special listing of these application activities follows the table of contents. In addition, each chapter contains "For Your Portfolio" sections, which suggest materials students can include in their professional portfolios. Selected References guide students to additional reading.

TEXT ORGANIZATION

Chapter 1 addresses observation of teaching and other school procedures, orientation to the school's facilities and policies, extracurricular activities, self-understanding,

and practices related to good teaching—all background issues students need to know about before engaging in teaching activities.

Chapter 2 focuses on the relationships among a student teacher or practicum student and other people in the school. Student diversity also receives extensive attention because of the movement toward inclusion to create a positive learning environment for all students.

Chapter 3 provides information on several classroom administration issues: grouping, scheduling, keeping records, supervising students, and managing the classroom environment. It offers practical suggestions about discipline—the main worry of many student teachers.

Chapter 4 offers practical suggestions about planning for both instruction and evaluation.

Chapter 5 discusses language skills, literal and higher-order thinking skills, and study skills.

Chapter 6 describes supporting the curriculum through instructional resources, including audiovisual materials, human resources, and community resources. Students should know how to use these resources to enhance their teaching.

Chapter 7 addresses using computer resources to support the curriculum and contains updated information on computer applications in teaching.

Chapter 8 focuses on classroom teaching and assessment strategies and contains practical strategies for daily use in student teaching.

Chapter 9 addresses legal and ethical issues that affect teachers, which are of great concern to all educators.

Chapter 10 offers advice on finding and applying for a teaching position, as well as continuing your professional growth after obtaining a position.

Three appendixes offer helpful information: Appendix A, Assessment Instruments; Appendix B, Sample Unit and Lesson Plans; and Appendix C, Sample WebQuests.

CHANGES IN THE SIXTH EDITION

This sixth edition has been reorganized to cluster related material more closely and to elaborate more on areas that are of great concern to student teachers and practicum students. The chapters on relationships with students and diversity have been combined to eliminate some redundancy, as well as those chapters on classroom management and discipline.

Instructional resources has been divided into two chapters to focus attention to computer uses while elaborating more on other types of resources. A chapter is devoted to legal and ethical issues and another chapter to becoming a professional educator to adequately cover these important topics.

Some additions or expansions to various chapters are particularly noteworthy. Chapter 1 includes information about INTASC principles and discusses the importance of developing dispositions to teach. Chapter 2 incorporates material on diversity and on students with average abilities. Chapter 3 emphasizes the importance of flexible grouping in addition to many other suggestions for effective classroom management. Chapter 4 includes revised material on lesson planning that places more emphasis on curriculum standards. Chapter 5 features additional material on writing skills and types of writing, as well as brief coverage of literal thinking skills to go with the lengthy treatment of higher-order thinking skills. Chapter 6 provides updated material on audiovisual media. Chapter 7 features a new list of criteria for evaluating websites, new material on computer simulations and other software, information about MOOs, and discussion of WebQuests. The chapter also addresses the hazards of instruction with computers, including e-cheating. Chapter 8 combines ideas for teaching and assessment strategies as various techniques are discussed with an emphasis on helping all students learn. Chapter 9 provides an anticipation guide on legal issues that readers are encouraged to complete before reading the chapter. After reading the chapter, students can check their answers, using the answer key. Chapter 10 emphasizes the importance of professional growth, with new information on National Board Certification, as well as other opportunities.

Appendix C addresses a more current instructional strategy—WebQuests.

THEORETICAL AND CONCEPTUAL FRAMEWORK

This text follows a widely accepted research-based framework. Because theory is of little use unless accompanied by practical applications, this text provides both theory and practice activities to involve prospective teachers in implementing theory.

Students should be at the center of learning. Therefore, this book focuses attention on student diversity, learning styles, and motivation to help all students become lifelong learners. The text also highlights relationships and interactions among personnel at all levels, and stresses awareness of the role everyone plays in the education of all students. This text emphasizes learning through technology as computers are and will continue to be an essential element of society. Believing that students learn best through an integrated curriculum, we stress connections among the language arts and all subjects across the curriculum. We also believe that a prospective teacher's education should not end at the conclusion of student teaching, so we support the idea of future professional development throughout an educator's career.

ACKNOWLEDGMENTS

We thank Douglas M. Brooks, Miami University, Oxford, OH; Harriet Morrison, Mary Baldwin College; Barbara Sandall, Western Illinois University; and Sara M. Sage, Indiana University–South Bend, for their helpful reviews of this manuscript. Their insightful comments were greatly appreciated.

We appreciate the assistance of Ben Stephen and Mary Morrill with our publication questions.

A special word of appreciation goes to Mike Roe, who helped with proofreading, computer problems, and permissions.

We are grateful to Alice Pleming and Kathy Dooley for permission to use excerpts from their student teaching journals; and to Laura Beaty, Janet Wheeler, Catherine Massengill, Emily Habegger Partin, Cindy McCloud, Kimberly Williams, and Tezra Volkmar, who allowed us to use their lesson plans and unit plans. Dr. Pam Petty, who allowed us to use her WebQuests as examples, has our gratitude.

Brief Contents

Contents

CHAPTER 4

Planning for Instruction   94

CHAPTER 5

Integrating Language, Thinking, and Study Skills   118

CHAPTER 6

Supporting the Curriculum Through Instructional Resources   142

CHAPTER 7

Supporting the Curriculum Through Computer Resources   162

Note: Every effort has been made to provide accurate and current Internet information in this book. However, the Internet and information posted on it are constantly changing, so it is inevitable that some of the Internet addresses listed in the textbook will change.

Application Activities

About the Authors

Betty D. Roe is Professor Emerita at Tennessee Technological University in Cookeville and was Director of Doctoral Studies for the College of Education. She has taught courses in reading and language arts methods, library science, and computers, and has supervised reading practicum students and student teachers across all grade levels and all subject areas. She received her Ed.D. in Curriculum and Instruction from the University of Tennessee, Knoxville. She is a former classroom teacher and has worked with diagnosis and remediation of reading difficulties for students in all grade levels in clinical situations. Betty has authored or co-authored 45 books, most of which are college methods textbooks, and numerous professional journal articles. She gives professional presentations on reading and language arts instruction, as well as storytelling presentations for all age groups. She is active in several professional organizations at local, state, national, and international levels.

Elinor P. Ross, Professor Emerita from Tennessee Technological University, taught reading methods and children's literature courses for 31 years. She has authored or co-authored 21 books and has presented papers regionally, nationally, and internationally. She coordinates the Reading Is Fundamental program, edits two newsletters, and tutors at a local elementary school.

Sandra Hope Smith, Assistant Professor in the Department of Curriculum and Instruction at Tennessee Technological University, received her MA in Special Education in 1981 and Specialist in Education Degree in Curriculum/Reading in 1989. She is currently completing her doctoral studies at Tennessee State University. Sandra currently serves as the Director of Teacher Education and coordinates all of the field and clinical experiences for preservice candidates in licensure programs. She also teaches courses in literacy and assessment, and facilitates the introduction to teaching course in the Department of Curriculum and Instruction. She presents regularly at numerous state and national conferences and has co-authored books in the fields of storytelling, literacy development, and the teaching of reading in elementary and middle school grades.

Student Teaching and Field Experiences Handbook

Chapter 1 Getting Ready

Case Study 1.1: What Am I Supposed to Be Doing?

Mr. Wiley is the mentoring teacher; Mr. Allen is his student teacher; Mrs. Paris is the principal.

Mrs. Paris: Mr. Allen, I just received a call from Mr. Wiley. He's having car trouble and won't be able to get here on time. I realize you didn't expect to be in charge of the class this morning, but, since you have been observing for a week, you should be able to take care of the attendance and lunch records with no problem. He said the first two classes will be easy to handle, too. In one, you just have to give the test he left in his file cabinet, which is already duplicated. He should be here before the students finish the test. Good luck! Call on me if you have any problems.

Mr. Allen: Thank you, Mrs. Paris. I'll do my best. (Mrs. Paris exits. Mr. Allen goes to Mr. Wiley's desk and begins searching for the register. He finds it and looks at it in dismay. He can't remember how to fill it out. Although he had watched Mr. Allen do it before, he hadn't observed carefully enough. Embarrassed, he goes next door to ask another teacher, rather than sending a student to get the principal. In the meantime, the students, left alone in the classroom, go wild. They run around the room, throw things, and yell. When Mr. Allen returns to the room with information about how to fill out his records, chaos reigns. "How does Mr. Wiley quiet them down?" he thinks in panic. "I have to do something fast.")

Mr. Allen (in a loud voice): Class! Be quiet! Return to your seats! (Mr. Allen's voice is hardly heard above the noise and has little effect. He suddenly remembers what he has seen Mr. Wiley do before, in a less chaotic situation. Mr. Allen walks to the front of the room, extends his right arm with his palm facing forward, and looks directly at the class without speaking. The noise and movement slowly begin to abate. Now his voice can be heard.)

Mr. Allen: Go to your seats, and listen for your name as I call the roll. (To his surprise and relief, the students comply. The record keeping proceeds smoothly, and Mr. Allen feels more confident. Then he realizes that he doesn't remember which lesson is first on Thursday mornings, since every day is not the same. Once again embarrassed, he turns to the students.)

Mr. Allen: What do we do first on Thursdays?

Chorus of answers: Spelling! Recess! (Mr. Allen knows recess isn't first, so he looks for the spelling book, wondering what activity to do on Thursday. Then he remembers the lesson planner Mr. Wiley keeps in his desk drawer. He finds the planner and verifies that the spelling lesson comes first. He also discovers that Mr. Wiley has planned a trial test for today. He saw Mr. Wiley give a trial test last week, but he doesn't remember the exact procedure. He leaps into the activity anyway, giving each word and a sentence with it, as he vaguely remembers Mr. Wiley doing.)

Randy: You're supposed to say the word again after you give the sentence. That's the way Mr. Wiley does it.

Mr. Allen (frustrated and upset): Well, I'm doing it today, and I'll do it my way.

Rachel: What was the word again?

Mr. Allen: Clothes.

Randy: Mr. Wiley never repeats a word after we've passed it.

Rachel: Like you close a door?

Mr. Allen: Didn't you listen to my sentence, Rachel? Just do your best. (The test proceeds along these lines until it is finished.)

Mr. Allen: Pass your papers to the front.

Joe: But we grade our own trial tests so we'll learn the words better. (Suddenly remembering that this is so, Mr. Allen decides to do it the way Mr. Wiley would. Half the papers have already been passed to the front.)

Mr. Allen: Okay. I'll let you check your own papers. Pass them back to their owners. (Papers are passed back, amid much murmuring. While this is happening, Mr. Wiley walks in.)

Mr. Wiley: I'm sorry I'm late. I had car trouble. How did things go?

Mr. Allen: OK.

Mr. Wiley: If you've finished that English test, that's perfect. We can go right on to math.

Mr. Allen: We didn't get to the English test yet. These are the spelling papers.

Mr. Wiley: That's a great deal of time to spend on spelling. We'll discuss your lesson, and I'll offer some suggestions to help you budget your time better.

Mr. Allen: Yes, sir.

1. What is the difference between just watching and truly observing?
2. Was Mr. Allen an effective observer? Why do you say so?
3. Do you observe classroom routines and procedures carefully enough to be able to perform them alone, if necessary?

THE CHALLENGE OF TEACHING

You are at a transition point in your teacher education program. Your student teaching or clinical experience will bridge the gap between what you have learned as theory as a preservice candidate and what you need to know for effective professional practice. Often teacher education candidates rank student teaching or their clinical experiences among the most meaningful events in their teacher preparation programs.

The National Council for Accreditation of Teacher Education (NCATE), a national accrediting agency for teacher education programs, identifies field and clinical experiences as one of its six standards. NCATE also describes quality experiences as systematic processes that place teacher education candidates in a variety of settings with diverse populations.

During student teaching you will work with diverse student populations who have a variety of learning strengths and needs. With the guidance of a mentoring teacher and support from your teacher education program, you will apply the knowledge and skills you have gained and add to your expertise through collaboration and cooperation with colleagues. You will also explore your teaching style and develop your competence as a professional educator through self-assessment and reflection. Your gradual introduction to teaching will prepare you to assume the additional responsibilities you will encounter.

Teaching is both a wonderful opportunity and a serious responsibility. The countless minute-by-minute decisions that teachers make, along with the kind of support and instruction they provide, can make the difference between students' success and failure. Teachers never really know the extent of their influence. What you teach may affect students in such a way that they will, in turn, influence others. Be sensitive to the needs and feelings of your students, and let them know that you believe in their ability to succeed.

SOME PRACTICAL MATTERS

Undoubtedly, you will have a lot of questions as you begin student teaching or a practicum in teaching. Once you are aware of your assignment, visit the school's website and secure a school policy handbook. Familiarize yourself with the school's policies and procedures. If there is no planned orientation, try to find answers to these questions:

- Where should I park?
- What time should I arrive, and when should I leave?

- Do I need to sign in at the office when I arrive?
- Do I need a visible form of identification? Should it be a photo ID?
- What responsibilities do I have for lunch and bus duty?
- When and where may I make personal phone calls?
- What should I do in case I must be absent because of illness or an emergency?
- Is there a professional dress code for teachers that I must follow?

You may also need to resolve some personal circumstances that might interfere with your effectiveness as a teacher. The following case studies present some potential conflicts to consider; you are likely to know of others.

CASE STUDY 1.2

Job Conflict

Nathan works after school at a child-care center to pay for tuition and living expenses. School ends at 3:00 and his job begins at 3:00, so there is no time for after-school activities or planning sessions. What are his options?

CASE STUDY 1.3

Sick Child

Ashley, a single parent, has a 6-year-old daughter who has chronic ear infections with high fevers. Ashley has no family nearby and feels that she must stay home when her daughter is ill. What are some other options for Ashley?

CASE STUDY 1.4

Missed Connections

Nicole's husband works the night shift and gets home around 7:00 in the morning, unless he misses the bus. When he is late, Nicole is late to school because she cannot leave their baby alone. What can Nicole do if her husband is late?

CASE STUDY 1.5

Car Pool

Sally, Joe, and Curt ride to school together. Sally and Joe are nearly always on time, but Curt keeps them waiting. Then all three are late for school. What should they do?

CASE STUDY 1.6

Personality Conflict

No matter how hard he tries, Cody cannot seem to please Miss Logan, his mentoring teacher. Cody realizes that they are quite different; she is structured and formal and he is holistic and less formal. He tries to be pleasant, prepared, and conforming, but she always finds fault. What should Cody do?

CASE STUDY 1.7

No Clothes to Wear

Tyler has had to work hard to pay for school expenses. His wardrobe consists of jeans, T-shirts, and not much else. He realizes he needs better clothes but cannot afford them. What choices does he have?

OBSERVING THE CLASSROOM TEACHER

When you begin a practicum or student teaching, you will probably spend most of your time observing. It is important to learn as much as you can during this time. You may want to keep a journal of your thoughts during observations and continue it as you move into teaching. As a student teacher, recording your reactions, exploring your beliefs, and reflecting on your development as a teacher in your journal can be one of your most valuable activities.

What Is Observation?

To benefit fully from your observation period, you need to have clear expectations that define what you are looking for during your student teaching. Observation is an effective tool for gathering information and reflecting on your professional growth. Observation involves

paying close attention to detail, analyzing and evaluating what is happening, and assimilating new ideas.

In this chapter's opening vignette, although Mr. Allen had spent a week looking at what was going on in the classroom, he was not carefully observing it. Therefore, he did not gain the maximum benefit from his observation time. If you are to use your observation time to best advantage, you need to know what to look for and how to look at what you are observing.

On your first day of student teaching, your mentoring teacher will probably introduce you to the class and suggest that you spend the next few days observing to get the "feel" of the classroom and learn the routines and procedures of a typical day. The mentoring teacher may mention that you should become aware of the teaching and classroom management techniques in use, with a view toward developing your own approach to teaching. Whether or not this is mentioned, you should be alert for these techniques, examining them analytically and critically as you consider them for possible use.

On your first day, ask your mentoring teacher for a seating chart that you can use as you observe. If a chart exists, make a copy, take it home, and study it at night. If a chart is not available, construct one with your teacher's help, before the next observation. Learn the students' names so you can develop rapport with them and create a positive learning environment. At the middle and secondary level, with several different sets of students' names to learn, you should apply yourself immediately to the task. Learning names, usually easier in a self-contained setting because you see fewer students each day, is important to your success.

There will be many routines and procedures that you want to observe during your first week. Get a daily schedule from the mentoring teacher so you will be aware of the order of classes, times for breaks and special activities, and beginning and dismissal times. Various organizational structures exist in school settings and each presents different challenges. Middle schools are often arranged with teams, and each day of the week may offer a different schedule. Secondary student teachers may find that each day's schedule is essentially the same except for variations for assembly schedules, test schedules, and other special events, or they may find that block scheduling results in days that look very different. Elementary student teachers in self-contained classrooms often have a different schedule for each day of the week. Familiarize yourself with the schedule as quickly as possible. Don't be left, as Mr. Allen was, wondering what comes next.

Areas of Observation

As your mentoring teacher begins to teach, observe carefully how specific teaching methods are utilized. Notice how your mentoring teacher organizes the students and plans for transitions. Pay close attention to how the students respond to the teacher and what routines and procedures are incorporated throughout the day.

Activity 1.1 can help you focus on important aspects of your observations. It covers 11 observation areas. Complete it for one of the observations that you do as your mentoring teacher presents a lesson.

You can facilitate note-taking as you observe by making a separate page for each of these 11 observation areas. Carefully recording the details of the lessons you observe will be beneficial, but it is not enough. At this point, you must analyze what you have seen and evaluate it critically. Below the notes you make on each observation area, write a brief analysis and evaluation (or do this mentally). Once again, some structure may help. Here are some questions you can ask yourself about each of the 11 observation areas.

Area 1. Did the students seem to grasp how the lesson was tied to previous learning? Did the motivational activities seem to engage students' interest? Why do you think they did or did not accomplish their goal?

Area 2. Were the purpose and relevance of the lesson made clear to the students? Why or why not? How might they have been better clarified?

Area 3. Were the teacher's procedures for presenting the content effective? Might some other procedures have been more effective? Why do you think so?

Area 4. Were the lesson materials appropriate and effective? Would other materials have been more effective? Why do you think so?

Area 5. Was the teaching style effective with this particular group and for this particular lesson? Why do you think so? If the style was ineffective, what might have worked better?

Area 6. Did the teacher seem to have adequate knowledge of the subject matter or content? Was enough outside knowledge brought into the lesson? If not, what else should have been included? Was content effectively related to the students' lives? If not, how might this aspect of the lesson have been improved?

Area 7. Were adequate provisions made for individual differences? If not, what steps might have been taken to improve the situation?

Area 8. Were classroom management techniques appropriate and effective? Why do you think so? If they were inappropriate or ineffective, what techniques might have been better?

Area 9. Did the teacher's personal qualities effectively advance the lesson? Why do you think so? Might changes in this area be helpful to future lessons?

Area 10. Was the conclusion of the lesson effective? Why? If not, what might have been done to improve it?

Area 11. Were the teacher's evaluation techniques appropriate and effective? Why do you think so? If not, what techniques might have worked better?

Following this analysis and evaluation, examine each observation area again and reflectively ask yourself these questions: "How can I incorporate this into my teaching? Will I want to use this technique, or an alternative I think would be better? How does what I have seen fit into what I have learned in methods courses during my teacher preparation program? Are there areas in which I need clarification? If clarification is needed, what resources might I investigate for further information?"

Policies, Routines, and Procedures

During student teaching, you should be observing more than lesson presentations. Upon arrival at your assigned location, you should inquire about school-wide policies if you have not been supplied with a handbook outlining them. Take notes on what you see and hear so that you can adhere strictly to school policy in the future.

Teachers are expected to attend faculty meetings, parent-teacher meetings, and professional development meetings. You may be expected to attend these with your mentoring teacher to observe them. Your mentoring teacher may be asked to chaperone a school dance or assist in the organization of an extracurricular activity, such as a play, concert, dance, or athletic event. Observing these activities will help you understand what working as a teacher entails. It also provides an opportunity to interact with your students outside the classroom and to meet their families.

Throughout the day, many routines and procedures will be implemented. Your mentoring teacher will have already introduced many of these, and you will be expected to continue with their implementation. Make a list of the small details such as how students enter and

ACTIVITY 1.1 | *Observation Form*

Answer the questions or place a check beside the appropriate responses.

Date: _____   Class observed: _____

Area   1   How did the teacher:

   1.   Start the lesson?   _____

      _____

   2.   Tie it to previous learning?   _____

      _____

   3.   Arouse students' interest?   _____

      _____

Area   2   How did the teacher make the purpose and relevance of the lesson apparent?

   1.   By making direct statements _____

   2.   By eliciting reactions from students _____

   3.   Other (Specify) _____

Area   3   What procedures were incorporated into the body of the lesson?

   1.   Lecture _____

   2.   Discussion _____

   3.   Audiovisual presentation _____

   4.   Demonstration _____

   5.   Student activities _____

Area   4   What materials were used in the course of the lesson?

   1.   Textbooks _____

   2.   Supplementary books _____

   3.   Films _____

   4.   Computers _____

   5.   Audiotapes _____

   6.   Videotapes _____

   7.   Television _____

   8.   Concrete objects _____

   9.   Transparencies _____

  10.   Illustrations _____

  11.   Models _____

  12.   Videodiscs _____

  13.   Other (Specify) _____

Area   5   What was the teacher's style of teaching?

    1.   Direct _____

    2.   Indirect _____

Area   6   Did the teacher show a broad knowledge of the subject area? _____ Did she or he stick to the textbook or bring in information from other sources as well? _____ Did she or he relate the subject matter to other content the students had studied, to current events, or to students' personal interests? _____ If so, how was this accomplished? _____

    _____

    _____

Area   7   What provisions were made for individual differences?

    1.   Small-group work _____

    2.   Individualized assignments _____

    3.   Differentiated reading materials _____

    4.   Other (Specify) _____

Area   8   What disciplinary techniques did the teacher use?

    1.   Flipping the light switch _____

    2.   Penalty points _____

    3.   Deprivation of privileges _____

    4.   Reward system _____

    5.   Time-out _____

    6.   Other (Specify) _____

Area   9   How did the teacher's personal qualities help advance the lesson?

    1.   Dressed appropriately, so that apparel did not distract from subject matter _____

    2.   Displayed no distracting mannerisms _____

    3.   Used correct grammar _____

    4.   Used appropriate voice volume and pitch _____

Area   10   How did the teacher end the lesson?

    1.   Summarized the day's learning _____

    2.   Assigned homework _____ If so, specify the kind of assignment. _____

    3.   Other (Specify) _____

Area   11   What evaluation techniques did the teacher use in the course of the lesson?

    1.   Oral questions _____

    2.   Written questions _____

    3.   Observation of students' verbal responses _____

    4.   Observation of students' application skills _____

    5.   Other (Specify) _____

leave the classroom, how completed work is turned in, and how attendance is collected, to name only a few. The successful implementation of routines and procedures assists in the creation of an effective learning environment and a successful classroom management plan. If you observe carefully, you won't end up like Mr. Allen, and you'll be more ready for teaching when your opportunity comes.

EXTRACURRICULAR ACTIVITIES

Typically, students participate voluntarily in a number of school-sponsored activities. School sponsorship makes faculty involvement in these activities important. As a student teacher, you will probably be involved in the extracurricular activities in which your mentoring teacher is involved. You may, however, be asked to help with other extracurricular activities in which you have special interest or expertise. You may be asked to do something as simple as taking tickets or chaperoning a dance or something as difficult as directing a dramatization or coaching defensive ends.

Some extracurricular activities center around clubs (science, photography, mathematics, computer, drama, foreign language, community action, future teachers, etc.); school publications (magazines, yearbooks, newspapers); athletic teams (football, basketball, soccer, baseball, track, golf, volleyball, wrestling); musical groups (marching band, jazz band, orchestra, chorus); and scholastic honor societies (Beta Club, Quill and Scroll, National Honor Society). School-sponsored dances, carnivals, and festivals also qualify as extracurricular activities. This variety provides a wide range from which to choose if you are asked to participate. The list of possibilities for after-hours involvement seems endless. You may help with science fair projects or work at a book fair; you may judge a storytelling contest or a debate; you may coach intramural sports, accompany students on special trips, mend costumes for a play, paint sets, move band equipment, organize the safety patrol—the list goes on and on.

You may think of extracurricular activities as just another intrusion on your already vanishing free time, or you may remember that extracurricular activities were really important to you when you were your students' age. Contribute some time and effort to give your students valuable experiences.

If your school has a handbook, read the section on extracurricular activities. Find out what roles faculty members play and each activity's rules and restrictions to help you choose activities or assist with assigned activities.

When you apply for a job, be sure to mention any extracurricular activities you supported during student teaching. Direct experience with editing the

Student teachers may be asked to help with extracurricular activities.

school paper, constructing sets for a play, or sponsoring the computer club may make you a more valuable candidate.

SELF-ANALYSIS

As you move through your practicum or your student-teaching experience, constantly reflect upon and evaluate your own progress. Although your mentoring teacher and the supervisory personnel with whom you work are providing feedback on your performance, your self-analysis is invaluable in fully assessing your progress. You can analyze the effectiveness of your lessons in a variety of ways.

Videotaping and Audiotaping

If videotaping equipment is not available, record your lesson on an audiotape and listen to it later at home. By going over tapes of your lessons, you can become aware of your voice control (audibility, pitch, expression), speech patterns (overuse of certain terms, such as "OK?"), use of praise and positive reinforcement, and clarity of directions. You can determine the kinds of questions you ask and the proportion of "student talk" to "teacher talk" during your lessons. You can also use a videotape to become aware of your nonverbal communication, such as encouraging nods, nervous gestures, or facial expressions.

Peer Coaching

Instead of having only one person critique the lesson, you may cooperate with other teacher education candidates in critiquing each others' lessons, or you may want to critique your own lesson.

Critical Analysis of Lesson Success

You and your mentoring teacher may collaborate on evaluating certain lessons by using a form such as that in Activity 1.2. You should agree on the components to be evaluated and then separately rate a lesson or series of lessons. Then you should get together to compare notes and reconcile any differences. Over a period of time, you should work on those components that are needing improvement.

Other components to include for certain lessons are giving clear directions; considering individual differences; implementing an effective classroom management plan; organizing activities well; modeling or demonstrating desired learning; using technology, audiovisual aids, and resources appropriately; maintaining a positive classroom environment; asking higher-order questions; promoting positive self-concept in all students; encouraging wide student participation; using differentiated teaching strategies; communicating effectively with students; and showing evidence of preparation.

Student Analysis

Your students' daily observations of your teaching may provide a great deal of information about your effectiveness. They may volunteer remarks such as "Can we do that again?" or "Tell us more about whales," that can guide you in planning subsequent lessons. The students may also give you insights into your effectiveness by answering questions such as "What did you learn today?" and "Did you do better when you worked with a partner?"

A checklist can provide a more formal type of evaluation from your students. For younger children, you may use a format similar to that in Figure 1–1. For older students, the format in Figure 1–2 is appropriate.

CASE STUDY 1.8

A Challenge to a Student Teacher's Evaluation

A student teacher, Ms. Downey, was teaching a chemistry class and trying to keep a close record of students' performance in her class. Through observing and analyzing students' responses, she quickly noted that three students seemed uninterested in the subject. Also, their early work was of rather poor quality. After she checked the results of a couple of tests (each covering 2 weeks of instruction), it seemed clear that the students did not grasp the content presented during that period of time. Ms. Downey thought student-teacher conferences might be helpful, and brought her concerns to the conferences. During the three conferences, the students responded with comments such as these:

1. The tests were too hard, so I just guessed.
2. Most of the students missed the same questions I missed.
3. Chemistry is mostly for brainy students.
4. You don't make it clear what I'm supposed to learn.
5. You talk all the time.
6. You don't show much interest in us.

What objective data could Ms. Downey present to respond to each of these comments? What could she learn from these responses?

ACTIVITY 1.2 | **Rating Key Aspects of Instruction**

Using the form below, rate yourself for each component of instruction according to the following symbols: plus (+) for *good,* zero (0) for *no evidence,* or minus (−) for *needs improvement.* You may want to make a copy for your mentoring teacher to complete so that you can compare ratings. You may also want to make extra copies so that you can rate yourself periodically as you grow in your ability to teach.

COMPONENT	RATING	COMMENTS
1. Gaining and holding student attention		
2. Telling students what they are expected to learn		
3. Reminding students of related knowledge or skills		
4. Presenting new stimuli for learning		
5. Guiding students' thinking and learning		
6. Providing feedback about correctness		
7. Judging or appraising the performance		
8. Helping to generalize what is learned		
9. Providing practice for retention		
10. Other:		

FIGURE 1–1

Rating Instruction by Younger
Students

A.   Marking Responses:

1.   My teacher usually looks like this:

2.   When I ask the teacher for help, he or she looks like this:

3.   After I finish the lesson, I feel like this:

B.   Oral Interview:

1.   If I were the teacher, I would:

2.   When I go to the teacher for help, he or she:

3.   I would understand my lessons better if:

Reflective Teaching

Although reflective teaching, a thoughtful analysis of your actions, decisions, and results in the classroom, requires time and effort, it can provide insights about your effectiveness as a teacher. It can also cause you to question your procedures and consider alternatives, change any nonproductive routines, and try new ideas. Activity 1.3 gives some reflective questions to ask yourself about one of your lessons.

Reflection can occur through many types of educational experiences—viewing a videotape of yourself, discussing your performance during a conference with your mentoring teacher, reviewing feedback from students, conducting observations of other teachers in which you compare their strategies with your own, discussing your performance with a peer coach, and journal writing. Journal writing may be an extremely helpful way to reflect on your teaching performance. When you first begin your journal, you may feel that you

are rambling and just putting down random thoughts. As you continue writing, however, you may find that you begin to question, explore, and, finally, focus.

To get the most from your journal writing, write about incidents, problems, or issues that truly concern you—not your lesson plan or a list of the day's events. Express your feelings about your frustrations and triumphs. Think deeply about their causes and consider what you need to do now. Writing can help clarify your thinking and enable you to reach conclusions about your teaching. (See Figure 1–3 for a sample journal entry completed by a teacher education candidate during a reading methods field experience.)

Your mentoring teacher or supervisory staff may assign journal writing, not only for your personal benefit, but also to help someone with more experience understand your needs and concerns. Similarly, you may want to do journal writing with your students in order to get to know them better. To ensure that they won't

FIGURE 1–2
Rating Instruction by Older
Students

Student Opinion Questionnaire

A. Circle the best answer.

   1. Are assignments and explanations clear? Are assignments reasonable?

        Rarely   Sometimes   Usually   Almost Always

   2. Is treatment of all students fair? Are students' ideas treated with respect?

        Rarely   Sometimes   Usually   Almost Always

   3. Do students behave well for the teacher?

        Rarely   Sometimes   Usually   Almost Always

   4. Is the teaching interesting and challenging?

        Rarely   Sometimes   Usually   Almost Always

   5. Do you feel free to raise questions?

        Rarely   Sometimes   Usually   Almost Always

B. Write a short answer.

   1. Mention one or two things you like about this teacher.

   2. Mention one or two things this teacher might do to help you be a better
        student.

FIGURE 1–2
Rating Instruction by Older Students

simply recall the day's events, you may need to model a sample journal entry based on your own reflections about the lesson. You may do this on the board, a chart tablet, or a transparency, or project it from the computer. Then discuss what you wrote and why. A practical procedure is to provide time each day for students to write in their journals and for you to respond to them about once a week. These guiding questions can help your students determine what to write in their journals:

1. What did I learn?
2. What do I want to know more about?
3. What don't I understand very well?

PORTFOLIO DEVELOPMENT

Portfolios—paper, electronic, and web-based versions— are used as professional growth and employment tools. In recent years there has been an increased emphasis on performance-based assessments in teacher education programs. Candidates complete authentic tasks and provide evidence of performance mastery. A portfolio, an organized collection of artifacts, provides evidence of a teacher education candidate's knowledge, skills, and dispositions. As a performance assessment tool, it can provide evidence of a candidate's competency from multiple sources and field experiences. As an employment tool, a portfolio can be shared during a job interview to reflect the work you have done in your teacher preparation program. Development of a professional portfolio is discussed in Chapter 10. As you move through teaching and other educational activities in the schools, you should be collecting your best unit and lesson plans; examples of your involvement with extracurricular and professional development activities; examples of your evaluations from supervisors and students; and your personal reflections on your experiences. Don't forget to save artifacts, such as audiotapes, videotapes, disk copies of websites you have developed or helped develop, and sample work from your students. At the end of your student teaching experience, you should have abundant evidence that you can perform the jobs for which you apply.

ACTIVITY 1.3 | **Questions That Reflective Teachers Ask Themselves**

Date: _____

Lesson: _____

Read and seriously consider the following questions. Choose several that pertain to your lesson and write answers for them.

1. Did the students learn anything? If so, why? If not, why not?

2. Did anything significant occur? If so, what and why?

3. Was the strategy I used the most effective one? What other strategies might have been effective?

4. How well did I relate the lesson to the students' knowledge, experiences, and interests? How might I have done this better?

5. How flexible was I in modifying the lesson according to the students' responses?

6. How well did I manage classroom behavior? What other behavioral techniques could I have used? What technique worked best and what didn't work? Why?

7. What connections were there between teaching strategies and students' learning? What does this tell me about what I need to do in the future?

8. What are some alternatives for conducting today's lesson?

9. How did I motivate the students? What are some other ways I might have motivated them?

10. Did I consider learning theory in preparing and implementing the lesson? If so, what theories worked? If not, what theories should I have considered?

11. Did I give students opportunities to direct their own learning? If so, how? If not, how could I have done this?

12. As a result of this lesson, what have I learned about teaching? How might I change to become a better teacher?

Teacher's signature _____

FIGURE 1–3
Excerpts from a Reading
Practicum Student's Journal

Oct. 19
I had to *reteach* what I taught yesterday. I really had to discipline a lot too. I feel that they understood the content of what we were doing better after we went over it again. We went over question by question to ensure that everyone was listening—learning? I really want to establish myself before I get off the strict basal lesson. When they deserve to do something fun, we will. I'm enjoying this. This is a real-life classroom. I am learning so much!

Oct. 20
They were so "bad" today, or was it me? It seemed those same three boys always cause so much trouble. I gave them something that really challenged them—it was obvious that they are not often challenged. They acted so completely confused. I took it up and they were doing, mostly, okay on it. The ones with the lower grades were obviously intentionally not trying. I will go over it tomorrow.

Nov. 4
I have to constantly tell them to be quiet!! Why won't they learn—they are going to get into trouble when they're loud. I gave them a skills test—they did great! No one has to retake it!! I felt so proud of my teaching!

Nov. 13
I almost lost it today. I had assigned them homework. Five of them had it and even remembered it. They never stopped talking! I didn't know what to do. It is so discouraging. Forget all the good stuff I've learned and heard to say and do. It makes me feel so bad.

Nov. 14
We started back on basal. Boy, did they hate it. This class is definitely "dynamic" and likes something besides plain old reading class. This will challenge me to add more creativity to these lessons.

Nov. 19
We had an interesting class today. First, Tommy was sent to alternative school . . . today. The teacher was out of the class at a meeting because of that. Another lady sat in while she was gone. Two girls from my class observed me. I got evaluated. The principal came in and out about Tommy. That makes five extra people in the classroom besides myself and the students. They managed to stay tuned in fairly well. And I think I had them challenged with interesting issues about the story.

FOR YOUR PORTFOLIO

INTASC Standards: 1, 2, and 9
(see p. 20)
To start your portfolio, choose one or more of the following items:

1. An artifact from an extracurricular activity with which you are working—a program from a play you directed, a diagram from a marching band show you helped develop or field, a copy of a school publication for which you were an advisor, or something similar.
2. A videotape of a lesson you have taught.
3. The results of an evaluation by your students, your mentoring teacher, or your college supervisor.
4. A self-reflection about your teaching, similar to Activity 1.3.

MANAGING STRESS

As a student teacher, you feel a high degree of anxiety when coping with the demands of stressful situations. Although too much stress can cause physical and emotional problems, a certain amount of stress is desirable and necessary to give you the impetus for involvement in a task. With the right amount of stress, you will put forth the extra energy to accomplish the challenging tasks that teaching presents.

Teachers undoubtedly encounter stressful situations in their profession. The difference between job satisfaction and burnout is the way teachers cope with these situations. Stress for student teachers often results from situations like those encountered by substitute teachers, as reflected in the ZITS comic on page 19. Figure 1–4 describes several stressful

FIGURE 1–4
A Day of Student Teaching

Time	Stressful Situation	Reactions	Rating	Avoidance/ Management Strategies
6:30 A.M.	Can't decide what to wear. Out of cereal for breakfast. Can't find car keys.	Felt rushed, tense, annoyed at self, hungry.	4	Decide what to wear the night before; check food supplies and keep adequate stock; always put car keys in same place. Set alarm clock 15 minutes earlier to allow for unexpected problems.
7:20 A.M.	Have to wait 10 minutes for car pool passenger.	Hated to waste time, especially after rushing around to get ready.	5	Use waiting time productively. Check over lesson plans; think about what to do about the problems Marty is having.
9:15 A.M.	Fire drill while introducing lesson. Students are excited and won't settle down again.	Felt angry with school for ruining my lesson. Why can't they have fire drills when nothing is going on?	8	Can't avoid fire drills. Need to stay more relaxed, give students more time to get back to the lesson. Don't push them—or myself—so much.
11:30 A.M.	Jack pulled a knife on Eddie. Kids gathered around. Looked as though a mean fight was coming.	Panic! Didn't know how to handle this one. Stood there like an idiot. Principal stopped it.	8	Must check with teacher about what to do. Need to be prepared to deal with such situations.
1:45 P.M.	Spied the university supervisor out of the corner of my eye as he entered to observe my lesson.	Couldn't remember what I was supposed to say next. Worried about the students' restlessness.	9	Be well prepared and know exactly what to do. Don't let the students get out of control. Do the best job I can and forget about Mr. Henry's being there.
3:00 P.M.	Cliff's mother accused me of being unfair to him. She claimed Cliff says I am "picking on him."	Felt unjustly accused, completely bewildered by her unfair statement. Wanted to shout, "It's not true!"	9	There has been a misunderstanding. Discuss the matter calmly. Find out why Cliff feels this way. Possibly include him in our conversation. Don't get angry!
7:30 P.M.	Left my teacher's manual at school. Will have to wait until morning to plan my lessons. Probably won't do well.	Felt disgusted with myself for forgetting it, worried about not being prepared for tomorrow's lesson.	5	Can I find an extra copy of the manual in the storeroom to keep at home? Need to put everything to take home in a special place so I won't forget. Get some any-occasion ideas to fill in.
10:00 P.M.	Just realized I have to put up a bulletin board tomorrow! I'll have to make it tonight.	Felt overwhelmed with so much to do and not enough time, angry at cooperating teacher for making so many assignments.	8	Keep a calendar of due dates. Try to keep ahead on assignments. Must get my sleep or I'll be a nervous wreck the next day.

Zits Partnership © Reprinted with permission of King Features Syndicate.

situations, reactions to them, stress ratings, and strategies for their avoidance and management. The ratings rank from 1 (lowest stress) to 10 (highest stress). Make a similar chart for one day of your student teaching, including your own avoidance and management strategies (see Activity 1.4). If four or more stressful situations are rated 8 or above, you will need to give serious attention to reducing your stress.

Some tips for dealing with stress include:

- Keep a positive attitude about yourself.
- Recognize and accept your strengths and areas to strengthen.
- Be prepared for each lesson.
- Try not to worry about things you cannot change; do something about the things you can change.
- Schedule time to be with friends outside of the school setting.
- Maintain open communication with your mentoring teacher and supervisory personnel.
- Take time to make a list of things to do, in order of their importance.
- Set deadlines for getting things done. Check off each task as you complete it.
- Break large tasks into smaller, more manageable chunks. Work on them one piece at a time. Do the hardest part first, and save the most interesting tasks until the end.
- Feel free to say "no" to others when you feel you can't handle another responsibility.
- Stay physically active by exercising, walking, or playing a sport.
- Get plenty of rest and sleep.
- Maintain your involvement in a hobby or relaxing mental activity.
- Keep your sense of humor.

The questionnaire in Activity 1.5 may help you analyze how you manage stress. Most reactions to stress fall into one of four categories: freeze, flee,

fight, or compromise. Learn your most effective ways of dealing with stress, and use these techniques to relieve future stressful situations.

DISPOSITIONS TO TEACH

NCATE, in one of its six standards for accreditation, describes dispositions as "values, commitments, and professional ethics that influence behaviors." These qualities have an impact on how you, as an educator, interact with students, families, communities, and other professionals and are guided by your attitudes and beliefs. Appropriate dispositions are so highly valued that they are included in NCATE's Standard 1: Candidate Knowledge, Skills, and Dispositions, and are expectations for all teachers.

NCATE accredited programs that prepare teachers and other school personnel must provide evidence that all of their candidates have the knowledge, skills, and dispositions necessary to help all students learn. The admission to the teacher education program process includes an assessment of your dispositions to teach as you continue throughout your approved program of study. As you exit your preparation program, you should be able to move successfully into the teaching setting and create positive and supportive environments for student learning.

Identifying your dispositions to teach requires a level of self-reflection and assessment. As your dispositions evolve throughout your preservice experiences, you should have opportunities to maintain a journal of your thoughts and reactions to your experiences. Opportunities to discuss your observations of school-based experiences also can assist in the development of your dispositions. Challenging your beliefs when involved in a real-life field experience is a powerful tool for developing self-awareness of your dispositions. For example, many preservice educators will respond positively to the statement that "all students can learn." However, in practice, an educator's actions when presented with a student for whom learning may be a challenge indicates the educator's disposition.

PRACTICES RELATED TO EFFECTIVE TEACHING

Identifying effective teaching has been the focus of much research and discussion. (See Activity 1.6.) The National Board for Professional Teaching Standards (NBPTS) set forth five propositions of effective practice for experienced teachers. They are used to assess educators who choose to pursue National Board certification, an optional, advanced certification for teachers with a minimum of 3 years of experience. Similarly, the Interstate New Teacher Assessment & Support Consortium, a Program of the Council of Chief State School Officers, has crafted professional standards for the licensing of beginning teachers. The INTASC standards include the knowledge, performances, and dispositions necessary for all beginning teachers regardless of their specialty areas and grade levels. The INTASC standards provide teacher education programs and candidates with the language to describe expectations for effective beginning teachers.

The following outlines the 10 INTASC principles:

1. The teacher understands the central concepts, tools of inquiry, and structures of the discipline(s) he or she teaches and can create learning experiences that make these aspects of subject matter meaningful for students.
2. The teacher understands how children learn and develop, and can provide learning opportunities that support their intellectual, social, and personal development.
3. The teacher understands how students differ in their approaches to learning and creates instructional opportunities that are adapted to diverse learners.
4. The teacher understands and uses a variety of instructional strategies to encourage students' development of critical thinking, problem solving, and performance skills.
5. The teacher uses an understanding of individual and group motivation and behavior to create a learning environment that encourages positive social interaction, active engagement in learning, and self-motivation.
6. The teacher uses knowledge of effective verbal, nonverbal, and media communication techniques to foster active inquiry, collaboration, and supportive interaction in the classroom.
7. The teacher plans instruction based upon knowledge of subject matter, students, the community, and curriculum goals.
8. The teacher understands and uses formal and informal assessment strategies to evaluate and ensure the continuous intellectual, social, and physical development of the learner.
9. The teacher is a reflective practitioner who continually evaluates the effects of his/her choices and actions on others (students, parents, and other professionals in the learning community) and who actively seeks out opportunities to grow professionally.
10. The teacher fosters relationships with school colleagues, parents, and agencies in the larger community to support students' learning and well-being.

A full copy of the INTASC core standards may be found at *http://ccsso.org/projects/Interstate_New_Teacher_Assessment_and_Support_Consortium/Projects/Standards_Development/*

SUGGESTIONS TO HELP YOU BE SUCCESSFUL AS A STUDENT TEACHER

During your first days in the classroom, you may feel somewhat unsure about what is expected of you. Following these general tips will help alleviate some of your anxiety.

- Be pleasant and polite to students, parents, your mentoring teacher, other teachers, administrators, support personnel, and others. Although you may be nervous, don't forget how to smile.
- Be enthusiastic about teaching. Show your mentoring teacher that you are energetic and willing, rather than lethargic and reluctant. Volunteer to help with tasks such as grading papers, giving individual assistance, and making instructional aids as the opportunity arises. The greater and earlier your involvement, the more comfortable you will be when you begin teaching.
- Be punctual. Punctuality reflects a professional attitude.
- Dress professionally. If you don't look like a teacher, the students won't treat you like one. In most cases, you can take your cue from your mentoring teacher or other teachers in the school.
- Check with your mentoring teacher about school policies before a crisis occurs in which you need to know those policies.

ACTIVITY 1.4 │ ***One Day of Student Teaching***

TIME	STRESSFUL SITUATION	REACTIONS	RATING	AVOIDANCE/ MANAGEMENT STRATEGIES

ACTIVITY 1.5 | *Analyzing Stress*

1. Identify a recent stressful situation. _____
   _____
   _____
   _____

2. Why did this particular situation cause you to feel stress? _____
   _____
   _____
   _____

3. How did you react? _____
   _____
   _____
   _____

4. Could the situation have been avoided? If so, how? What else could you have done? _____
   _____
   _____
   _____

5. Should you have reacted differently? What else could you have done? _____
   _____
   _____
   _____

6. What was most effective in helping you overcome your feelings of stress? _____
   _____
   _____
   _____

7. Could you have used this situation in a positive way? How? _____
   _____
   _____
   _____

8. How could you have reduced the intensity of the stress? _____
   _____
   _____
   _____

9. If the same thing happens again, how can you manage the stress better? _____
   _____
   _____
   _____

ACTIVITY 1.6 | *Practices for Effective Teaching*

Read the list of guidelines related to good teaching practices near the end of the chapter. Periodically, consider your quality of performance in each of these areas and rate yourself on a scale of 1 (lowest) to 5 (highest) for each guideline.

GUIDELINES	RATING PERIODS			
	1	2	3	4
1. Organize content around concepts.				
2. Support and respond to students.				
3. Encourage meaning making.				
4. Make authentic assignments.				
5. Integrate thinking skills.				
6. Create a learning community.				
7. Stress conceptual understanding.				
8. Use teachable moments.				
9. Relate material to prior knowledge.				
10. Actively engage students.				

For each rating period, identify your strengths and weaknesses according to the guidelines. Consider how you might develop your strengths and reduce your weaknesses.

First period:

Strengths:

Weaknesses:

Second period:
  Strengths:

  Weaknesses:

Third period:
  Strengths:

  Weaknesses:

Fourth period:
  Strengths:

  Weaknesses:

Reflect on your overall teaching style and identify those guidelines that you follow most closely.

- Learn the students' names quickly. This helps you both to build rapport and to create an effective learning environment.
- Always model appropriate language and grammar for the students. Take care to meet this responsibility in speaking and writing.
- Write legibly. You may be asked to construct worksheets or study guides for the students or write assignments on the board. Use the form of writing appropriate for your students (manuscript or cursive), and make sure that you form the letters properly, that the spacing and size of letters are appropriate, and that the overall product is legible. Once again, you are a model for the students.
- Keep calm. Do not allow yourself angry outbursts in school, even if things are not going well.
- Never criticize your mentoring teacher to another teacher or criticize other teachers in the school to each other. This is unprofessional behavior.
- Become familiar with the school's resources well before you are expected to take charge, so that you will be able to locate the things you need when you need them. You must be able to integrate technology into the teaching and learning process. Make sure you are aware of the available technology resources and support.
- Learn the daily routine thoroughly, so that you can manage it smoothly when you take over responsibility.
- Speak with pride about becoming a teacher. In these days of criticism of education, you should stand up for your chosen profession.

Later, when you begin teaching, you will need to remember the preceding tips, which apply to all your field and clinical experiences, including student teaching, plus the following additional tips, which apply to your direct teaching activities. Learn them so that you can perform acceptably.

- Be aware of the students' physical comfort. Adjust the temperature and lighting so that they support the learning environment. Make sure that there is adequate ventilation.
- Don't make a presentation or lecture about something you have written or drawn on the board while standing in such a way that you block the students' view of the material.
- Use your voice well when teaching. A droning monotone bores students. An overly loud voice may intimidate some students, especially younger ones. A too-quiet voice may not carry well enough to reach students at the back of the room.
- Use only classroom management methods sanctioned by your mentoring teacher.
- Distribute classroom participation as evenly as possible. (Recognize a variety of students when calling on them during class time.)
- Vary activities to keep students interested and engaged. Avoid relying exclusively upon one teaching approach.
- Plan each lesson thoroughly, no matter how well you think you know the material. Consider the instructional needs of all the students, and adjust your explanations and procedures accordingly.
- Make clear and unambiguous assignments, and give students an opportunity to ask for clarification if they need it.
- Grade and return all assignments promptly. Students will learn more from assignments with immediate feedback.
- Make sure that all assignments contribute appropriately to instructional and curricular goals.

DISCUSSION QUESTIONS

These discussion questions and those near the end of the other chapters may be handled in different ways. Questions may be discussed by the entire class, shared with partners, considered in small groups, or adapted for role-playing.

1. What are some things that cause stress? What are some ways you can reduce the effects of these stressors? Can you think of a time when you handled a stressful situation especially well?
2. What are some common areas of stress that you can share with other practicum students or student teachers? Can any changes be made in policies or assignments to reduce the stress?
3. Consider the guidelines for good teaching (Activity 1.6, and the fuller list in text). What are your reactions to them? Which ones are in accord with your personal philosophy of teaching? Which ones might cause you difficulty?
4. Think of the teachers you have had. Which characteristics of good teaching did they possess? Which characteristics were often lacking? Do you think you would have learned more if your teachers had implemented the guidelines in this chapter?
5. What can you do to help with extracurricular activities? What have you done so far? Can you

think of a way to help that no one else is doing? What is it?

6. What special talents or interests do you have that could help you become involved with extracurricular activities?

7. How can you make your observations of your mentoring teacher or other teachers most useful to you? Would it help to keep a log of ideas for future use?

8. Do all the teachers you have observed use the same teaching and disciplinary techniques? Why do you believe this might be so?

9. What are the most effective ways for practicum students and student teachers to evaluate their own teaching?

10. How valid are students' evaluations of teachers' performance?

11. How important is it for you to start developing a portfolio now? Why?

Chapter 2

Working with Students, School Personnel, and Parents

Case Study 2.1: Self-Improvement Activities

*M*rs. Sanchez is a mentoring teacher. Miss Mosley is her student teacher.

Mrs. Sanchez: Miss Mosley, there is a special inservice education program at the teacher center Thursday evening at 8:00. Would you like to attend with me?

Miss Mosley: What's the topic?

Mrs. Sanchez: Our reading program. Although you aren't required to attend, this is an excellent opportunity for you to learn about the materials you'll be using for the remainder of the semester. I thought you'd want to take advantage of it. I'll be glad to drive you over there, if you need transportation.

Miss Mosley: Yes, I'd like to go. Thank you for inviting me. (At the end of the semester, Mrs. Sanchez makes the comment in Miss Mosley's evaluation: "Interested in self-improvement of teaching skills.")

1. Did Mrs. Sanchez have a good basis for her evaluative comment? Why or why not?
2. Do you show interest in self-improvement of teaching skills when opportunities are presented?

FOCUS ON SPECIFIC RELATIONSHIPS

Student teaching and other field experiences involve developing appropriate relationships with a variety of people—students, college or university supervisors, mentoring teachers, other school personnel, other student teachers, and parents. These interactions can be a major factor in your overall success as a student teacher or practicum student. Let us look at these relationships separately.

STUDENTS

Student teachers or practicum students are involved in important and demanding relationships with their students. Therefore, it is important to develop a positive and cooperative relationship with each student in the class. Some student teachers and practicum students misunderstand this relationship and try to be "buddies" with the students in order to be liked. Unfortunately, being liked is not sufficient for this relationship; respect is also important, as is recognition of the student teacher as an authority figure. The students' respect must be earned, and that takes time. It is not automatically accorded. Development of a "buddy" relationship can undermine the students' respect for you as an authority figure, and thus adversely affect classroom control.

What, then, should be the relationship between you and your students? An appropriate relationship will require a great deal of perceptiveness and understanding on your part.

General Guidelines

First, you must treat each student as a worthwhile individual. That means reacting positively to all students and showing them you care about their progress and well-being. Simply learning the students' names quickly can have a positive effect on your relationships with them, as can mentioning that an absent student was missed. When students perform well, your approving comments help establish a positive relationship.

Let students know you respect them as individuals by listening to their opinions and expressions of feelings and responding to them in a way that shows you have given them careful thought. Dismissing students' ideas as trivial or worthless suggests that they are unable to contribute effectively to the class. Such actions can cause students to withdraw from the learning environment, rather than participate in classroom activities.

Nonverbal behavior can also promote good student relationships. Smile at students to show that you enjoy them. Listen to them when they voice problems, and try to help each one. Let them know that you are on their side.

To show respect for students' individuality, avoid labeling them according to racial, ethnic, socioeconomic, or sex stereotypes. Expectations should not be the same for all Asian Americans, all African Americans, all whites, all Hispanics, all people whose ancestors were of any particular nationality, all poor people, all rich people, all boys, or all girls. Each group member should be looked upon as an individual with a variety of traits acquired through interaction with the environment. As a student teacher, you help to shape some of the traits your students develop within that environment. Don't be so narrow-minded as to expect all members of a group to be alike.

Avoiding Sexism. The following case study involves sex stereotypes.

CASE STUDY 2.2

Sex Stereotypes

Miss Chambers, a student teacher in a fifth-grade class that was studying Mexico, thought that staging a fiesta would be a good teaching device, because it would give the children an opportunity to sample many Mexican foods. She told the boys to plan and construct a set to look like a festive Mexican home, while the girls located and prepared the foods to be tried. Darren, who liked to cook at home, wanted to prepare the tamales. Miss Chambers responded, "Surely you don't want to cook with the girls. You need to help the boys with the construction."

1. What is your analysis of Miss Chambers' reply to Darren?
2. What would you have said?
3. Do you suppose some of the girls might have enjoyed the construction project better than the cooking?
4. How would you have handled the entire project?

Sex stereotypes, such as the one Miss Chambers demonstrated, unfortunately still exist in some places. Certain activities, toys, and manners of speaking are arbitrarily attributed to boys and others to girls. Teachers sometimes discourage boys from cooking or sewing, indicating that these are not appropriate activities for boys, just as other activities are considered inappropriate for girls. Grant and Cooper (2003, p. 35) cite Wotorson (2001) as saying that students "should be encouraged to cross boundaries and participate in activities that challenge the way that they have previously thought about things (e.g., boys as athletes and girls as onlookers cheering the boys)."

You should avoid sexist practices when you choose materials and work with male and female students. Sexist practices can restrict what a person becomes by limiting behavior and career choices. Congress enacted Title IX of the Education Amendments Act of 1972 to prohibit discrimination against males or females in federally assisted education programs. Even though it is no longer legal to discriminate, many people continue to do so through their attitudes toward sex roles.

Some of the gender differences that appear to exist may be the result of different cultural expectations for boys and girls as they grow up. You may inadvertently be helping to cause the differences, rather than helping both boys and girls recognize the breadth of their behavioral and career choices. Boys should be permitted to cook and sew, as well as perform carpentry. They should also be allowed to show emotions, ask for help, and be gentle and cooperative without having their masculinity questioned. Girls should be encouraged to engage in athletic activities or use computers. They should also be encouraged in their study of math and science, as this acknowledges that girls may want to enter technical fields requiring knowledge of these subjects. Orlich and others (2004) point out the need for you, as a teacher, to provide leadership opportunities for students of both sexes.

Both men and women are found in careers, such as nursing and construction work, that were once considered the domain of a particular sex. Therefore, a girl who wants to be an airplane pilot should be given as much reinforcement as a boy who wants the same thing.

In addition, girls and boys should receive equal attention from you. All students need to be given chances to respond and receive teacher feedback.

Your language may unintentionally support sexist stereotypes. When the builders of our nation are referred to as forefathers, for example, young children may feel that women had no part. Use of the generic *he* may also cause young, and even adolescent, students to assume that only males are the topic of conversation. Terms such as *mailman* and *policeman* seem to close the careers of letter carriers and police officers to females. You must eliminate such usages from your speech patterns.

Dealing with Cultural and Linguistic Diversity

You are likely to teach culturally diverse classes. Therefore, you must help each student develop a positive cultural identity and accept classmates with other cultural backgrounds. Students need opportunities to read material by and about people from their own cultural backgrounds and from a variety of other backgrounds. This will help them see that people from other cultures are like them in many ways: they often share similar dreams, emotions, and experiences. Students also need help in understanding why some differences exist and learning to value those differences for their contributions to our nation and the world.

Teachers in culturally diverse classrooms should direct attention to the contributions and values of all represented cultures, as well as some that are not. This allows students to feel a part of the educational experience and to experience an increased sense of self-worth. In social studies classes, for example, inclusion of such material should be a natural occurrence. Emphasize contributions to our society, other societies, and the world at large made by people from different cultures, as well as difficulties faced by these people, as you teach history, geography, political science, and current events. In science, emphasize scientific contributions of people from varying cultures. You may need to point out the cultural background of the scientist in question; otherwise, the students may simply assume that the person was from their own culture or a culture stereotypically expected to produce scientists. In literature, include selections by and about people from different cultures. You may also want to locate books in the primary languages of your ESL students; the Internet can help you locate appropriate books. For example, the Center for the Study of Books in Spanish for Children and Adolescents' website, *www.csusm.edu/campus_centers/csb/*, can help you locate books in Spanish. Use a search engine to find sites for books about different cultures, by authors and illustrators from different cultures, or written in different languages. (Complete Activity 2.1 to see how your classroom rates in this area.)

FOR YOUR PORTFOLIO

INTASC Standard: 3

Include a copy of Activity 2.1 in your portfolio, along with evidence of adjustments in materials that you made, if any were needed, to help combat any cultural bias that you detected.

On special occasions, students from different cultural backgrounds should be allowed to explain, if they wish, how those occasions differ for them or how they celebrate similar things at different times of the year. Special attention to the effects that Columbus's landing in the New World had on the indigenous people, for example, or consideration of the points of view that groups such as the Tories, Native Americans, British, and French had toward the American Revolution may be appropriate in expanding multicultural awareness and understanding.

Classroom materials should be free of cultural bias. Even math activities may show cultural bias by the situations described in statement problems. Teachers must be vigilant and de-emphasize material that could cause some children to feel that they do not "fit in" with the class.

Cooperative learning groups (described in detail in Chapter 3) should be multicultural. In such situations, the students will learn from each other and come to respect the contributions made by the other group members.

In classrooms with little or no cultural diversity, an even more urgent need exists to make students aware of the ways in which people may be different from them, while sharing some characteristics with them. They need to realize that all kinds of people have influenced their world. Printed materials, as well as multimedia resources, will help make the discussions of other cultures vivid and complete.

Understanding of the culture or cultures represented in your classroom is very important for you as a student teacher. For example, a child from one culture may look down and fail to meet your eyes as a sign of respect, but your cultural background may cause you to interpret this action negatively. One beginning teacher was upset when she saw a group of Navaho children helping each other on a test. She interpreted their actions as cheating, but in their culture cooperation and helping others are considered desirable. However, there is much diversity within cultural groups, and you should not expect all students from a particular group to respond to the same situation in a similar manner. (Complete the Class Culture Survey in Activity 2.2 to help you plan ways to adjust for multicultural class membership.)

Some of your students may speak little or no English; likewise, you may not speak their language. However, you can relate positively to such students through persistence and effort. From the first moment they enter the classroom, include these students in classroom activities that require little language. At the elementary level, these activities may include playing active games at recess, drawing and painting, and viewing displays and demonstrations. At the secondary level, the activities may include almost all aspects of a physical education class or some vocational classes and viewing displays and demonstrations in other areas. You should attempt to communicate with each student through gestures, pictures, and any words you know from her or his language. Even though attempting to communicate with these students may be frustrating, always be positive. Encourage other students to include a new student in their activities, explaining that they can make the new student comfortable by helping him or her learn the standard procedures and popular activities. Students often take behavioral cues from their teachers.

CASE STUDY 2.3

Making a Breakthrough

In January, Carlos, a 9-year-old boy from Puerto Rico, enters a mostly white, middle-class suburban school near a northern U.S. city. Carlos is a shy child who knows only a little English. Mrs. Hearn, the mentoring teacher, and Carol Vaughn, the student teacher, encourage the class to make Carlos feel part of the class. Sam Ray is a student teacher in another fourth-grade class.

At recess, John, an outgoing boy, asked Carlos to play kickball on his team, but Carlos refused. He told John, in broken English, that he didn't play ball. Even though a couple of boys were willing to show him how, he would not play. He moved away from the boys and stood by himself off the field.

At lunch, Hank asked Carlos if he brought his lunch, and Carlos replied, "Sí." However, when Hank invited Carlos to sit at his table, Carlos shook his head and sat down by himself.

After a week, Miss Vaughn told Mrs. Hearn that she was worried about Carlos. She explained that the class made some initial attempts to make him feel welcome, but had started to ignore him. "He just stays by himself and looks so sad and lonely. We should be able to do something," she said.

Mrs. Hearn indicated that she was concerned about him too, but she didn't know what to do. The children have told her that he never wants to do anything with them, so they don't ask him anymore.

Miss Vaughn pointed out that some children laugh at Carlos because of the unusual food he brings to lunch and his strange actions. She told Mrs. Hearn that she would talk to Carlos to see how he felt about the class. When Miss Vaughn asked Carlos how he was getting along, he replied, "Not so good. Boys and girls, they no like me."

Miss Vaughn assured him that the other students liked him and wanted to be friends, but he responded, "No they don't. I no like them either." Miss Vaughn gave up on the conversation unsatisfied.

A few days later she ran into a fellow student teacher and had an idea. She asked, "Sam, aren't you teaching a unit on Mexico?"

Mr. Ray replied, "I'm right in the middle of it."

ACTIVITY 2.1 | *Checking for Cultural Bias and Stereotypes in Reading Materials*

1. Are a variety of cultures represented in the illustrations in the materials? _____

2. Are a variety of cultures represented in the written texts of the materials? _____

3. In the illustrations, are the people from any particular cultures shown in stereotyped occupations or activities? _____ If so, which ones? _____

    _____

    _____

    _____

4. In the written texts, are the people from any particular cultures described or represented in stereotyped occupations or activities? _____ If so, which ones? _____

    _____

    _____

    _____

5. From what cultures do the main characters in stories or featured characters in expository text come? _____

    _____

    _____

    _____

6. Are any of the materials written by people from other cultures? _____ If so, which ones? _____

    _____

    _____

7. Are any of the materials illustrated by people from other cultures? _____ If so, which ones? _____

    _____

    _____

8. What do the results of your analysis of the reading materials in your classroom indicate that you need to do in order to provide your students with positive multicultural reading experiences? _____

    _____

    _____

    _____

ACTIVITY 2.2 | **Class Culture Survey**

1. What different cultural backgrounds are represented by the students in your classroom?

	CULTURES	NUMBER OF STUDENTS
a.		
b.		
c.		
d.		
e.		
f.		

2. What are some important holidays or events for the various cultural groups in your class?
   a.

   b.

   c.

   d.

   e.

   f.

3. List any students in your class who speak a language other than English as their primary language. Make a checkmark by the language if you can speak it.

	STUDENT'S NAME	OTHER LANGUAGE	CAN YOU SPEAK IT?
a.			
b.			
c.			
d.			
e.			
f.			

"Great!" she said. "How would you like for your students to learn some Spanish words?"

Mr. Ray liked the idea, so Miss Vaughn told him about Carlos. She said, "He is having a really hard time fitting in. I thought maybe you could ask him to help you with some Spanish words to make him feel better about himself."

Mr. Ray agreed and set a time for Carlos to visit his class.

Back in her own class, Miss Vaughn told Carlos that the class down the hall was learning about Mexico, but the teacher didn't speak Spanish. "Could you go there and tell them some Spanish words?" she asked.

Carlos was reluctant, stating that they wouldn't like him, but Miss Vaughn persisted and told him that she was sure that they would. She got his attention when she said, "Anyway, you know Spanish words, and they don't know any."

Finally, Carlos agreed to try. When he went to Mr. Ray's class, Mr. Ray introduced him and told the class, "He knows how to speak Spanish and is going to tell us some words we need to know."

One girl burst out, "Terrific! I'm working on a scrapbook. I can put in some Spanish words. Carlos, how do you say family in Spanish? How about dinner? And school?

A boy called out, "Can you teach us how to count in Spanish?"

Several students demanded, "Say something to us in Spanish!"

Mr. Ray called the class to order, then said, "Give Carlos a chance to answer. Carlos, can you tell Jean the words she wants to know first?"

Quietly Carlos said, "Sí. Word for family is familia. What else you want to know?"

Carlos answered more questions, gradually building confidence and volume as he proceeded. A big grin broke out on his face as he noticed how interested the students were in what he was saying.

When the period was over, Mr. Ray thanked Carlos for his help and asked him if he would come back again.

Carlos smiled shyly and replied, "Sí."

John heard about Carlos's visit to the other class from a friend and approached him again. "Hey, Carlos," he said. "I hear you've been teaching the kids down the hall to speak Spanish. How about teaching us?"

Carlos looked surprised. "Sí. If you want."

John said, "You teach us some Spanish, and we'll teach you how to play kickball. Is it a deal?"

Carlos agreed with a nod, and the boys walked off talking together.

1. Why do you think Carlos had trouble getting along with the other students in his class?

2. What were some indications that he was beginning to feel more comfortable in his new school?
3. Why did Miss Vaughn's idea about having Carlos teach Spanish to a group of children seem to help him when other attempts to help had failed?
4. Can you think of other plans that might have helped Carlos adjust to his new class?

Students differ in their ancestry, language, religion, physical characteristics, or customs. Some are not native to the United States, or come from the inner city or from rural areas, such as parts of Southern Appalachia. Various groups exist within a larger, dominant society, but they exhibit different language patterns, attitudes, or behaviors from those in the mainstream population. Teachers should be aware of concerns related to culturally diverse students.

Your knowledge of the language and culture of ethnic groups, such as Hispanics, African Americans, Asian Americans, and Native Americans, can be valuable. Research reveals typical learning patterns exist within cultural groups. For example, many Mexican Americans seek close personal relationships with their teachers and prefer learning general concepts to learning specific facts; African Americans tend to like discussion, collaborative work, and active projects; and many Native-American students value quiet times for thinking and the use of visual stimuli for creating images. Remember, however, that variations among students within any cultural group are as great as similarities, so avoid the temptation to stereotype by ethnic group (Guild, 1994).

Because Latino cultures value interactions among family members, children are taught to work together and be helpful to others. Therefore, instead of expecting all independent work, try letting students work in pairs, do choral reading, and discuss answers to homework questions before writing them on their own. Because each school setting will have a different cultural mix, try to familiarize yourself with the cultural backgrounds of the specific students you are assigned to teach.

Multicultural Education. Multicultural education affirms the value of various groups within the schools. Supporters of multicultural education believe that material related to a wide variety of cultures should be an integral part of the curriculum, beginning in kindergarten and continuing throughout the other grades. In social studies, have students study world events from different perspectives. Instead of having the students consider only prevalent U.S. views, you can lead them to consider how people from other countries view international events. In literature, have students read stories with varied cultural content. You can also incorporate multicultural themes into art, music, science, mathematics, and physical education.

A much less effective approach some teachers take to multicultural education is the "heroes and holidays" observance. Two or three times during the year, certain periods are set aside to celebrate a particular event related to a specific culture. For example, at Thanksgiving children may dress as Native Americans and construct tepees, or in observance of Martin Luther King's death, students might prepare a "soul food" meal. Such observances do little to promote understanding of other cultures, but rather reinforce misconceptions and stereotypes. As a student teacher, you should consider taking a more meaningful approach to multicultural education.

Multicultural content in the curriculum can offer relevant reading material for students of particular ethnic groups. Many African-American students will be more interested in reading stories about Harriet Tubman's heroic efforts to free slaves or George Washington Carver's ingenuity in finding ways to use peanuts than about situations not involving African-American characters. When students have greater interest, they will be more enthusiastic about learning.

In recognition of the learning preferences of non-mainstream cultural groups, Coelho (1994) recommends that you consider two major educational strands when planning instruction:

- Cooperative learning for developing both social and academic skills
- Exploratory talk to connect language and learning

Many studies indicate that cooperative learning is particularly beneficial for minority students, for promoting race relations, and for enhancing self-esteem. Here are some strategies you can use with students of varying cultural backgrounds (Garcia, 1994).

1. Hold high achievement expectations for all students.
2. Focus on teaching reading, writing, and math.
3. Maintain an orderly, safe environment.
4. Provide continual feedback on academic progress.
5. Give recognition for academic success.

Be conscious of ways to use multicultural content in your lessons. Keep in mind that multicultural education involves more than occasionally adding a bit of information about a minority group to your lessons. It means presenting material from a global perspective that values the contributions and cultures of each group.

You might want to subscribe to *Teaching Tolerance,* a free semiannual journal designed to combat racist attitudes (Education Department, Southern Poverty Law Center, P.O. Box 548, Montgomery, AL 36101–0548). Used in about 55,000 schools, it includes practical materials, resources, and strategies for elementary and secondary classroom teachers. Free materials, such as a book entitled *Responding to Hate at School* and video-and-text teaching kits, are also available through mail order.

Attitudes Toward Cultural Diversity. Be sensitive to the special needs of the culturally diverse students in your classroom, and respect their ethnic and racial backgrounds. While some students have no problems with their ethnicity, others feel insecure and ill at ease

Students with culturally different heritages may be assigned to work together.

in a different culture. You should respond to students with ethnic adjustment problems in helpful and constructive ways.

Several strategies are available to encourage students to accept peers who have different cultural origins. Role-playing can help students understand how it feels to be a member of a different cultural group. Assigning children of different heritages to work together on a committee helps them realize that each member of the group can make an important contribution. You can create other situations in which problems can be solved only through the cooperation of each member of a culturally mixed group.

Culturally different students need to acquire the values and behaviors essential for success in the dominant society while retaining important aspects of their own subcultures. Whereas you cannot do a great deal to further this ideal in a short period of time, your awareness of cultural differences, your attitudes toward your students, and the focus of your lessons can make a difference (see Activity 2.3).

FOR YOUR PORTFOLIO

INTASC Standard: 3

Put your lesson plan from Activity 2.3 in your portfolio. Comment on the success of your adaptations for students with special needs.

Language-Minority Students. Every year, many non-English speakers enter the United States from a variety of nations. Miller and Endo (2004, p. 787) point out that "educators need to provide an environment that reduces stress and anxiety and also increases immigrant students' motivation and self-esteem." Students who exclusively speak a language other than English need to learn English quickly in order to benefit from the educational experiences offered in an English-speaking school. Don't be too concerned about these students acquiring mastery of English grammar and rules. English language learners learn English best through hearing it in normal conversations and read-alouds of literature, seeing it in classroom materials, and using it purposefully in actual classroom activities, rather than through a grammar-based instructional approach.

You should refer to a foreign-language dictionary when communicating with students who are learning English. If a student reads her or his own language fluently, you should provide a dictionary with English equivalents of familiar words for that student.

In the primary grades, you can construct a picture dictionary of English words for such a student. You may make use of pictures and concrete objects to supply needed vocabulary words. For example, you may show the student a picture of a dog or an actual dog and point to the picture or animal while saying the word *dog.* Coloring books and picture books were successfully used with an 8-year-old child from Thailand, whose vocabulary grew rapidly due to her desire to communicate. Classmates spent countless free hours identifying objects in these books for her, listening to her repeat their names, and helping her correct her pronunciation. In return, she translated the items into her own language for her highly receptive classmates. The result was mutual respect and enjoyment. Grant and Cooper (2003) validate the use of this approach, pointing out that the students' own language should be used as an instructional resource.

When providing information or giving directions in class, teachers can explain the material in simpler terms for English language learners or rewrite the material in simpler words and shorter sentences. They can also preteach any difficult vocabulary terms (Miller & Endo, 2004).

You may want to assign buddies, such as students who speak the new students' languages, to students who speak little or no English. Including new students in cooperative learning groups and classroom activities in which they can listen to the language being used is also a good practice. Garcia (2002, p. 356) found "use of a thematic curriculum and collaborative, small group instruction to be helpful." As the students learn English, they can help familiarize other students with a second language, as Carlos did in his school and as the Thai girl did in her class.

CASE STUDY 2.4

Learning English Through Collaboration

Lori, Mr. Chowdhuri's student teacher, observed that there were several Korean students in her second-grade class. Although they were eager to learn English and were making good progress, Lori wanted to help them feel more comfortable with their new language.

Aware of the benefits of cooperative learning for language-minority students, Lori decided to form groups, each of which would include a Korean child, so far as possible. Lori knew the children loved the big books that Mr. Chowdhuri shared with them during reading lessons, so she asked each group to make an original big book to share with the rest of the class. Since the children were enthusiastic about the project, Lori got the supplies they needed and let them get to work.

As she listened in on the groups, she heard the children eagerly suggesting ideas. The Korean children listened carefully, joined in, and gladly accepted the corrections in language usage that their native-English speaking peers offered. Whewon was especially full of ideas, and Lori noticed that he wanted to dictate the text. As he spoke the lines, group members approved his ideas, but sometimes changed verb endings and word order to correspond with English usage.

As a result of this collaboration, the Korean children learned many of the fine points of English—without a grammar book and in a mutually satisfying endeavor. Lori felt that she had taken a big step toward realizing her goal.

1. What are some other ways to help language-minority children learn English in a constructive, purposeful way?
2. Compare the advantages of teaching English to non-English speakers through purposeful conversation rather than grammar rules.

Students Who Speak Nonstandard Dialects. Some of the students in your class are likely to speak non-standard dialects of English. Part of your job as a teacher is to expose these students to standard English, since most employment opportunities require it. You must model standard English for students and reinforce its use in school settings without discrediting their home language. In other words, the home language should be treated as one communication system and standard English ("school language") as an alternative system. Students should not be reprimanded for using their home language in informal settings, but they should practice standard English in formal situations, such as giving oral reports and producing written reports. All teachers must approach this task with understanding and sensitivity.

Showing Respect for and Fairness to All Students

You will find all types of students when you enter the classroom. Current concerns about the need for inclusion (placing individuals with disabilities in regular education settings) have resulted in many students being placed in regular classrooms, regardless of physical, intellectual, or emotional disabilities (Orlich, Harder, Callahan, Trevisan, & Brown, 2004). Students will probably be culturally diverse and range in ability from academically gifted to slow learning. Some may be learning disabled and some may be physically challenged. There are likely to be students whose first language is not English. You must give your best efforts to challenge, help, provide for, and understand these students.

Instead of focusing on differences, however, recognize the many ways in which these students are alike. They have many of the same needs in terms of acceptance, achievement, and interactions, and their interests are also likely to be similar, centering around friends, ball games, music, popular television shows or films, and the like. You should help each student reach his or her potential and find a niche in the classroom.

You can show respect by allowing your students to take on responsibilities. Giving students tasks, no matter how small, shows that you trust them to fulfill the duties and recognize their ability to do so. This attitude can have an enormous effect upon the way a student responds to you. Let us look at the case of Randy as an example.

CASE STUDY 2.5

Showing Respect for Students

Randy, a sixth-grade student, had been retained in two previous grades. As a consequence, he was a 14-year-old in a classroom with many 11- and 12-year-olds. Naturally, he was larger than the other students and had different interests. Furthermore, he was poor, and most of his clothing was worn and faded. The heels of his boots were worn out, and his sleeves were a little too short for his arms.

Randy was generally quiet and obedient in class, but rarely made any attempt to do his assignments. He displayed an extremely negative self-concept, informing the student teacher, Miss Davis, "I'm too dumb to do that," when she encouraged him to try some of the work.

Miss Davis tried very hard to treat Randy the same way she treated the other students. She called on him to respond in class and listened respectfully to his replies. She greeted him when he entered the classroom in the morning and smiled and spoke when she passed him in the hall. In addition, she gave him much encouragement and assistance during directed study periods. Still, she felt she was making little headway. To be sure, he talked a little more in class than he had previously, and turned in a few more assignments, but Miss Davis still did not feel she had reached Randy.

One day, as Randy was leaving the classroom to go home for lunch, Miss Davis realized she needed to mail a letter and remembered that Randy passed by a mailbox on his way home. She asked him if he would mail the letter as a favor. Randy looked at her in disbelief, since nobody at school had ever trusted him to take responsibility for anything. He hesitated and said, "You want me to mail it?"

ACTIVITY 2.3 | *Adapting Lessons to Students with Special Needs*

Briefly outline a lesson plan for a subject you are teaching.

How would you adjust this plan for the following students? (You may consider other types of diversity, particularly those of students you are teaching.)

Students with Hearing Impairments:

Students with Visual Impairments:

Students with Limited Use of English:

Learners Who Are Academically Challenged:

Gifted Students:

Miss Davis replied, "I'd appreciate your doing it, if you don't mind."

Randy walked over and picked up the letter, glancing around to see if others had heard this exchange. "I'll be sure it gets mailed," he told Miss Davis rather loudly, and walked out of the room proudly holding the letter.

Upon returning to the room after lunch, the first thing he told Miss Davis was, "I mailed your letter." He said it with a smile of satisfaction.

Thereafter, Randy began to respond more and more to Miss Davis's encouragement to do assignments. He seemed to try much harder to do what she thought he could do. He did not become a scholar overnight, but he improved in all his work and once even earned a 100 in mathematics. And he continued to carry Miss Davis's letters with pride.

1. What is your analysis of the way Miss Davis handled Randy?
2. Would you have treated the situation differently in any way?
3. Would it have been wise for Miss Davis to give a crucial piece of mail, such as a bill payment, to Randy before she was sure that he was trustworthy?

All students must receive attention; do not favor a few and ignore or avoid others. This may be difficult, because some students are not as appealing as others. Some dress carelessly or shabbily, fail to wash, or have belligerent attitudes. Your challenge is to be equally accepting of and positive about these students' behaviors and those of the neat, clean, cooperative students. Although you should not accept behavior that deviates from school rules, you should show acceptance of the individual, regardless of her or his behavior. You should also find traits in each person to which you can react positively. Try to develop a sense of community in your classroom in which all students can feel they are valued class members. Activity 2.4 will help you focus on this behavior.

To have a good relationship with your students, absolute fairness is important. Enforce rules equally for all students, because any hint that you have "teacher's pets" will cause poor relationships between you and the majority of the class.

Honesty is also important in your student relationships. Students quickly recognize insincerity and resent it.

Therefore, to establish good relationships with students, you should do the following:

1. Treat each student as a worthwhile individual, worthy of respect.

2. Use appropriate nonverbal behavior in your student interactions.
3. Avoid labels and stereotypes when working with students.
4. Offer students chances to take on responsibilities.
5. Give attention to all students.
6. Be positive toward all students.
7. Be fair to all students.
8. Be honest with all students.

Challenging the Gifted Student

Gifted students often make much faster academic progress in a year than do average students. Usually, they have some of these characteristics:

1. Interest in books and reading
2. Large vocabularies and the ability to express themselves verbally in a mature manner
3. Curiosity and long attention spans
4. High levels of abstract thinking
5. Wide ranges of interests

Whereas gifted students are able to direct many of their own activities, some direction from the teacher is needed. Marty Williams describes her experiences in teaching some gifted students in Figure 2–1.

Within the school program, look for opportunities to challenge gifted students. Here are some ideas.

1. Make available a wide selection of resource materials.
2. Develop theme studies that provide opportunities for in-depth and long-term learning experiences.
3. Create a kit of challenging problems, puzzles, riddles, and the like.
4. Support students in creating and directing their own projects.
5. Encourage students to prepare oral and written reports on current theme studies.
6. Place gifted students in cooperative learning groups where they can work with less able students.

As a student teacher, you should begin collecting a file of creative and unusual ideas to use with gifted students. Figure 2–2 shows one card with which you can start your file.

Educational opportunities beyond regular classroom instruction may be available for gifted students in your school. These options may include special programs outside the classroom, use of resource teachers, minicourses, summer programs, independent study, advanced placement, community programs, curriculum compacting, and study groups. In addition, your school system may have a

FIGURE 2–1
Math Wizard: A Course in Informal
Geometry

During the summer, I taught a minicourse in informal geometry geared to gifted children in grades 4–6, as part of the Summer Enrichment Program. Since geometry is an indispensable tool of humankind, used constantly in many professions—by the builder, the engineer, the navigator, the astronomer, the artist, the musician, the inventor—gifted children should learn this material to have a solid foundation on which to build more complex geometric skills as their education progresses.

Some of the concepts taught and investigated in this minicourse were the three basic shapes; the ideas of proximity, separation, order, and enclosure; the relationship of sides and angles; the ideas of congruent, similar, and different; the Platonic Solids and Euler's Formula; and the visualization and creation of two- and three-dimensional objects.

Gifted children need to begin by working with concrete objects, even though these students are quick to perceive the abstract. From concrete objects they can move to semiconcrete or pictorial representations and then to abstract thinking.

Integration of mind and body is also essential for the gifted student, and with this in mind, I made it a point to involve the students physically with the concepts we studied. For example, they used their and/or other students' bodies to demonstrate the ideas of proximity, separation, order, and enclosure, and we had a relay race as a follow-up to the section on visualization and creation of two- and three-dimensional objects.

Every few days we had a "Tricky Puzzle"—a mathematical brain-teaser—to serve as a follow-up of the lesson. These puzzles also served as a lesson carry-over to get things rolling the next day by having the students present their solutions of the previous day's puzzle. "Tricky Puzzle" time was definitely the highlight of the day!

As the culminating experience for this minicourse, the students created box sculptures from "trash" they had been collecting since the first day of class. The only criteria were that (1) the students have a "guiding idea" for their construction, and that (2) they be able to name the geometric shapes involved in their sculptures. This exercise served as a good way to wrap up the course and ended things on a pleasant note.

FIGURE 2–2
Sample Activity Card for
Gifted Students

BOX O' BALLADS

Have a copy available of Carl Sandburg's book *The American Songbag*. Provide time and materials for students to do one of the following related projects after discussing and enjoying some of the ballads:

1. Draw a panorama representing one of the cowboy ballads.
2. Write some imaginative ballads of your own about the pioneers or the railroad workers.
3. Create a shoe-box diorama representing one of the lumberjack ballads.
4. Plan and present a short creative drama representing the ballad of your choice.
5. Read in several sources about the historical period represented and prepare a report.

special teacher for the gifted and talented, who can give you a great deal of help with materials and program planning.

As the student teacher, you can enjoy learning from gifted students as you become involved in their projects and support their efforts. Respect their ideas and encourage a wide range of activities. As you work with these students, you will certainly need a sense of humor. It is helpful to be able to admit mistakes and laugh at yourself!

ACTIVITY 2.4 | *Valuing Students' Diversity*

Refer to the Class Culture Survey that you did in Activity 2.2 to focus on students who represent various ethnic backgrounds. Plan some experiences for valuing the diversity of students in your class. Briefly describe them here.

Experiences:

Reflection: How effective were the experiences? What else could you try?

Helping the Student Who Is Academically Challenged

The main characteristic of students who are academically challenged is that they do not learn as quickly as do others of the same age. You will have to make some adjustments for instructing these students, such as:

1. Carefully developing readiness for each learning task
2. Moving through instructional material gradually and thoroughly
3. Developing ideas with concrete, manipulative, and visually oriented materials
4. Using simplified materials
5. Varying activities to accommodate short attention spans
6. Relating learnings to real-life experiences (such as school, lunchroom, gymnasium, current events, community projects, and holiday celebrations)
7. Providing for large amounts of practice to master new learnings
8. Reviewing with closely spaced, cumulative exercises to encourage retention

If a student who is academically challenged is having difficulty with a particular concept or idea, you may need to use corrective exercises and materials, such as the one shown in Figure 2–3.

Many such students, accustomed to years of placement in low groups, have negative self-concepts. It is important for them to experience success in some way—perhaps through athletics, art, or some other talent or skill. Consider those students in your class who have less academic ability than others, and then do Activity 2.5.

FIGURE 2–3

Sample Corrective Exercise for Students Who Are Academically Challenged

If you re still having trouble with these words . . .

The sun is high in the sky.

That s my son.

sun
A

son
B

1. Do <u>sun</u> and <u>son</u> sound alike?
2. What is different in the spelling of the words?
3. Draw a picture to fit these sentences.
   a. The <u>sun</u> is shining.
   b. Mother is with her <u>son</u>.
4. Write a sentence using the word <u>sun</u>. Then write a sentence using the word <u>son</u>.
5. Circle the picture word that fits these sentences.
   a. The _____ was behind the clouds.
      (sun, son)
   b. Bill is Mr. Brown s _____.
      (sun, son)

To develop and maintain positive attitudes toward school subjects, provide students who are academically challenged with situations that relate not only to their experiences, but also to the real world in which they live. Identify basic life skills, and relate them to subject content. For example, in math, teach skills related to such everyday tasks as reading price tags, calendars, road maps, recipes, coupons, timetables, thermometers, clocks, and sales slips; understanding money values and measurement units; and making change. Similarly, you can present subject matter concepts through such readily available materials as newspapers and magazines, "how to" books, telephone directories, mail-order catalogs, television guides, scouting manuals, menus, greeting cards, hobby materials, food and medicine containers, road signs, and nature guides.

Some secondary school programs focus instruction for the student who is academically challenged on practical applications, such as planning a budget; filling out job applications; learning social skills needed in family and job situations; and using independent living skills, such as food preparation, home management, attention to personal hygiene practices, and safety practices. Other functional curriculum programs incorporate career education, specific vocational skills, or on-the-job training in certain areas.

Providing for Students with Learning Disabilities

Students with learning disabilities usually demonstrate a significant discrepancy between intellectual potential and actual level of performance. They have some sort of difficulty learning in one or more subjects, but they are usually average or above average in intelligence, and not visually or hearing impaired, or educationally deprived.

The following guidelines may help you understand how to work with students who have learning disabilities.

1. Increase attention span by removing distractions, including any materials other than those necessary for the assigned task.
2. Teach the student how to organize his or her desk, belongings, and materials.
3. Try to improve one behavior at a time, rewarding appropriate behavior and involving the student in recording progress.
4. Carefully create a positive learning environment and tasks with specific standards, limits, and rules, and be consistent in your expectations. Make consequences for violations clear.

5. Assign one task at a time, at first using a step-by-step procedure. Use short, sequential assignments, with breaks between tasks.
6. Find a variety of media to present content (such as computer programs, videos, audiotapes, and transparencies), and use active methods (such as simulation games, experiments, and role-playing) as instructional strategies.

Practices frequently used with secondary students who have learning disabilities include teaching generalized learning strategies (such as note-taking, test-taking, outlining, and study skills), putting greater emphasis on multimedia presentations of material than on lectures or textbooks, and making provisions for alternatives (such as oral instead of written tests).

Students with Attention Deficit Disorder (ADD).
Attention deficit disorder (ADD), a form of learning disability, can occur with or without hyperactivity. ADD is most common among elementary school children and tends to slow down by adolescence. The child with ADD is likely to:

1. Be inattentive and unable to remain "on task"
2. Become impatient while waiting for his or her turn during games
3. Blurt out answers to questions
4. Fidget with his or her hands or feet
5. Be easily distracted
6. Turn in careless or incomplete work
7. Talk excessively and interrupt others
8. Lose things necessary for school tasks (e.g., pencils, books, assignments)
9. Engage in potentially dangerous acts without considering the consequences (e.g., darting into the street without looking)
10. Shift from one activity to another without completing anything

Since this disorder occurs in about 3% of children, you are likely to have an ADD child in your class—one who constantly disrupts the class and has several of these 10 characteristics. A guidance counselor or your mentoring teacher may have some suggestions for dealing with such a student. The following ideas can also be helpful:

1. Reward the child for remaining on task and completing work.
2. Set up study carrels or private areas where the child can work without distraction.
3. Keep lessons short.
4. Use progress charts and contracts.
5. Ignore inappropriate behavior whenever possible.
6. Stick to schedules and routines.

ACTIVITY 2.5 | *Building the Self-Esteem of Less Able Students*

Some students in a class may be less able than others. List ways that you can help the less able students build their self-esteem and succeed, and try these techniques in the next 2 weeks.

Two weeks later: Identify the techniques that were most effective by putting an asterisk (*) in front of them. Put an "X" in front of the least effective techniques. Can you think of other strategies to use?

Helping At-Risk Students

Educators often use the term *at risk* when referring to certain students. What does *at risk* mean, and what can you do to help these students?

At-risk students lack the necessary skills for succeeding in school and later life. They are likely to become dropouts, runaways, delinquents, or teenage parents. Family or societal conditions are generally the reasons why students are at risk; these include:

- Homelessness
- Abuse
- Poverty
- Unstable family situations
- Immigration, involving students who have trouble adapting to the language and behaviors of typical classrooms in the United States
- Persistent health problems and malnourishment
- High rate of absenteeism

These students will need a great deal of support and understanding. Although you may not be able to become directly involved in such issues as a student teacher, here are some ways you may be able to help.

- Be a good listener.
- Intervene when you sense a problem developing.
- Offer encouragement for efforts.
- Give positive reinforcement to build self-esteem.
- React sensitively to situations.
- Visit homes or meet with caregivers to understand family situations, if possible.
- Assign a buddy or a tutor to a student who needs help.
- Develop a sense of community within the classroom so that all children feel welcome and respected.
- Provide opportunities for achieving success.

FOR YOUR PORTFOLIO

INTASC Standards: 2, 3
Write a case study of a specific student who may be at risk. Describe ways you tried to encourage and support the student.

Providing for Students with Physical Disabilities

Some students have visual, auditory, or other physical disabilities. Students with visual disabilities should be encouraged to wear corrective lenses as appropriate, should be seated in positions that allow them to see visual displays clearly or given enlarged printed material, and should be given opportunities to learn through auditory and kinesthetic modes. Students with auditory disabilities should be encouraged to wear hearing aids as appropriate, should be seated where they can hear instruction clearly, and should be given opportunities to learn through visual and kinesthetic modes. Students with other physical disabilities should be provided with adaptive materials and assistance to allow responses to be given in alternative formats. Some can be helped by computers with special software; others may need to have paraprofessionals to assist them in completing activities.

Literature depicting students with physical disabilities in a positive light can help such students gain self-esteem. The literature should not have the disability as its primary focus, but should give individuals with disabilities a chance to show what they are capable of doing. They are neither hailed as superheroes nor treated as helpless victims (Landrum, 2001). A few books that you might want to try are:

Banks, Jacqueline T. (1993). *Project wheels.* Boston: Houghton Mifflin. (wheelchair)

Blatchford, Claire H. (1995). *Nick's mission.* Minneapolis, MN: Learner. (deaf)

Bloor, Edward. (1998). *Tangerine.* New York: Scholastic. (visually impaired)

Inclusion

Inclusion refers to including students with exceptionalities in the regular classroom. In an inclusion classroom, students with disabilities remain in the regular classroom for the entire day, and specialized teachers come into the classroom to provide support services. Because students with special needs are now being integrated into regular classes, you will probably be responsible for a number of students with exceptionalities. (See Chapter 9 for the legal issues connected with including individuals with disabilities in regular classrooms.)

Test materials and appropriate records are used by an Individualized Education Program (IEP) team to evaluate each student with disabilities. The team is composed of the student's teacher, one or both of the parents, and a representative of the local education agency (other than the teacher). It may also include the student and additional professional personnel, and you may also be invited to participate.

The team writes an IEP, which provides assessment information, as well as classroom modifications and instructional plans that you should know about when you work with these students. The format will probably include items such as these:

1. Student's present levels of educational performance
2. Student's learning style

3. Annual goals
4. Short-term instructional objectives
5. Specific educational services needed
6. Date when those services will begin and length of time the services will be given
7. Evaluation of student's ability to meet goals and objectives

---

FOR YOUR PORTFOLIO

INTASC Standards: 2, 3

If you have the opportunity, be a member of an IEP team. Include a copy of the IEP, with the student's name deleted, that you helped to create.

The following ideas may be useful in teaching included students:

1. Build rapport with the students. Let the students know that you are genuinely interested in helping them overcome difficulties. A comfortable, relaxed atmosphere also enhances rapport.
2. Make a plan for alleviating their difficulties as much as possible. Tailor instruction to meet the needs of each individual student, and relate instruction to the student's learning characteristics and potential. Different approaches may succeed with different students, so you must be familiar with many different approaches and flexible in your use of them.
3. Adjust the length of the instructional sessions to fit the students' attention spans. In fairly long sessions, you will need frequent changes of activities.
4. Learn the students' interests and use them as the focus of your instruction. A student will tend to put forth much effort to master a particular concept or skill that relates to a special interest. Give authentic, meaningful assignments and emphasize the values and usefulness of completing tasks.

Special education teachers and other personnel can offer you help when you work with students who have exceptionalities (see Activity 2.6). A paraprofessional may be available, and peers, either students from the same classroom or students from higher grades, may act as tutors.

CASE STUDY 2.6

Planning for Differences

Mr. Hernandez, a student teacher, is planning a study of the Civil War for his American history class. He is aware of the need to adjust instruction for varying

achievement levels and personal needs. He plans to encourage several advanced students to read widely and present information to the class in the form of reports, panel discussions, and dramatizations.

Some students will read chapters from the textbook and search for answers to a list of questions. Mr. Hernandez will prepare study guides to help these students focus on particular information.

Several students who learn more slowly will use some easy-to-read books and other supplementary materials to prepare for a group discussion about the Civil War. They will also view a video as part of their study. Mr. Hernandez will assign a student tutor to help when difficulties arise.

During this theme study, Mr. Hernandez plans to place students in cooperative learning groups with each group consisting of an advanced student, a student who learns more slowly, and two or three students of average abilities. Working as a team, these students will investigate different aspects of the Civil War and share their findings with the rest of the class.

Other students will read about Harriet Tubman and role-play her efforts in freeing the slaves. One student with ADD will work on short, sequential assignments, with a specific "date due" schedule. Mr. Hernandez will help Felipe, a student who is visually impaired, by providing audiotapes and asking a proficient reader to read key information aloud to him. In these and other ways, Mr. Hernandez hopes he has made appropriate adjustments for the needs of the students in the classroom.

1. What is your opinion of the way Mr. Hernandez adjusted assignments to meet differing needs?
2. What additional ideas can you suggest for meeting individual differences?

COLLEGE OR UNIVERSITY SUPERVISORS OR LIAISONS

Your relationship with your college or university supervisor or liaison is also important. He or she has the responsibility for overseeing and critiquing your classroom work. Your supervisor will help you throughout the student-teaching experience, as well as determine your grade at the end. Therefore, your supervisor will be offering, either orally or in writing, suggestions for improving your teaching. These suggestions are intended to help you analyze what you are doing and make the most of your field experience. They are not meant as personal attacks upon your competence. Try to consider the suggestions objectively and ask questions about points that may be unclear, rather than react defensively and produce excuses for mistakes you may have made. If you show your supervisor that you are open to suggestions and

ACTIVITY 2.6 | *Support Personnel for Students with Special Needs*

Identify a student with special needs in your class, and identify several people who might help you work with this student, such as your mentoring teacher, a resource teacher, or a guidance counselor. Interview them, and then write an informal plan for helping the student.

Comments from support personnel:

Informal plan:

Reflection: How effective is my plan? Who else might be able to help? What else could I try?

will welcome constructive criticism, your relationship is likely to be a good one.

A way to show that you are eager to improve and that you welcome your college or university supervisor's help is to put his or her suggestions into practice as soon as possible. When your supervisor makes a suggestion and subsequently sees no attempt on your part to change, he or she is likely to view your behavior negatively. However, if your supervisor sees you working to incorporate the suggestion into your teaching, he or she is likely to perceive you as a serious student with a desire to become a good teacher.

FOR YOUR PORTFOLIO

INTASC Standard: 9

Put one of the written evaluations from your college or university supervisor in your portfolio, along with a written explanation of how you changed your teaching practices as a result of this evaluation.

Asking pertinent questions of your college or university supervisor shows a desire to improve and an interest in seeking new knowledge—desirable attributes that are likely to be appreciated. After observing your teaching, your supervisor will probably hold a conference with you or with both you and your mentoring teacher. It is a good idea to take the written comments your supervisor makes about your performance to these scheduled conferences. If conferences are not automatic, don't hesitate to request them if you feel the need for more feedback.

CASE STUDY 2.7

Fear of Exposure

Dale Martin, a secondary school student teacher, was assigned to two classes of algebra, a class of plane geometry, and a class of trigonometry. His university supervisor visited him several times, but always during one of his algebra classes. Dale was very confident and comfortable teaching the algebra classes, resulting in positive comments from his university supervisor. However, he struggled with the trigonometry class, and could sense that his mentoring teacher was displeased with his efforts. Dale confessed his concern to Alvin James, a student teacher in physical education.

Alvin suggested that Dale ask Mr. Walsky, their university supervisor, to sit in on the trigonometry class during his next school visit, so that he could give Dale

some feedback. Dale replied that Mr. Walsky had only seen him in successful experiences, and if he saw the trigonometry class, Mr. Walsky's overall evaluation at the end of the quarter would be lower. Therefore, Dale said nothing to Mr. Walsky.

1. How do you feel about Dale's situation?
2. What is your opinion of Alvin's advice?
3. What would you have done?
4. What is likely to be the result of Dale's decision?

When you are speaking with your college or university supervisor, be straightforward about your problems. He or she can act as a liaison between you and your mentoring teacher or other school personnel if the need arises. Your honesty will make the supervisor's job easier and will probably ultimately improve your situation. Furthermore, your openness about problems or concerns will also improve the rapport between you and your supervisor.

Your supervisor is there to help you. Your openness, honesty, and willingness to accept suggestions will create a good relationship that makes it easier for your supervisor to help.

MENTORING TEACHERS

A good relationship with your mentoring teacher is vital for achieving maximum benefit from the student-teaching experience. Whereas your college or university supervisor may be in contact with you once or twice a week for a period or two, your mentoring teacher is with you every day. You and your mentoring teacher will be working together for the best interest of the students.

Remember that the mentoring teacher has ultimate responsibility for the classroom to which you are assigned. She or he is legally responsible; therefore, some mentoring teachers are more hesitant than others to relinquish control. The way you conduct yourself initially will strongly influence how the mentoring teacher feels about leaving you in control. Taking an interest in everything that is going on in the classroom, asking questions about appropriate procedures and classroom rules, and making notes on information the mentoring teacher offers may be helpful. Being responsive to requests for assistance (putting up bulletin boards, grading test papers, etc.) will show the mentoring teacher that you are a willing worker.

Your appearance and manner are also important. Your mentoring teacher will feel more comfortable entrusting you with her or his charges if you dress appropriately (look more like a teacher than a student), speak correctly (use standard English), and exhibit self-confidence.

CASE STUDY 2.8

Appropriate Dress

Susan Granger was in a secondary English practicum class. Her mentoring teacher was Mrs. Barfield, a 50-year-old English teacher.

On the first day of her practicum, Susan reported to her assignment wearing a pair of jeans, a T-shirt, and a pair of tennis shoes. Before Susan had a chance to introduce herself, Mrs. Barfield made the mistake of asking her if she was a new student in the class. When Mrs. Barfield learned who Susan was, she said, "Ms. Granger, I believe you need to dress more appropriately for teaching in the future."

Susan, who noticed that Mrs. Barfield was clad in casual slacks and shirt, was furious. Later that day she said to her roommate, "Who does she think she is, telling me what to wear? She had on pants herself."

1. What do you think about Mrs. Barfield's comment to Susan?
2. Was it justified?
3. Was there a difference in Mrs. Barfield's dressing as she did and Susan being dressed as she was? If so, what was the difference?
4. Might Susan's attire affect her relationship with Mrs. Barfield? Might it affect her relationship with her secondary students?

You must conform to the dress code for teachers, if one is in place. Your college or university supervisor may provide you with information about the dress code for the school to which you are assigned, or you may be expected to discover it by reading the school's handbook for teachers or visiting the school's website. Do not assume that there is no dress code. Check to be sure before you cause yourself avoidable difficulties.

When you are given an actual teaching assignment, careful planning is likely to evoke a positive response from your mentoring teacher. Showing responsibility in small ways will encourage the mentoring teacher to give you larger responsibilities. (Chapter 6 has tips for good planning.)

Although you may be very eager to begin teaching, do not demand that your teacher let you start. Demonstrate your readiness, and then suggest that you are ready. If this fails, you may wish to consult your college or university supervisor, who can act as a liaison.

Your teacher may want to team-teach with you before letting you strike out on your own. Teaming with another teacher is a valuable experience, and it will prepare you for a possible future organizational plan. Team-teaching allows teachers to take advantage of team members' special skills. For example, if you have musical knowledge and skill, you may help drama students add a dimension to their production that the classroom teacher could not have supported. However, the classroom teacher may be able to help much more with blocking scenes than your skills would have allowed you to do. Each of you may work with the students on the production, utilizing your unique talents. A team member with particular expertise may plan the lessons in that area and do the primary teaching in it, while the other team member provides support and follows the plan provided for specific activities.

You may find that your mentoring teacher does some things differently from the way you would do them or the way you have been taught. Do not criticize her or his methods; ask why she or he does things that way. Weigh the pros and cons of the teacher's method. If you feel it is not the best way, simply ask if you can try another way in which you have some background. Most mentoring teachers expect some experimentation and will allow this without conflict. This approach can certainly help your relationship with the teacher, and, upon examination, you may find things of value in the teacher's approach that you will also wish to use. Just because you have not been exposed to an idea or approach before does not mean it is not a good one.

Most programs have specified minimum requirements that student teachers are expected to meet. However, if you are only willing to do the minimum expected of you, your relationship with the mentoring teacher may be less than perfect. Dedicated educators do not settle for doing the least they can get by with doing.

Your mentoring teacher, like your college or university supervisor, will be providing oral or written suggestions (or both) and constructive criticism. Accepting these comments as avenues to improvement will enhance the rapport between you and your mentoring teacher. If the mentoring teacher sees that you are attempting to put the suggestions to work, she or he will be more likely to have positive feelings toward you as a prospective member of the profession. Ignoring suggestions or indicating that you cannot or will not change will not promote a good relationship.

CASE STUDY 2.9

No Desire to Change

In his first conference with his mentoring teacher, Leon Garritt was told, "Mr. Garritt, you must watch your English when you are speaking to the class. I noticed you saying 'he don't' and 'I seen' several times during this single lesson."

Leon responded, "That's the way everybody talks back home. I've talked that way all my life. It's too late to change now. Besides, I'm going back home to teach. I want to sound like everyone else."

1. How do you think Leon's teacher responded to Leon's explanation?
2. Do you think Leon's reaction affected his relationship with the teacher? In what way?
3. How would you have responded if you had been in Leon's position?
4. How would you have responded if you had been Leon's teacher?
5. Does where Leon plans to teach have any relevance to the issue at hand? Why, or why not?

FOR YOUR PORTFOLIO

INTASC Standard: 9

Put a copy of your mentoring teacher's written evaluation of your teaching in your portfolio along with an explanation of your adjustments in response to this evaluation.

Taking the initiative and offering assistance before it is requested shows the teacher that you are ready to take part in classroom activities. Waiting to be told every move to make displays immaturity and lack of confidence.

Showing the mentoring teacher your preparedness, willingness, and ability to perform in the classroom can enhance your relationship. Appropriate reactions to suggestions and criticism and willingness to work cooperatively are also important.

OTHER SCHOOL PERSONNEL

In addition to building a good relationship with your mentoring teacher, you must develop positive relationships with other school personnel, including other teachers, administrators, counselors, supervisors, secretaries, the custodial staff, and cafeteria workers. From time to time you will interact with all these people.

On your first day in the school, introduce yourself to the school personnel you encounter. Tell them that you are pleased to meet them, explain that you are a student teacher or practicum student, and indicate that you may need their assistance in the future. They will appreciate your acknowledgment that you may need their help, and they may seek opportunities to help you. Even if you do not need their aid, just knowing them and realizing that they know who you are will make life in the school more comfortable.

CASE STUDY 2.10

Pleasantness Pays Off

Miss Garcia, a student teacher in first grade, went out of her way to meet and be pleasant to the school custodian, Mr. Nabors, although some of the teachers thought he was uncooperative. However, she was glad she made the effort on the first day her mentoring teacher left her in charge of the class.

The children were moving down the hall toward their classroom following a milk break, when Mario started throwing up. The children squealed and scattered as Mario's snack gushed onto the floor. Mario burst into tears.

Mr. Nabors, hearing the commotion, hurried over to help Miss Garcia. He made certain that the remainder of the class lined up again and became quiet, while Miss Garcia calmed Mario. Then he assured Miss Garcia that he would take care of clearning the hall immediately, while she continued with her normal procedures.

1. Do you think Miss Garcia's friendly approach to the custodian worked in her favor?
2. In your opinion, is it possible that the custodian's reputation is unjust?
3. How might the other teachers elicit more cooperation from him?

Other teachers may offer valuable suggestions about teaching or disciplinary actions and may provide you with support and counsel in the absence of your mentoring teacher. Administrators can help you become acclimated to the school and school policies and may also offer useful information about your professional responsibilities. Supervisors may offer critiques of your teaching procedures, or they may provide materials that will be helpful in your lessons. Custodians may help with incidents such as the one cited in the previous case study, as well as with major and minor spills of food, paints, or other classroom materials.

Cafeteria workers may alert you to problems developing in the cafeteria before they are beyond control.

In brief, you should be pleasant to all school personnel and cooperate with them as necessary. Your friendliness and cooperation will be returned in kind.

OTHER STUDENT TEACHERS AND PRACTICUM STUDENTS

Other student teachers or practicum students are probably assigned to your school; if not, you have probably been assigned to a seminar with student teachers or practicum students from other schools. These peers are facing the same challenges that you are, even though different situations make each assignment unique. If you are willing to collaborate and share your experiences openly, you may find that these peers can help you analyze and solve the problems you face. At the same time, solutions you have discovered may benefit others in the group. Openness and willingness to cooperate can make your relationships with the other student teachers or practicum students very rewarding.

Just because another student teacher or practicum student is teaching in an elementary school and you are teaching in a secondary school, or another teacher is a physical education teacher and you are a chemistry teacher, do not assume that you cannot learn from each other. Regardless of level or subject area, many of the problems student teachers and practicum students encounter, especially in human relations, are similar.

CASE STUDY 2.11

Learning from Others

Troy was assigned to a secondary geography class for his student-teaching experience. He had planned for and taught several lessons but had trouble estimating the amount of time his plans were going to take. As a result, he had twice run out of instructional material before the period ended. He hadn't known what to do, so he had just let the students have a study period each time. He mentioned his problem in his student-teaching seminar.

Carol was teaching in a sixth-grade self-contained classroom but was expected to conduct certain classes during specified periods of the day. When she had run into the same problem that Troy had, her mentoring teacher had suggested planning several extra filler, or sponge, activities for each subject area in case her lessons did not take as much time as she expected. The practice had worked well for her. She mentioned several

filler activities she had used for social studies, including blank outline maps to be filled in with data pertinent to the current topic, vocabulary card games, and construction of time lines. Troy adapted several of her ideas to meet the needs of his particular class and found that they worked well for him too. (See Chapter 4 for suggestions for filler activities.)

1. Do elementary and secondary student teachers and practicum students have many common concerns such as the one Troy and Carol shared?
2. What are some of the common concerns?

Treat your fellow student teachers and practicum students with the same respect you show the other teachers you encounter. Listen to what they have to say in your seminars, and share your knowledge with them. The relationships can be mutually beneficial.

PARENTS AND OTHER CAREGIVERS

As a practicum student you probably will not have much contact with parents and other caregivers. As a student teacher, you may or may not have much contact. If such contact occurs, however, it is vitally important that you develop good relationships with parents. (Although we use the term *parent* for convenience, some students will have other members of the family, foster parents, or others as caregivers who have the main contacts with the school. All need to be treated similarly.)

One factor in effective interaction with parents is knowing about the community in which you are teaching. Awareness of the types of businesses, industries, and recreational facilities in the community will give you some insight into the background from which the parents come. Awareness of the general socioeconomic, racial, and ethnic balance of the community also will be helpful. Knowing that the people in the town generally are avid football fans and enthusiastically support the local high school team or realizing that many work in the coal mines and may have associated health problems can give you a basis for interacting with community members with greater understanding and empathy. For this reason, it is a good idea to spend some time familiarizing yourself with the community and its people. Walk around the downtown area and observe the businesses and the people. Attend recreational activities, such as ball games, concerts, dances, and festivals, and note community interests. Drive around the residential section, and observe the types of homes in which your students live. These experiences will help prepare you for encounters with parents.

Many parents are uncomfortable in the school environment, so when parents come to the school to discuss their child's progress, the teacher (or possibly you as the student teacher) must make an effort to put them at ease. Open the conversation with a nonthreatening comment, perhaps about the weather or some recent local event. Then express your appreciation to the parent for taking the time to come to the school. It is difficult for many parents to schedule such visits, and your acknowledgment of this fact may put the parent more at ease. It is also best to begin the discussion about the student on a positive note. Almost all students have praiseworthy attributes—a pleasant manner, creativity, talent in art or music, athletic ability, cooperativeness, or excellence in a particular academic area. When called in for a conference, however, many parents expect the worst, as appears to be the case in the Sally Forth comic strip below.

Be honest with parents about problems, but do not be abrupt or unkind in your comments. Have documentation relating to the problems you are describing; for example, portfolios that contain samples of the student's work, test papers, records of homework, or records of disciplinary conferences with the student. Explain the procedures you plan to implement to correct the problems, and express anticipation of improvement. Try to end the interview with another positive note. Always stress your desire to help the child in any way you can, and urge the parents to consult you if they have any concerns. Throughout the conference, remain pleasant, calm, and objective.

If you can think of ways that parents can help with educational activities, suggest them to your mentoring teacher. Some parents may be able to serve as resource persons and provide information to the students during a special unit; for example, a parent who is a doctor might come to school to talk about a particular disease, the importance of sanitary practices to healthy living, or the importance of immunizations. A police officer, firefighter, or public official may be able to share information in a social studies class. Some parents may be able to share cultural information from their heritages during a unit on other countries. Some may be able to share knowledge of foreign languages, music, dances, and art forms that they know. Others may be able to perform needed tasks, such as building a piece of scenery or making costumes for a play, chaperoning a field trip, listening to students read orally for practice, reading to students, and teaching team sports to students. If you make parents welcome to participate in your classroom in various ways and show your appreciation for their knowledge and helpfulness, they will tend to look favorably upon you as their child's teacher.

It is important that parents perceive you as a competent professional who is truly concerned about their children. If you put your best foot forward in any encounter with parents, they are more likely to be supportive of your plans for the students.

Listen to what parents tell you about their children. They can often supply information that will help you understand the students' strengths and weaknesses and thus help you plan instruction that will be most beneficial to the students. Parents will also be favorably impressed with your willingness to listen to them.

If you meet parents outside the school setting, smile and speak to them. Do not bring up problems at

chance meetings; these should be covered in carefully planned conferences.

CASE STUDY 2.12

Careless Comments Cause Problems

Mr. Meadows, a student teacher in a junior high school, saw the father of Joe Mills, one of his general science students, in the supermarket. Mr. Meadows walked over to Mr. Mills and said, "If Joe doesn't start coming to class more regularly, I will have to give him a failing grade. I think he cuts class to sneak off and smoke."

Mr. Mills was visibly upset. "Why haven't I been notified of this?" he demanded. "Why don't you keep parents adequately informed?" Then he turned and stalked away.

The next day, Mr. Meadows' mentoring teacher, Mrs. Daily, told him that Mr. Mills had called the principal and spoken angrily to him about the way the general science class was being handled. The principal demanded an explanation from Mrs. Daily. Now Mrs. Daily demanded an explanation from Mr. Meadows.

1. What mistakes did Mr. Meadows make in his contact with Mr. Mills?
2. What should he have done instead?
3. What would you have done?

Parents are potential allies. If you make an effort to communicate with them appropriately, they can help you better understand your students. Parents have their children's best interests at heart and will respond favorably to you if they believe you do, too.

DISCUSSION QUESTIONS

1. What conditions could cause problems in developing good relationships with your students? How might you work to overcome these difficulties?
2. Are there any special problems in developing good relationships with students of racial or ethnic groups different from yours? What are they? How can they be overcome?
3. How may knowing that the college or university supervisor is giving you a grade affect your relationship with him or her? Should this happen? Why or why not?
4. Why should you avoid criticism of your mentoring teacher's methods?

5. Why is it a good policy to develop positive relationships with many school personnel?
6. How can your relationships with other student teachers benefit your student teaching?
7. How could your poor relationships with parents inhibit a student's progress?
8. What will you do if:
   a. You are a student teacher in second grade, and an apparently bright and curious Vietnamese boy, who speaks no English, is in your class. Your mentoring teacher has ignored him, letting him entertain himself during lessons. The boy's father, an engineering student at a university, speaks broken English. The boy's mother is free during the day, but she speaks only a few words of English. No one in your school speaks any Vietnamese.
   b. You are student teaching in sixth grade, and a girl in your class comes from an impoverished home with no running water. The child's clothes are filthy. Her face and hands are encrusted with grime, and she smells bad. The other children make fun of her and refuse to sit next to her.
9. A student teacher in a secondary school located in an area with little racial diversity wrote the following entry in her journal of reactions to daily events at school: "Students from other countries were visiting the school for some FFA event. One of my students walked out in the hallway (before class) and spoke to a visiting student, using a racial slur. I'm so tired of all these racial problems. They seem to get worse every year." How should she have handled this situation?
10. The student teacher in Question 9 was told by her supervisor, "You could approach a situation like this by asking the student to put himself in the other person's place and think how the remarks would make him feel."
    a. Do you think this advice would work? Why or why not?
    b. What other advice could have helped her to deal with such a situation?
11. How could you identify the following types of students: (a) gifted; (b) learning disabled; (c) culturally diverse?
12. Consider one content or subject area. How would you challenge the gifted student?
13. How can you consider the needs of culturally diverse students in the instructional program?
14. What are your responsibilities toward the included student?
15. How can you and special resource personnel cooperate to ensure the best program for students with exceptionalities?

16. In the ninth-grade history class where you are a student teacher, a student named Roberto speaks fluent Spanish but refuses to try to learn more than the small amount of English he already knows. Many of the other students are Mexican Americans like Roberto, but unlike him, they are learning English rapidly. When it is time to give a test over the unit you have been studying, Roberto is the only one who has difficulty reading the questions. What would you do? Would you translate into Spanish for him (assuming you can), read the questions to him in English, or let him do the best he can with the test on his own? Explain your answer.

17. What things could you do that would keep parents from always expecting the worst when they are asked to come to school for a conference, as was the case in the Sally Forth comic strip in this chapter?

Chapter 3

Creating a Learning Environment

Case Study 3.1: Chaos in the Classroom

Miss Collins, a student teacher, has been successfully using the Newspaper in Education program with her ninth-grade students. As a culminating unit activity, she expects the students to publish a newspaper of their own. She has divided them into groups for writing their paper.

Li-Jan: Miss Collins, what am I supposed to do?

Miss Collins: What is your job?

Li-Jan: I'm supposed to be the sports editor.

Tony: Miss Collins, where are we supposed to work?

Miss Collins: What is your group, Tony?

Tony: Feature stories.

Miss Collins: Well, try to find a place over by the bulletin board.

David: That's where you said we could work, Miss Collins.

Miss Collins: Well, find another place then, Tony. What is your group, David?

Li-Jan: Miss Collins—

Miss Collins: Just a minute, Li-Jan. What did you say, David?

David: We're writing the ads.

Miss Collins: Oh, that's right. Now, Li-Jan, what did you want?

Li-Jan: What is the sports editor supposed to do?

Miss Collins: Look at the sports section of the paper, and see if you can figure out what's supposed to be in there.

Li-Jan: Who's supposed to be in my group? I can't find anyone to work with me.

Miss Collins: Let's see. I know I have that list here somewhere. It must be under these papers.

Linda: Miss Collins, Joe says he's in charge of the news stories, but yesterday you said I could do that.

Miss Collins (to the whole class in a raised, agitated voice): Everyone be quiet! We can't work in here with all that noise. Get busy now.

Li-Jan: Is it okay if I just write something about what our softball team did over the weekend?

Miss Collins: Yes, that'll be fine, Li-Jan. Just do that. I can't seem to find who the other members of your group are.

Phil and Steve: Miss Collins, you said we needed to go interview some other teachers. Is it okay if we do that now?

Miss Collins: I'm not sure.

Joe (approaching Miss Collins angrily): How come Linda says she's supposed to do news stories? I thought you told me to do that.

Linda (addressing Joe): She told me to do them!

Miss Collins: Why don't you two work together on them?

Joe (shuffling off and muttering under his breath): I can't stand that girl. She's a creep. She can do it by herself for all I care.

Phil and Steve: What about it? Can we go?

Miss Collins: Go where? Oh, yes, I remember. Did you make appointments with anyone?

Phil and Steve: No, were we supposed to?

Miss Collins: Well, you really should.

Diane: It's almost time for my bus. May I be dismissed?

Miss Collins: I had no idea it was that late already. Yes, go to your bus.

Miss Collins (addressing the class): Class! (No one hears.) Class! (Still no one hears amidst the laughter, talking, and running around the room.) Everyone! (now shouting to be heard) Clean up your work, and get in your seats. We will be dismissing soon.

The students finally hear her and begin to gather their things together. School is dismissed before they finish, and Miss Collins must straighten up the rest of the room herself. At this point, her mentoring teacher walks in and asks, "Well, how did everything go?"

Miss Collins (with a heavy sigh): I'll never try that again. These kids don't know how to work in groups.

1. Was Miss Collins' idea for a culminating activity a good one? How might it have been handled more successfully?

2. What mistakes did Miss Collins make in assigning group activities? How could she have prevented some of the problems?

3. Why do you think Miss Collins ran out of time? What factors should be considered when scheduling activities such as this one to be sure there is enough time?

4. What could Miss Collins have done to get the students' attention instead of shouting at them? How could she have reduced the noise level while the students were working?

5. Do you agree with Miss Collins that these students can't work in groups? Do you think she was right to say she'll never try group work again?

SUPPORT SYSTEM FOR TEACHING

Although knowing your subject and how to teach it is important, students won't learn if your plans go awry because of poor classroom management. The Interstate New Teacher Assessment Support Consortium (INTASC) has identified an expectation for beginning teachers regarding skills in classroom management. Beginning teachers "use an understanding of individual and group motivation and behavior to create a learning environment that encourages positive social interaction, active engagement in learning, and self motivation" (INTASC, 1992).

As a practicum or student teacher, you have numerous opportunities to apply your knowledge of human development and learning. You are responsible for establishing nonthreatening climates where all students are comfortable and engaged in purposeful learning tasks. Classroom management includes all of the teacher's efforts to organize the learning environment or create a learning community so that learning is purposeful and productive. It involves the management of learning materials, resources, time, classroom space, and students (Wong and Wong, 1998).

CLASSROOM MANAGEMENT

Classrooms range along a continuum from highly structured to extremely flexible. While one teacher may assign seats arranged in perfect rows, another may have a room filled with clusters of chairs for small-group work and areas designated for learning centers. Regardless of the structure or flexibility in your classroom, you must do a great deal of planning and classroom management.

In order to create a positive learning climate, a positive student-teacher relationship must be established. When teachers provide a collaborative, supportive student environment, there are fewer disruptions and discipline problems (Thompson, 1998). Planning for effective instruction involves developing and implementing a classroom management plan and knowing how to organize the classroom environment for optimal use of resources and time.

Wong and Wong (1998) describe a well-managed classroom as one with a high level of student involvement in the tasks, clear expectations, few disruptions and little wasted time, and a task-oriented but comfortable climate. Wong and Wong suggest that teachers who create a positive learning climate and demonstrate effective classroom management begin by laying the foundation on the very first day of school. At this time it is extremely important to create a sense of security and acceptance. Effective teachers spend time on class-building and team-building activities while sharing their expectations. Many times students provide valuable input in the formation of classroom expectations. It is also important to identify routines or procedures and discuss acceptable methods for completing them, which may involve simulating them during the beginning of the school year. Clear expectations for procedural tasks can eliminate confusion and wasted classroom time.

ORGANIZATIONAL PLANS

Individualization

Each student has a unique personality, experiential background, level of language facility, degree of academic potential, attitude, cultural background, and home environment. Ideally, teachers would work with each student individually, but this arrangement is impractical, of course. Nevertheless, teachers should provide students with opportunities to work individually at times in order to pursue special interests and proceed at their own paces. Some ideas for independent activities follow.

1. Sustained silent reading (SSR)—In this program, students, teachers, and perhaps the entire school staff read materials of their choice during an agreed-upon period each school day (generally between 15 and 30 minutes long).
2. Journal writing—Each student writes a daily entry in a notebook. Entries may consist of reactions to lessons, communications with the teacher, or special concerns. Teachers may read the journal entries and respond to them.
3. Computer-assisted instruction—Students work on computer programs to practice skills, play games, write compositions, or solve puzzles.
4. Differentiated learning centers—Students work independently on special projects at specially created learning centers. These centers give students choices of activities that extend classroom learning based upon previously taught concepts.
5. Research reports—Students choose topics to investigate, find reference materials in the library, organize the content, and prepare oral or written reports or multimedia presentations.

Flexible Grouping

Grouping is a compromise between totally individualized and whole-class instruction. Individual differences can be reduced to some extent by achievement grouping, but many differences still remain.

Other forms of grouping serve other functions. You will be concerned primarily with intraclass groupings

(groupings within the classroom). Your mentoring teacher may use small groups for instructional purposes. As you teach, try flexible grouping as a way to meet your objectives.

Groups can serve different purposes. During some reading instruction, such as guided reading, children with similar attributes meet together. Groups may also be formed for students having difficulty with particular skills in specific subject areas, such as math or writing. In social studies, students may work together in research groups, while groups in science classes may perform experiments that illustrate certain concepts. Physical education classes may be divided into homogeneous groups according to skill level, or into heterogeneous groups so that less able students can benefit from interaction with more proficient students. Groups may be short-term or long-term, depending on the time required to meet standards.

You may wish to try interest grouping. Ask students to list topics of interest or complete an interest inventory; then identify the most popular topics and ask students to sign up for their first, second, and third choices. Form groups based on your findings.

Achievement groups can reduce the range of individual differences that the teacher must meet in a specific lesson and help the teacher focus on each group's strengths and needs. However, when groups are set up on the basis of achievement levels, low-achieving students often develop poor self-concepts. By forming project and interest groups, you encourage students of differing achievement levels to work together, and students contribute according to their particular knowledge, skills, or talents.

The groups you form and the way you conduct them can make an impact on the way students respond to tasks. Read the following case studies and notice the way each teacher uses groups.

CASE STUDY 3.2

Let's Find Out About Dinosaurs!

After surveying his students' interests, Mr. Barnes places the children in groups according to their preferences. One group, consisting of three children from the low-achievement group, two from the middle group, and three from the high group chooses dinosaurs. Their assignment is to create a room display and give a presentation after 2 weeks of work.

Almost immediately, the students are excitedly delving into books, working on drawings, sharing models from home, and planning their presentations. Jessica suggests

they contact the librarian, who may have some videos. Seth wants to share a kit he got for Christmas for the display. Amy offers to draw a backdrop for the display, and Andy says he'll find some leaves and moss to make the display look more natural. Robert is studying dinosaur habitats so that the display will be as accurate as possible, and Ruth is outlining topics for a report she plans to write. At least during this period, achievement levels are forgotten.

CASE STUDY 3.3

Which Invention Will It Be?

Ms. Ting wants to get all her students involved in a unit on inventions, so she forms groups, each consisting of one or two leaders and three or four students who have not been participating actively in class. Each group must decide which invention has had the greatest impact on the progress of the human race.

Working secretly in their groups, the students investigate inventions, select the ones they feel are most influential, and find information to support their choices. They know they'll have to support their selections with facts, so they seek evidence from many library sources, as well as from teachers and others they consider authorities. Instead of only a small number of students participating, everyone works creatively to prove that his or her group's invention is most significant.

1. How did Mr. Barnes and Ms. Ting use grouping? How successful were they? What benefits resulted from such groupings?
2. What are some ways you have observed groups working well? How could you organize your class into groups that would actively involve all students?

The preceding case studies demonstrate the importance of getting all students involved as active and productive participants in the learning process through effective grouping. Here are some guidelines to help you form and manage groups.

1. Don't begin impulsively. Think your plan through carefully before you start.
2. Try to make your groups a workable size, small enough that everyone must participate but large enough to develop a worthy project. Generally, four to six students will work well.
3. Avoid putting students who cause trouble when they are together in the same groups.

4. Be sure that resource materials—references and supplies—are available and that students know how to use them.

5. Establish clear expectations so that students know their privileges and limitations. Make sure before starting that all the students understand exactly what they are to do. Allow them freedom to talk quietly and move around the room. If possible, let them go to the library or media center for additional information.

6. Assign roles that have clearly defined responsibilities and also design an accountability measure, such as a rubric for scoring, so that the students know what standards the final projects or products should meet.

7. Experiment with the length of time for maintaining groups; allow enough time to get something accomplished but not so much that students lose interest and stray off task.

8. Give each group space to carry out its activity without interfering with the other students.

9. Be available to facilitate and offer ideas.

Complete Activity 3.1 on grouping patterns to help you analyze the uses of grouping in your classroom situation.

Cooperative Learning

In cooperative learning, students work in groups or as teams to help each other acquire information. Sometimes students discuss material or practice skills that the teacher has presented; at other times they use cooperative methods to discover information on their own. Two key elements are individual accountability and positive interdependence (Slavin, 1990, 1991).

Cooperative learning has been used successfully at all grade levels and in every subject area. Its benefits include increased self-esteem, better intergroup relations, more positive attitudes toward school, higher academic achievement, and acceptance of students in an inclusion setting. Cooperative learning is especially effective with students from diverse cultural backgrounds, including English language learners (ELL), who acquire social behaviors, learn content, and practice English during group interactions. Also, for students from many cultures cooperative arrangements seem to be more natural than competitive situations.

Because cooperative learning has possible academic and social benefits, you may want to try it with your classes. Although workshops and courses can provide training, some self-study and guidance from other teachers may be enough to help you get started. Become familiar with some of the most widely used

cooperative learning models so that you can choose an appropriate one. Figure 3–1 shows five methods of student team learning (STL), a type of cooperative learning.

Here are some features of effective cooperative learning.

1. Appropriate room arrangement to facilitate group work.

2. Reasonable time period set for reaching goals.

3. Group size appropriate for the task (usually four to six students), with more complex tasks requiring more members.

4. Understanding of goals, procedures, tasks, and methods of evaluation by each group member.

5. A teacher who facilitates by circulating, first by checking to see that everyone understands, then by asking individuals questions about content.

6. A problem, goal, or task that requires higher-order thinking skills and is viewed as important by the students.

7. Active participation by each group member, often by assignment of specific roles or responsibilities.

8. Individual accountability by having each member complete a test, make a presentation, write a paper, or provide a product.

9. Positive interdependence by making group members dependent on each other for meeting goals.

10. Heterogeneous group composition, with members from high-, low-, and average-achievement levels.

11. Acceptable social behaviors and interactions.

12. Thoughtful group discussions in which members provide reasons for their responses.

CASE STUDY 3.4

Cooperative Learning— What Went Wrong?

After a lesson about the signing of the Declaration of Independence, Ms. Grady formed groups of five students each to reinforce the lesson. She asked them to use the textbook to answer factual questions on a worksheet. One student from each group would be responsible for finding the answer, and another would be the recorder.

As the students began working, Ms. Grady checked to see if they were finding the answers. The first group was on task, but the second group was having some problems. Ms. Grady sat with this group for the remainder of the class period, helping them locate answers in the text. Whenever the class got too noisy, she reminded the students to work quietly.

ACTIVITY 3.1 | *Grouping Patterns*

Place a checkmark (✓) beside each type of grouping that is currently being used in your classroom. Place a plus sign (+) beside any type of grouping not currently being used that you intend to try. Note your reasons at the bottom of the page.

_____ Achievement grouping to put students of similar achievement together

_____ Needs, or skills, grouping to correct problems

_____ Research grouping to investigate topics or themes

_____ Project grouping to perform experiments or carry out construction activities

_____ Interest grouping to allow students to pursue special interests

FIGURE 3–1
Methods of Student Team
Learning (STL)

Student Teams-Achievement Divisions (STAD)—After the teacher has presented the lesson, four-member student teams of mixed ability help each other learn the material. Each member takes an individual test, and scores are computed to arrive at team scores. Teams that meet certain criteria earn rewards, which are usually certificates.

Teams-Games-Tournament (TGT)—This procedure begins like STAD, but weekly tournaments replace quizzes. Groups of students of similar achievement levels, representing their home team, compete at tournament tables. Points earned in the tournment are taken back to home teams. Points of team members are averaged.

Team Assisted Individualization (TAI)—Combining cooperative learning with individualized instruction, TAI is used to teach math to students in grades 3 through 6. Team members usually work on different units but help each other with problems and check answers. Groups earn points as members complete units and do extra work.

Cooperative Integrated Reading and Composition (CIRC)—Teachers use CIRC to teach reading and writing from literature-based readers to students in grades 3 through 5. Students work in pairs as they read to each other, make predictions, write responses to stories, and so on. They take quizzes and may also "publish" team books.

Jigsaw—The teacher divides information to be studied into categories and puts students in home groups, with each student responsible for learning a different category. Expert groups, consisting of all students who have studied the same category, meet to review content and prepare to teach it. Experts return to their home groups and take turns teaching the material.

At the end of the period, each group turned in a worksheet. Ms. Grady marked their papers, with each group member receiving the group's grade. Some students complained that the grading wasn't fair because they didn't have a chance to participate, but Ms. Grady said that's the way cooperative learning works.

1. Was this task appropriate for cooperative learning? Did it cause students to think, or was it simply a literal question-answer exercise? How could Ms. Grady create a stimulating task from this topic for cooperative learning?
2. How did Ms. Grady perform as a facilitator? What could she have done differently to be more effective?
3. Was each student actively involved? Why did some students resent the grading procedure? How could each student have been an active participant?
4. Was there evidence of both individual accountability and positive interdependence? If so, what evidence was there?
5. Considering your answers to the previous questions, did Ms. Grady understand how cooperative learning works?

Whole-Class Instruction

Whole-class instruction is often most effective for specific purposes. Appropriate activities for the entire class include listening to a resource visitor, contributing ideas for a theme study, viewing a video or multimedia presentation, participating in a discussion, watching a demonstration, listening to an ongoing story, brainstorming ideas, writing a language experience story, and creating a semantic map. Whole-class activities build a sense of belonging.

Integrated Curriculum

Believing that students learn best when concepts are interrelated and reinforced, many teachers implement theme studies that span the curriculum. Instead of fragmented, isolated subjects taught throughout the day, these teachers identify worthy themes that enable students to see real-world connections. Students use reading and writing all day in authentic situations as they investigate topics related to themes. Chapter 4 features more on theme studies.

If you want to teach through themes, consult your mentoring teacher and the curriculum guide to select a significant topic. Be sure that your theme merits the time that you will need to give it! Then plan extensively, considering ways to apply the theme to different curriculum areas. Involve your students in planning, gathering resources, researching topics, learning concepts, designing projects, developing a culminating activity, and evaluating their progress. Ideally, teachers should carry out theme studies throughout the entire day, but you may feel more comfortable starting in a limited way, perhaps by integrating language arts and social studies and teaching other subjects separately.

FOR YOUR PORTFOLIO

INTASC Standards: 1, 5, 7

Outline a unit in which you integrated learning across much of the curriculum. Even if you teach a single subject, you may still have been able to integrate other subjects, particularly language skills.

CASE STUDY 3.5

To Integrate or Not to Integrate

As Kathy Jenkins sat in a seminar listening to a discussion of integrated curriculum, she reflected on her two student-teaching experiences. Her first assignment had been in the second grade at Spring Street School. She recalled planning lessons for handwriting, spelling, grammar, and reading. Each subject was taught from a different book, and no lesson related in any way to another. She remembered doing a unit on forest animals, but it didn't tie in with what the students were doing in any other subject. Her lesson plan book had been filled with small blocks of time, each centered on a different subject or skill.

In her current fifth-grade class at Northside School, her teacher was centering instruction around the theme of survival. Kathy was amazed at the way Mr. Sundaram was able to connect nearly every subject, although he did teach math lessons from the math book. "Perhaps what impresses me most," thought Kathy, "is the way the children are planning so many of the activities themselves. They are discovering material on adventurers, on national heroes, and on people who showed courage in various ways. They're creating projects on endangered plants and animals in the rain forests, and they're writing books on survival skills in the wilderness. They've found dozens of books—fiction, nonfiction, and biography—to use as resources. They've invited a forest ranger to speak on survival in the woods and a nurse to speak on health hazards. They've learned new words related to the theme— and how to spell them. I never imagined there were so many ways to tie survival skills into the curriculum." Comparing the two experiences, Kathy remembered how the second-graders sat quietly in orderly rows as the teacher did the talking. These fifth-graders, in contrast, were constantly moving about and talking with each other.

Listening to a visiting storyteller is a large-group activity, sometimes involving whole classes.

It was hard to tell exactly what they were doing some-times. "Even though I find theme studies exciting," Kathy thought, "I'm not sure I could manage them successfully."

1. Compare the advantages for the students of a segmented and an integrated curriculum. In which of Kathy's classrooms do you believe the students were learning more? Why do you think so?
2. What are some problems created by integrating the curriculum? How can you be sure you are covering everything if you don't follow a textbook in each subject?
3. What are some ways to involve students in planning and implementing theme studies? How can you use their ideas?

SCHEDULING

Time affects nearly every phase of your teaching, from how much you accomplish and how well you hold the interest of your students to how you feel as you proceed through the day. Good time management is a characteristic of an effective teacher.

Flexibility Within a Routine

A well-planned routine helps you identify what you need to accomplish, builds student security by letting the students know what to expect next, and provides you with a structure for the day.

You will probably begin teaching by following the schedule already set by your mentoring teacher. Don't be a slave to your schedule, however; it is for your convenience. Don't let it become an obstruction to learning. Sometimes, to develop a concept fully, you will need more time than what is scheduled. You may want to use multimedia, invite a resource person, or take a field trip. You may get into an activity and realize that some really creative experiences are taking place. Whenever possible, allow these learning experiences to continue, even if it means extending them beyond the scheduled time limit.

One way to have flexible scheduling within a fixed schedule in a self-contained classroom is to plan on a weekly instead of a daily basis. For example, you may spend 20 minutes extra on math today because you are working with manipulative materials and cut 20 minutes out of language arts. You can pay back this time later in the week. Some schools offer flexibility through block scheduling, in which blocks of time are skillfully arranged to meet instructional needs. When considering scheduling, be aware that some students report to supportive classes. A handful may go to reading lab from 10:10 to 10:40 three times a week; another group may go to a class for gifted students from 1:15 to 2:15 every Friday. Don't plan an activity for the whole class when some students will be elsewhere.

Using Time Effectively

Your time, both in and out of the classroom, is precious. Many of the procedures that have become habitual for experienced teachers will require detailed planning for you. In order to have time for yourself, make use of planning periods during school. Don't depend on this time, however, as unexpected interruptions frequently occur throughout the school day.

Evenings and weekends are not entirely your own during student teaching. You may be working with your mentoring teacher on the yearbook, sharing late afternoon bus duty, or coaching the football team well into the evening. Sometimes you will have a parent-teacher conference after school or a meeting in the evening. Record keeping also takes a great deal of time. For these and other reasons, many universities do not permit student teachers to take additional courses. If you have held a part-time job during your college years, you may have to quit or reduce your hours. Avoid committing too much time to extracurricular or social activities, because full-time student teaching is generally much more demanding of your time than 15 or 18 hours of coursework.

Because of demands on your time, you must plan well ahead. Order or reserve materials in advance. If you need to make several games or posters, buy all the materials at once. A single trip to the library or media center can serve many purposes if you get resource material you will need over a period of time. In addition to searching through curriculum guides for ideas, brainstorm for a few minutes. Your own ideas are often as good as or better than those you find elsewhere.

The following tips will help you keep things moving in the classroom:

1. Have learning centers ready for action, fully equipped and neatly arranged.
2. Put markers in your books so that you can turn quickly to the right pages.
3. Be sure all needed resource materials are readily available, including supplies you will ask students to distribute.
4. Make sure students can transition from one activity to the next with little disruption, wasted time, or confusion.
5. Prepare for the next day's lessons before you go home unless you are an early riser and prefer to come in and get things ready early in the morning.

No class always operates on schedule. Sometimes something funny happens, and everyone needs to take time for a good laugh. Although you may lose some time from a scheduled activity by taking advantage of a "teachable moment," this time is well spent. For instance, when the first snow falls, let the students go to the window and watch. Then share a poem or a song about snow, or talk about how snowflakes form, and note their delicate beauty. After a particularly tense test-taking session, students may need time to relax.

Remember—schedules do keep things moving along, but they are not cast in concrete.

Filler, or Sponge, Activities

Even the most experienced teacher cannot predict exactly how long a lesson will take. As a relatively inexperienced teacher, you will often find yourself running out of time—or having time left over. The best filler (or sponge) activities when you have extra time are those that directly relate to your lesson or unit and are age/grade appropriate. For instance, if you are teaching a unit on energy, the students could brainstorm several ways to conserve or produce energy. Try to plan one or more filler activities for each lesson in case you have time left over. Chapter 8 provides specific examples of filler activities.

RECORD KEEPING

Every teacher is responsible for keeping records. Since the amount and type of record keeping varies from one school system to another, your mentoring teacher will show you what records your school requires. When you are responsible for keeping records, record the information promptly so that you don't forget to do it later. Keeping accurate records is an important aspect of professionalism.

School Records

The attendance register is an important school record. Class roll must be taken daily or every class period, and all absences and cases of tardiness recorded. These records are used for various purposes, including computing average daily attendance for state funding. The state allocates a certain amount of money for each child counted in the average daily attendance record. Records are sometimes used in court cases to verify a student's presence in school on a particular day. Attendance information is summarized at the end of every month. Even though these records may be handled electronically or by office personnel, you should learn how to do them yourself, especially since you may need access to them when help may not be available. You need to know when students have been absent and may have missed an important lesson so that you can help them catch up.

As a student teacher, you will probably have very little responsibility for ordering books and supplies or keeping inventory. However it would be a good idea to learn these procedures for the future. Become familiar with school supply catalogs so that you know what materials are available, what they cost, and how to order them.

You will also have to keep records related to your teaching. Record in a daily lesson plan book brief outlines of your lessons and page numbers of material you expect to cover in each class. Since you can never be sure exactly how far you will get in your lesson, you will probably have to modify these plans slightly from day to day. If you schedule a field trip in connection with a lesson, you must keep records of parents' permission notes and any money you collect. Using audiovisual media may require completed request forms. You may want to give the school media specialist a list of topics you will be covering and request help in locating appropriate books and materials.

Reflective Record Keeping

As part of your student teaching or practicum assignment, you may keep a journal to record the lessons you teach, your feelings about teaching, or both, as well as some of the funny things the students say or insights about teaching you don't want to forget. Later, looking back, you will probably notice how your attitudes changed and your confidence grew as the weeks passed.

FOR YOUR PORTFOLIO

INTASC Standard: 7
Photocopy a page or pages from your daily lesson plan book when you were teaching full-time and include it in your portfolio.

Reporting Students' Progress

Keeping track of students' progress is another important form of record keeping. You should keep records of daily quizzes and completed daily assignments, as well as major test scores. Your mentoring teacher probably has a grade book with each student's grades before you arrived. You may be expected to record your grades in this book, or you may have your own grade book.

Some teachers keep student assessment results in folders or portfolios at school for monitoring each student's progress throughout the year. Parents should be kept aware of their child's performance; therefore, teachers often send tests and other papers home with students. If you decide to send papers home but are not sure all the students are showing the papers to their parents, ask the students to have a parent sign each paper and then return it to you.

Some computer-managed instructional systems in areas such as reading and mathematics generate reports on students' progress. These reports may indicate what skills each student needs, what skills have been mastered, and sometimes what assignments have been given. Some reports are for your use as a teacher, whereas other reports are for parents.

Reporting to parents can be done through report cards, descriptive letters, or orally at parent-teacher conferences. Your mentoring teacher may ask you to assist in assigning grades on report cards or to assume the full responsibility for grades during your student-teaching period. In either case, be sure you thoroughly understand the school's grading system. Most schools give grades according to achievement, while some grade on the basis of students' ability. Most report cards have a place for comments, which you may or may not wish to use. Putting grades on report cards requires some hard decisions. If the responsibility is yours, be sure to have good records of students' work and evidence on which to base your decisions. You may want to send notes to parents of students who have behaved or achieved unusually well. These notes are always welcome and help build positive relationships among the student, parents, school, and you. These notes will be especially appreciated by students who rarely receive praise and are often in trouble. If you regularly send favorable comments home, the students are likely to do better work for you.

CASE STUDY 3.6

No Records for Support

Miss Patel, a student teacher, has recently been concerned about Vinetta's behavior. Vinetta doesn't do her homework and doesn't seem to be doing good work in class. Miss Patel decides to ask Vinetta's mother, Mrs. Kolsky, to come for a conference. Mr. Kent is the mentoring teacher.

Miss Patel: *Good afternoon, Mrs. Kolsky, I'm Miss Patel, Vinetta's student teacher. I'm glad you were able to come to talk with me about Vinetta.*

Mrs. Kolsky: *Yes. I hope Vinetta is getting along all right.*

Miss Patel: *That's just it, Mrs. Kolsky. Vinetta doesn't seem to be doing as well as she could be.*

Mrs. Kolsky: *Why not? What's wrong? Is there a problem?*

Miss Patel: *She isn't doing her homework, and she isn't doing very well in her classwork, either.*

Mrs. Kolsky: *Well, this is the first I've known anything about homework. And what do you mean she isn't doing well in her classwork?*

Miss Patel: *I've been assigning homework for each night, but Vinetta never has hers done. As far as classwork is concerned, she just doesn't seem to be doing her best work any more.*

Mrs. Kolsky: *May I see her grades on her classwork and her test grades? I'd like to look at the tests to see what she is having trouble with, too.*

Miss Patel: *I'm afraid I don't have any records of her classwork. I've given some quizzes, but I've let the students take them home. I have the scores but not the papers. I can remember, though, that she didn't do very well on any of her classwork. And the test scores are low. Didn't she bring her tests home?*

Mrs. Kolsky: *No, she hasn't brought any of them home. It seems to me you don't really know what you're talking about. You say she isn't doing well, but you can't show me any papers. When I ask you what she isn't doing well in, you don't seem to have any definite answers. These test grades are just numbers. What is she having trouble with? I don't think there's anything wrong with Vinetta at all. I think you just don't have your facts straight. I'd better talk to Mr. Kent.*

1. Was it a good idea for Miss Patel to have a conference with Vinetta's mother if she felt Vinetta could be doing better work?
2. What went wrong with Miss Patel's conference?
3. What could she have done to back up her statements to Mrs. Kolsky?
4. Is there any way to make sure parents know their children have homework assignments? How can you be sure parents actually see the test papers you return?

You may want to record student information in an anecdotal report—an objective, detailed account of a student's behavior. Your reasons for selecting particular students to observe may vary; nevertheless, be accurate and objective in recording your observations. Write the date and time of each observation, and try to include everything that happens, both positive and negative. Ideally, the student won't realize what you are doing, and will continue to act naturally. Choose a student to observe and complete Activity 3.2, an anecdotal report.

A cumulative record file in the school office generally contains health and attendance records, comments by school personnel, various test scores, and all official student records. As a student teacher, you will probably be allowed to see this information, but remember that it is confidential.

CASE STUDY 3.7

To Look or Not to Look

Three student teachers—Miss Luke, Mr. Feinstein, and Mrs. Tsai—are talking while waiting for their seminar to begin. They have been student teachers for 4 weeks.

Miss Luke: *Do you know what cumulative records are?*

Mr. Feinstein: *I think they are some records in the office files that nobody ever looks at.*

Mrs. Tsai: *They are kept in the office, but I've looked at the ones on my students. My mentoring teacher took me right down on the first day I got my classes and told me where they were and that he expected me to read them all the first week. Some of them are really eye-openers, I'll tell you!*

Miss Luke: *What do you mean?*

Mrs. Tsai: *I really learned a lot about my students, and I knew just how to treat them right from the beginning. Linda's file said that one time they caught her stealing a CD player, so I don't trust her for a minute. Anytime anything disappears, I feel sure Linda had something to do with it. And Tad. They said all through the grades that Tad has been a discipline problem, and they're surely right. He's always causing trouble.*

Mr. Feinstein: *I'm not sure it's right to read all that personal information about your students. Doesn't that influence how you feel about them?*

Mrs. Tsai: *Sure, it influences how I feel. But this way I know right away all I need to know about the students instead of waiting until the end of the semester to find out.*

Miss Luke: *I'm not going to look at my students' cumulative records. I want to make up my own mind about them and not go by what other teachers have said.*

Mr. Feinstein: *But suppose there's something really important in there? Something we should know about? Maybe one of the students had psychological testing or something and the psychologist made recommendations about how he or she learns best. Wouldn't that be helpful?*

Mrs. Tsai: *Definitely! It said in one of the records that Chad's parents had been divorced a couple of years ago and he had a real emotional problem with that. The teacher suggested that we all be patient with him and consider his feelings.*

Miss Luke: *I'm just not sure if it's a good idea to read all those records. It still might do more harm than good.*

1. How do you feel about reading your students' cumulative records? If you feel you should read them, should you look at them as soon as you meet the students or at some later time?
2. How could the information in cumulative records be helpful? How could it be misused?
3. What is the purpose of keeping cumulative records?
4. Do you think Mrs. Tsai is able to treat Linda and Tad objectively? Would she have arrived at the same conclusions about these two students if she hadn't read their files? Do students tend to meet our expectations of them?
5. Who is allowed to read cumulative records? Do you know what the law says about this?
6. Did Mrs. Tsai breach confidentiality when she gave out personal information about her students to her peers? How could she have discussed this issue without violating confidentiality?

Before examining students' cumulative records, give yourself enough time to evaluate the students for yourself. Then look at the records to learn more about them. When you read the files, keep in mind that test scores do not always accurately reflect a student's capability. Also, be sure to look for information through observations of specific situations. Avoid being swayed by unsupported generalizations and opinions offered by previous teachers. Using cumulative records wisely can help you understand your students better and help you plan appropriate learning activities for those with special needs.

The Family Educational Rights and Privacy Act of 1974 (PL 93-380) governs the control of students' records. Students over 18 years old or parents of students under 18 may examine these records—they have access to all teachers' comments (except notes of teachers or administrators for personal use), test scores, and special reports in the file. However, the law forbids anyone else except those directly involved in the students' education to see the records without written consent.

SUPERVISION OF STUDENTS

You may share your mentoring teacher's assigned supervisory responsibilities, such as performing cafeteria, hall, or bus duty, or supervising study hall. Each school has its own policies regarding supervision of students waiting for buses, moving through hallways, eating in the cafeteria, and working in study halls. Observe your mentoring teacher closely, and learn the ground rules for these situations so that you can handle them properly.

You may have hall or bus duty. Hall duty simply means supervising students in the halls as they change classes. Teachers are expected to keep an orderly flow of traffic, direct new students, and help with problems in school hallways. In some schools,

ACTIVITY 3.2 | *Anecdotal Report*

Name of student selected:

Reason(s) for selection:

Types of information you are seeking:

Begin your anecdotal records below with your first entry. Be sure to include the date, time, and location of the observed behavior. If there is not enough room on the bottom of this page, use the back of the page to finish the first record. Continue with other entries on separate sheets of paper. Staple them, in order, to this cover sheet.

bus duty is handled by each student's homeroom teacher; in other schools, students assemble in a central location, where they are supervised by one or more teachers. If you must assist your mentoring teacher in supervising groups of students from different classes, you might suggest ideas for passing the time constructively.

CLASSROOM ENVIRONMENT

As a student teacher, you have some responsibility for the appearance and comfort of your classroom from the early days of your experience. When you take over full teaching responsibilities, the classroom's appearance and comfort will, in most cases, be completely your responsibility. Naturally, in most situations you will follow the procedures established by your mentoring teacher. In some areas, however, you may want to try variations, with the teacher's approval.

Seating Arrangements

Few classrooms today have stationary furniture. Movable furniture represents an opportunity for flexible arrangements for varied purposes. One arrangement may serve for whole-class instruction, another for small-group instruction, and still another when students are working on individual projects. If an instructional group requires a dry-erase board, the students can cluster around the board for that lesson, then disperse when another learning activity begins. Students can turn chairs to face a video or multimedia presentation shown on a side wall, a follow-up discussion using a dry-erase board on a different side wall, and a demonstration at the front of the room, all within the space of a single class.

With all this mobility, other considerations about seating must not be overlooked. Students with certain disabilities must be seated in the most advantageous positions possible. For example, students who have hearing difficulties should usually be seated near you; those who are nearsighted may need to be seated close to the board, displays, and demonstrations; and so on. Potentially disruptive students should also be seated where they are less likely to cause trouble; this may mean seating them near you or making sure that certain students do not sit beside each other. Activity 3.3 gives you a chance to work on seating arrangements in one of your classes.

In addition to the seating arrangement, make sure each student has a chair and desk of suitable size. Students in a single grade vary greatly in size, so one desk size will not be appropriate for all of them. If necessary, swap with other teachers to get a comfortable desk for each student.

The days of straight rows and alphabetical seating are behind us; current practice is much more flexible. Use this flexibility for your benefit and that of your students.

ISSUES IN DISCIPLINE

In every classroom, students occasionally misbehave, and dealing with them could be a problem. Consider the following situations. None of the answers is necessarily right; in fact, you might be able to come up with a better solution. In some cases, you might choose more than one answer. Consider what the circumstances might be and the probable consequences of each alternative.

1. Billy talks back to you, defying your authority. What do you do?
   a. Paddle him.
   b. Tell him to shut up and sit down.
   c. Ignore his behavior this time.
   d. Speak to him calmly, explaining why you cannot tolerate this kind of behavior.
   e. Punish him by making him stay in at recess.
   f. Laugh at him, because he really was sort of cute.
2. Chrissy throws something at Tammy and hits her on the head. What do you do?
   a. Check to see if Tammy is hurt. If not, ignore the situation.
   b. Let Tammy throw something at Chrissy and hit her on the head.
   c. Warn Chrissy that, if she does it again, she'll have to miss lunch for 1 week.
   d. Make an example of Chrissy. Reprimand her severely in front of the class.
   e. Stop what you are doing. Quietly point out that throwing things can be dangerous and that this behavior is unacceptable.
   f. Go on with your lesson as if nothing happened.
3. Two students are talking and giggling in the back of the room while you are trying to conduct a discussion. What do you do?
   a. Move closer to the students, pause, and look at them intently.
   b. Call on one of them to answer a question you have just asked.
   c. Stop and wait as long as necessary until everyone is quiet.
   d. Call them by name, and ask them to pay attention.
   e. Say in a loud and angry voice, "Your talking is disturbing to the rest of the class. I want you to stop this minute. If I hear one more word out of either of you, I'll send you both to the office."

f. Wait until after class; then talk to the students, and explain that their talking was very disturbing.

4. Carol is eating potato chips during reading group. You ask her to stop, and she defiantly tells you "No." What do you do?

a. Try to take the bag away from her by force.

b. Tell her that if she is going to eat chips in front of the other students, she will have to bring enough for everyone.

c. Tell her that if she'll put the chips away now, she can eat them during recess.

d. Ask her to return to her seat until she is finished.

e. Insist that she stop eating. Warn her that she will be punished if she does not stop right now. Continue until she complies.

f. Drop the request for the moment. Get the students interested in an exciting part of the story, and then quietly ask Carol to put the chips away for now.

5. Judy and Jerry are passing notes during math class. What do you do?

a. Pick up the notes from their desks, and read the notes aloud to the class.

b. Pick up the notes from their desks, tear them into shreds, and drop them into the wastebasket.

c. In front of the class, say sarcastically, "Judy and Jerry seem to know all there is to know about math, since they aren't paying attention." Then send them to the board, and give them a difficult problem to work in front of the other students.

d. Assign Jerry and Judy 10 extra problems for homework, and threaten to do the same to anyone else who doesn't pay attention.

e. Walk toward their desks; look at them intently until they understand that you are waiting for them to stop writing the notes, and then continue your lesson.

f. Have them stay after school and pick up all the scraps of paper in the room.

To deal with situations such as these, you must understand what discipline is and what it is not. Discipline is controlled behavior. It is also your ability to get attention when you need it. It does not call for an absolutely quiet and rigidly controlled class, although some degree of order is implied; in fact, quiet, purposeful talking can occur in a well-disciplined, or well-managed, classroom, with students moving freely about as they work on projects.

Discipline problems may be real or perceived (Thompson, 1994). Problems are real when students infringe on the teacher's freedom to teach and the other students' freedom to learn. For example, the teacher should be able to speak without interruption in order to teach, and students should be able to listen attentively without distractions caused by other students. When students' behavior interferes with these freedoms, discipline problems exist.

If a student is inattentive but not interfering with others, there is no real discipline problem; however, you may need to deal with this student's lack of attention at a later time. Teachers vary in their tolerance for students' talk and movement. By simply learning to accept reasonable student activity while they work independently or cooperatively, you may find that many perceived discipline problems don't really exist.

Teachers often consider discipline their number one problem, probably because of the complexity of discipline problems. You must consider the students' personalities and backgrounds, the type of learning situation in which they are involved, and the distractions that may interfere with their concentration. Disciplining students is also difficult because, in most cases, you must decide what to do on the spot, and you cannot always anticipate the consequences of your actions. Modeling respect for your students guides them toward appropriate interactions with others.

CAUSES OF DISCIPLINE PROBLEMS

All behavior has a cause or a purpose. Discovering and understanding the cause of an undesirable behavior may help you prevent its recurrence. Unfortunately, many causes are complex and difficult to analyze.

Many things may cause discipline problems: society, something in the classroom environment, the students themselves, or maybe even you! Let's look at some of the causes. Society may need to shoulder part of the blame. Observers of social institutions, such as schools, report that those institutions generally reflect the state or condition of society. Many educators feel that educators are change agents, and in order to cause change in society, you must change the factors you can control. Teachers make the difference in the classroom. You create your classroom environment. Analyze your classroom. Is there something in the room you could change that might reduce the number of discipline problems?

You may inadvertently be responsible for some of the discipline problems that arise. Can you answer all of these questions affirmatively?

1. Are my lessons well-planned and purposeful?
2. Am I meeting the interests and needs of all of the students? Are they motivated to learn?
3. Are the students actively engaged in learning?

ACTIVITY 3.3 | **Seating Arrangements**

Draw a seating chart for use with one of your classes during whole-group instruction. Circle the names of students with special needs who should have special consideration in seating arrangements. In the space below your seating chart, explain the reasons for the particular placements of these students.

4. Is the material at an appropriate level of difficulty, and do I have reasonable expectations for each student?

5. Do the students understand exactly how I expect them to behave and know the consequences of misbehavior?

6. Am I fair and consistent with discipline, and do I carry out my promises?

Being able to answer "Yes" to each of these questions will go a long way toward preventing discipline problems.

Students possess such a bewildering array of emotional, physical, and social problems that it is no wonder they sometimes misbehave. Sometimes you may be able to help students solve problems or accept what's troubling them. Sometimes just knowing that you care makes a difference to them. Students whose personal problems no longer interfere with their concentration are less likely to cause problems for you.

Students may misbehave to get attention, but giving attention to undesirable behavior only encourages it. As adolescents move toward adult independence, many take risks to see how far they can go, until their behavior becomes unacceptable and you must do something about it. Older students may be uncooperative because they resent being in school and attend only because the law requires them to be there until they reach a certain age.

Dreikurs believes that students are social beings who want to be accepted. When they misbehave, they believe that their actions will get them the recognition they crave. These students exhibit characteristics as follows: (a) attention getting, often in the form of disruption, wanting special favors and extra services, and irrelevant questioning; (b) power seeking, through arguing, lying, contradicting, and showing hostility; (c) revenge seeking, by hurting others through vicious or violent acts; and (d) displaying inadequacy, through withdrawal based on feelings of helplessness and failure. Dreikurs advises teachers to confront such a student: express the mistaken goal, discuss the faulty logic involved, and get the student to think about the reason for the behavior. He claims that this opens communication and allows the teacher to take constructive actions that will ultimately change the student's behavior (Charles, 1989).

Discipline problems may result from misunderstanding the traditions and behaviors of students from diverse cultures. For example, in many cultures students cooperate and work together at home, but in our schools, they are often expected to work individually, especially on tests. Thus, the teacher may regard students as cheating or disruptive when they are simply following their natural inclinations to help each other on such tasks. Providing cooperative learning activities helps these students adjust to the school's expectations.

Some students are at times simply unable to control their behavior. Students with attention deficit hyperactivity disorder (ADHD) are fidgety, easily distracted, inattentive, and often quite disruptive in class. Although medication may help these students, you can also reduce disruptions by assigning their most difficult work early in the day, giving explicit instructions, providing active involvement, assigning short tasks, and seating these students close to you.

Your situation as a student teacher or practicum student is slightly different from that of the classroom teacher. No matter who is doing the teaching, the discipline standards set by the regular classroom teacher usually prevail (see Activity 3.4). The students realize that even if you're in charge of this lesson, they will ultimately have to answer to their regular teacher. Since you don't have the experience of a regular teacher, you may fail to notice small incidents that could lead to big trouble in the future. You may also overlook occasional infractions because you want the students to like you; however, they will take advantage of you when they discover they can get away with misbehaving.

PREVENTION OF DISCIPLINE PROBLEMS

Preventing discipline problems is one secret of classroom management. A reactive approach to discipline fails to anticipate problems and offers no well-thought-out plan for responding to situations. Thus, discipline strategies vary from one case to another and may often be inappropriate. However, a proactive approach requires forethought. It involves anticipation and preparation, and it relies on consistent behavior by the teacher and consistent consequences for violations (Ban, 1994).

Relationships with Students

Your relationship with the students is of primary importance. They are amazingly perceptive and know how you feel about them. Here are some ways to develop a positive relationship.

Learn Students' Names.   Learn names and use them as soon as you can. Use a seating chart or name tags to help you. Calling students by name gets their attention quickly. Expect them to say Mr., Mrs., Ms., or Miss before your name when addressing you, to maintain a respectful relationship.

Check Seating Arrangements. See if you might eliminate some centers of disturbance by relocating a few students. Observe those who are likely to initiate trouble and keep them separated.

Avoid Confrontations with Students in Front of Their Peers. It is best to discuss problems rationally later, during a one-to-one conference. Whenever you can, help students work out their problems instead of sending them to an outside source.

Ignore Insignificant Infractions. Overlook minor misbehavior, such as rumpling paper and passing notes, rather than disrupting the entire class to call attention to these incidents. Deal with such matters later, if necessary, on an individual basis.

Maintain Self-Control. Remain calm when faced with discipline problems. If you yell and become excited, students will probably take advantage of you, because they will sense that you are losing control.

Be Fair, Firm, and Consistent. It doesn't take students long to figure out what kind of disciplinarian you are. Rubinstein (1999) describes a "real teacher" as one who, from the first day, dresses the part, verbally shares classroom management expectations, is decisive, uses materials effectively, and is explicit and direct.

Give Students Choices Whenever Possible. All students should be able to make some choices of their own—what books to read, projects to complete, interests to pursue, friends to work with, and behavior patterns to follow. The students should know and be prepared to accept the consequences of their choices. They should be granted privileges as long as they behave appropriately; if they abuse a privilege, you may need to take it away.

Encourage Students to Solve Their Own Problems. Instead of arbitrating conflicts yourself, turn some problems over to students and let them find solutions, perhaps during group or class meetings. In so doing, you help them develop responsibility and problem-solving skills. You may already be familiar with some conflict resolution strategies that help students deal with conflicts peaceably and avoid violence.

Involve Students in Making Classroom Rules. When students participate in setting rules and understand why these rules are necessary, they are likely to feel responsible for their actions. Although you will probably continue many of the classroom policies already in effect, you may negotiate some rules of your own to take care of new problems as they arise. Don't create too many rules, however, or you'll have trouble enforcing them all. Make sure that both rules and consequences are explicit; avoid vague requests such as "behave" or "cooperate" because students may not know what you mean. After rules have been established, help your students evaluate their effectiveness. If a rule is frequently violated, perhaps the rule is unnecessary, or if a penalty seems unfair, perhaps there is a more appropriate consequence.

Allowing for student choice and involving students in the construction of classroom rules are engaging and motivational strategies that can assist you in creating a respectful learning climate. However, remember that some decisions need to be discussed and negotiated, as demonstrated in the following Dennis the Menace comic.

"WE ALL VOTED, MISS BUTLER, AND IT WAS U-NANI-MOUS! WE'D LIKE MORE FREE TIME."

© Reprinted with permission of King Features Syndicate.

Presentations of Lessons

If you follow these suggestions, your lessons should give little cause for misbehavior: Make sure the classroom is as comfortable and free from distractions as you can make it. Get everyone's attention before you begin, and be sure that desks or tables are cleared of everything except what the students will need during the lesson. Be well prepared, and maintain good eye contact with students during a lesson. Know your lesson well enough that you don't have to read from the manual, or your written plans, while you teach. Watch for students who may have trouble understanding the work, and be ready to help them over their hurdles; otherwise, their frustration can erupt as behavior problems. Be ready to switch to another method if one strategy isn't working.

Start and end your lessons promptly and make transitions from one lesson to another quickly and

ACTIVITY 3.4 │ ***Observation Sheet for Classroom Management***

Carefully observe your mentoring teacher for management strategies. Note nonverbal behavior, preventive actions, and disciplinary techniques.

Management strategies:

Most effective strategies:

Least effective strategies:

Conclusions about strategies I may want to use with this class:

smoothly. In discussion lessons, let only one student answer at a time; this prevents the confusion that results when several students call out answers. Keep your lessons interesting and fast-paced. If you are enthusiastic, the students will catch your enthusiasm. Get them actively involved in your lessons and keep them motivated, since highly motivated students seldom cause discipline problems. Have more than enough material for the entire class period. In case you run short, keep ideas in mind for filling in the remaining minutes productively.

Give directions clearly and precisely. Reinforce important directions by writing them on the board. Be sure the students know what choices they have when they finish their work. If they don't know what to do next, they may become disruptive. If necessary, explain things more than once or provide written, as well as verbal, directions so that everyone understands. Put things in simple words for young students.

Your teaching style makes a difference in how students respond to you. Move around the room, and use nonverbal communication to interact with various students as you teach. Call on students who seem inattentive to get them involved.

The volume of your voice can set the noise level of the class. If you raise your voice to be heard, the students will only get noisier. If you lower your voice, they will become quiet to hear what you have to say. Be sure, however, that you can be heard in the back of the room and that you speak distinctly.

Reacting to Danger Signals

If you're alert to impending trouble, you can often stop problems just as they start. Boredom, daydreaming, restlessness, and long periods of inactivity breed discipline problems. Danger signals include a paper wad shot across the room, a half-smothered giggle, or a quick exchange of glances between students.

When you sense trouble brewing, move quickly to avert it. Try these ideas:

1. Change your tactics fast. Switch to a different approach, read a story, play a rhythm game, or discuss an event in which students share an interest.
2. Use nonverbal communication to arrest the problem. Catch and hold the instigator's eye. Pause in midsentence and look intently at the potential troublemakers. Shake your head slowly to indicate disapproval.
3. Remind the students of a privilege or reward that will be the consequence of good behavior, while looking in the direction of the potential problem.
4. Move closer to the source of trouble. Indicate that you are aware of what's going on.

5. Speak more softly and slowly. You will get the students' attention for the moment, as they try to figure out why you shifted your speech.
6. Refocus students when you sense impending problems by saying something like "Guess what is going to happen this Friday?"
7. Use humor. Laugh with the students and occasionally at yourself. A good laugh reduces tension. Laugh off a minor incident instead of making a big deal of it. For example, to a student who has just thrown a paper airplane, say "Billy, I'll bet the Air Force could use you to help design airplanes. Now let's get back to work."
8. Call on students you believe are about to cause a problem to answer a question, or simply insert a student's name in midsentence to bring attention back to the lesson; for example, "The next question, Johnny, is number seven."
9. Confiscate distracting materials, especially toys or food, that are diverting students' attention.

FOR YOUR PORTFOLIO

INTASC Standard: 5
Describe an occasion when you used a classroom management technique effectively, or discuss how you were able to improve a student's behavior by applying certain techniques (or do both).

DEVELOPING STUDENTS' SELF-DISCIPLINE

As long as students rely on you to control their behavior, they are likely to lapse into poor behavior if you do not constantly direct their actions. The objective of good discipline, according to Marshall (1998, p. 14), "is to increase self-responsibility, social awareness, and social responsibility." Rewards and punishments, or consequences, usually last only as long as they are in effect (Kohn, 1994). These extrinsic motivators do not change underlying attitudes and behaviors. Although rewards usually work better than threats and punishments, Kohn claims that they are both strategies teachers use to manipulate behavior. However, the child who finishes work in order to get a sticker or a piece of candy soon works only for the reward, instead of thinking creatively, exploring ideas, and taking risks.

As an alternative to rewards and punishments, Kohn (1993, 1994, 1996) recommends creating a classroom community featuring trust, shared responsibility, and active student participation in decision making. As part of the community, students feel valued and respected; they care about one another. They feel safe, both physically and emotionally. Because these students care about others, they are better at conflict resolution and there is little need for such disciplinary measures as rewards and punishments.

Students are often unaccustomed to being responsible for their own behavior because teachers have usually told them what to do and what not to do. Creating a democratic class community may take some time and patience, but your efforts will pay off in terms of building rapport with your students, gaining their respect, and decreasing disruptions. Teach them to be responsible for their actions by forming groups where they direct some of their own activities, expecting them to perform classroom duties, encouraging them to keep records of their progress, having them evaluate their own progress, and setting up a tutoring program where they guide other students' learning. Start with small tasks and work up to larger ones as students demonstrate readiness to assume more responsibility. Help them identify and set goals for themselves; then encourage them to find ways to reach their goals. If students believe that you think they are capable of directing many of their own activities, they are likely to live up to expectations.

FOR YOUR PORTFOLIO

INTASC Standards: 5, 9
Write your philosophy of discipline and include it in your portfolio. State your goals and the techniques you would use and those you would avoid.

DISCIPLINARY MEASURES

Some teachers seem to be aware of everything that goes on in the classroom, even when they don't appear to be looking. Effective teachers develop a sort of sixth sense that enables them to pick up the vibrations from their classes so that they usually know what's happening. You can acquire this ability if you develop sensitivity to sounds, movements, voices, and behavior patterns within your classroom.

Teachers with "eyes in the back of their heads" are usually effective classroom managers. In fact, it is difficult to observe the techniques they use because their methods are subtle and unobtrusive. A quiet nod, the mention of a student's name, or a warning glance usually suffices. Don't worry if you haven't yet mastered this technique—it often takes years of practice.

Since even master disciplinarians occasionally have problems that require more attention, you

probably will also. When problems do develop, consider several factors before taking action. Keep in mind the purpose of disciplinary action: to maintain or restore order by helping the student control his or her behavior, not to seek revenge for violation of the rules. You should also consider the reason for misbehavior and the personal circumstances of the misbehaving student. Appropriate disciplinary measures vary according to the student's grade level, special needs, degree of motivation for learning, ability level, and personality. As you can see, there is no single solution for any problem.

Before deciding what to do, consider your school's policy regarding discipline. Check with your mentoring teacher to find out what types of disciplinary action are permitted if a student misbehaves. Can you keep students after school, or do bus schedules prohibit this? Can you deny a student recess, or is a certain amount of free time compulsory? Is there a detention hall, and do you have the option of sending a student there? What do you do if a student doesn't have a hall pass, talks back in class, or destroys school property?

In cases of persistent inappropriate behavior or major infractions, you need to know what to do. You may need to keep dated, explicit records of incidents, which may be used for referrals or for decisions about placing students in an alternative school. You need to know when parents should be contacted and when suspension or expulsion is a consequence. Your mentoring teacher has the responsibility for contacts with parents in most cases and, along with the administration, for any decisions about suspension or expulsion.

Knowing Some Options

Despite your attempts to instill a sense of social responsibility and create a community, you may sometimes reach a point at which you must discipline a class or an individual student. You may want to ask your mentoring teacher for advice before choosing one of the following, but here are some potentially appropriate consequences for specific types of misbehavior:

1. If a student tries to be the class clown . . .
   a. Explain that there are times when that kind of behavior is appreciated, but it is not appropriate during class.
   b. Give the clown special assignments to show your confidence in her or his ability to assume responsibility.
   c. Praise the clown for completion of serious work, but ignore the clowning.
   d. If the behavior persists, isolate the clown temporarily.
2. If students talk at inappropriate times . . .
   a. Ignore the interruption, if possible.

b. Change the seating arrangement. Some students may encourage those who sit near them to talk during class.

c. Give students a few minutes of free time to get talking out of their systems.

d. Stop your lesson and wait until everything quiets down.

3. If students litter or mess things up . . .

a. Provide time for them to clean up their desks and work areas.

b. Provide incentives for neat work.

c. Brainstorm all the ways to make the room neater, cleaner, and more attractive.

d. Let students be messy sometimes; then give them a chance to clean up.

e. Confiscate articles left carelessly around the room. Return them at the end of the week.

f. Use creative dramatics. Turn young students into robots, and see how quickly they can put things away.

4. If students push, shove, and make noise when forming lines . . .

a. Appoint a different leader each week who is responsible for maintaining a disciplined line.

b. Dismiss one row or group at a time. Choose the best-behaved group first.

c. Have students line up according to some plan, such as alphabetical order, height, or color of clothing.

5. If a student tattles . . .

a. Explain that you don't want to hear personal information about another student (gossiping), but only news of rules that have been broken or of someone who has been hurt (reporting).

b. Ask the tattler to write down the information for you to read at the end of the day, because you do not have time to listen. Writing may discourage him or her.

c. If there are several tattlers in your class, ask them to save all their tales to tell on Friday afternoon. By then, they will probably consider the matters too trivial to share.

d. Role-play a tattletale incident so students can understand why this behavior is undesirable.

Testing the Technique

Some common disciplinary practices are considered generally effective; some are considered borderline, and may be good or bad depending on the circumstances; others are thought to be inappropriate.

Effective Techniques

Reinforcers. Both verbal and nonverbal reinforcers are effective for encouraging good behavior and discouraging improper conduct.

Restitution. A student who takes or destroys something should be expected to return or restore it. If this is impossible, the student should compensate for the loss in some other way.

Role-Playing. Students appreciate the feelings of other students and see incidents in a new light when they role-play.

Contracts. The use of contracts works well for intermediate and secondary students. Contracts are agreements that deal with specified behaviors, tasks, responsibilities, and rewards. They give the effect of a legal commitment and are signed by both the teacher and the student.

Group Discussions. Guided, open discussions are good ways to handle disputes and discipline problems. Students feel involved and responsible for carrying out their own recommendations.

Gripe Box. A suggestion or gripe box allows students to express dissatisfaction. After reading the students' notes, you might want to make some changes. Select one or two gripes for students to discuss in class in order to resolve the complaint.

Nonverbal Signals. Effective use of nonverbal signals and body language is one of the best forms of discipline. Examples include a frown, a smile, a nod, movement toward a student, an intent look, a raised hand, and a wink.

Time-Out. Time-out can be used to remove a student who is highly distracting to the rest of the class or who is acting in such a way that she or he could harm others. The teacher isolates the student from the rest of the class for a period of time until the student cools off and regains control. The isolation area should be secluded, quiet, and dull.

Appeal to Reason. When told why good behavior is necessary, students are often persuaded to act well. You might say, "Be careful with the equipment so we don't break anything" or "Work quickly so we'll have time to plan our party."

Approval of Behavior. This method generally works well in elementary school. The teacher notices students who are "ready to begin," are "sitting up nicely," or "have their books open to the right page." Other students follow suit because they also want recognition.

Grounding. This technique is effective for a student who doesn't work well or doesn't cooperate at a learning center. The student must return to his or her seat to work until ready to rejoin the group.

Matching the Penalty to the Offense.   A consequence should relate to the offense so that the student can see the reason for it.

Attention-Getting Signals.   Agree on a signal to get instant attention, such as raising your arm, ringing a bell, or saying "Freeze!"

Writing It Out.   When a student misbehaves, ask the student to write what happened, why it happened, and how the situation could be handled better next time.

Borderline Techniques

Planned Ignoring.   This technique may work for a while. Sometimes if you ignore a problem, it will go away; at other times, however, it only becomes worse, until you are forced to deal with it.

Apologies.   Genuine apologies are effective. If you force students to say words they don't mean, you are only teaching them to lie. Their apologies mean nothing.

Removal of Students from the Classroom.   Although you may be tempted to remove an out-of-control student, try to settle the matter yourself, since you and your mentoring teacher probably know the situation better than anyone else.

Merits and Demerits.   This system consists of awarding or taking away points for certain kinds of behavior. This technique may work well if it is carefully structured and used on a temporary basis. Students should eventually learn to control their own behavior, however, rather than rely on outside incentives.

Remaining after School.   Keeping a student after school, either in your own room or in detention hall, may have some value as a penalty for misbehavior. Unless some educational experience is planned for this time, however, this will waste both your time and the student's time. Remaining after school can also interfere with bus schedules or worthwhile extracurricular activities.

Denial of Privileges.   A denied privilege is usually an effective penalty. It can have a negative effect, however, if a student is being denied something that he or she really needs. For instance, denying a hyperactive child recess is detrimental, since he or she probably needs this outlet to burn off surplus energy.

Scoldings.   An occasional reprimand is often necessary, but a bitter harangue has a negative effect on the whole class. Avoid nagging, constant faultfinding, and long discourses on behavior.

Personal Conferences.   A one-to-one conference often clears up problems and helps the student and teacher understand each other. Privacy is necessary for a free exchange of views and for keeping a matter confidential. The teacher must listen carefully to the student's views. Conferences are ineffective when the teacher simply makes accusations and the student is unresponsive; they can be destructive if they deteriorate into arguments.

Inappropriate Techniques

Additional Classwork or Homework.   This practice generally results in the student's disliking the subject or content area.

Ridicule or Sarcasm.   Students who are embarrassed or humiliated by their teachers may suffer serious psychological damage.

Grade Reduction.   Grades for academic achievement should not be affected by behavior.

Threats.   It's usually better to act than to threaten. If you do make threats, be prepared to follow through. Generally, threats cause students to become upset and suspicious.

Corporal Punishment.   Corporal punishment rarely corrects a problem. Like threats, it usually has a negative effect on students and should be used only as a last resort, if ever. Improper use of corporal punishment can result in legal challenges. As a student teacher or practicum student you should never use corporal punishment.

EVALUATING FOUR CASE STUDIES

The following case studies are based on actual situations. Read them, and evaluate the teacher's action in each case. Were other options available? How would you have handled these students?

CASE STUDY 3.8

The Last Straw

Jeff, a twelfth-grade student, came from a low-socioeconomic-level home where he was taught the value of a good education. His parents were interested in his progress and encouraged him to do well.

In industrial arts class, Jeff was a reasonably good student, but he often caused minor disruptions. He would distract other students by sticking his foot out to trip them, making wisecracks, laughing raucously at nothing, and occasionally defying his teacher, Mr. Hamlin. Mr. Hamlin put up with his behavior for several weeks. He knew that Jeff was basically a good student and did not feel that Jeff's interruptions warranted a confrontation.

One morning, Jeff decided he would go to the cosmetology class to get a haircut during industrial arts; however, Mr. Hamlin refused to give him permission. Jeff cursed at Mr. Hamlin and said that he was going to get his hair cut anyway. At this point, Mr. Hamlin realized he had been too lenient with Jeff. He knew something would have to be done, or there would be a total breakdown in discipline in his class. Mr. Hamlin took Jeff to the office, where the principal suspended him for his defiant and discourteous behavior.

Following his suspension, Jeff returned to school with his father. During a conference with the guidance counselor, Mr. Carlin, the entire situation was reviewed and correct standards of behavior were discussed. A contract was drawn up, which allowed Jeff to return to class as long as he acted appropriately. Mr. Carlin went over the contract with Jeff and his father in detail. If Jeff failed to live up to his commitment, he would be dropped from the class roll. Jeff seemed to hold no malice toward his teacher or the counselor and willingly agreed to sign the contract, along with his father and Mr. Carlin. The counselor also requested that Jeff apologize to Mr. Hamlin and the rest of the class, but only if he felt he owed them an apology.

Mr. Hamlin later reported that Jeff had been much less disruptive in class and that he was behaving more maturely.

CASE STUDY 3.9

Moving Toward Acceptable Behavior

Jill, a fifth-grader who lives with her mother and step-father, abused by her father as a young child. Although her stepfather has helped her make adjustments, Jill and her mother do not get along well. Both parents are beginning to lose patience with her. At the beginning of the year, Jill threw temper tantrums when things didn't go her way. She nearly went into convulsions sometimes and had to be taken from the room. At other times, she was told to stand in the corner as punishment for her fits of temper. She hated standing in the corner, so the number of tantrums gradually decreased.

Jill was hostile toward the teacher, Mrs. Lynch, and the other children. She was loud and aggressive when she came to school in the morning. She called people names and frequently told lies. She was easily distracted and rushed through her work, not caring if it was done correctly. On the playground, she tried to get control of the soccer ball and take it away from the other children. She had no remorse about hurting people, even when she caused them to bleed. During the year, three things seemed to help Jill. First, Jill enjoyed getting the other students' attention. She discovered that when she was nice to them, they would be friendly toward her. To win friends, she began to change her attention-getting strategies to more acceptable behavior patterns.

Second, Jill's relationship with Mrs. Lynch helped her. Mrs. Lynch and Jill talked frequently in private about why Jill acted as she did and how she might get along better with the other children. Jill began to trust Mrs. Lynch and stopped feeling that Mrs. Lynch was picking on her.

Third, Jill was also helped by the school psychologist, with whom she met each week. The psychologist required her to earn points for satisfactory achievement. Jill's teachers had to sign a paper each time she earned a point. Jill then took the paper to the psychologist, who granted her a privilege if she had earned at least 16 points in a week.

Jill is still immature and demands attention in unacceptable ways, but her behavior is much better than it was at the beginning of the year.

CASE STUDY 3.10

Parental Restitution

Troy, a fifth-grader, is an unpopular boy with wealthy parents. His mother places a great deal of importance on wealth and continually brags about recent trips and acquisitions. It seems to Troy that money can buy anything.

Troy wanted desperately to be accepted by his peers. He decided to ask Sheila, the cutest girl in class, to "go with" him for $10 a week. This seemed like a lot of money to Sheila, but she was doubtful about the arrangement. She discussed Troy's proposition with her friends before deciding what to do. She really didn't want to be Troy's girl, even for the money. She finally agreed, however, and Troy brought $10 to school for her.

Until this time, Sheila had barely spoken to Troy, but now she occasionally sat with him during lunch and talked to him during the day. She allowed him to call her at night, but they never went anyplace together. However, this arrangement satisfied Troy, who boasted to his classmates about his new girlfriend. They were properly impressed, and Troy gained status among his peers.

After 2 or 3 weeks, Troy's teacher, Mrs. Hobson, became suspicious of the new relationship between Troy and Sheila. One day she saw Troy handing $10 to Sheila. She talked to the two quietly and found out about their arrangement.

Mrs. Hobson felt that the only thing to do was to bring both sets of parents to school and discuss the matter with them. During the conference, the parents agreed to talk to their children about ending the arrangement. Sheila's parents returned the money to Troy's parents, and the matter ended. Troy and Sheila resumed their original relationship, and Troy did not seem depressed over losing Sheila's attention.

CASE STUDY 3.11

Peer Pressure Works

Dan came from a high-socioeconomic-level home and had the support of his family. He didn't believe in law enforcement, school regulations, or God. He was an excellent student academically, but had begun using drugs as a high school sophomore.

As a junior, Dan became even more involved with drugs. His guidance counselor, Mrs. Tilton, was aware of Dan's dependence on drugs and talked to him about his problem on several occasions. Dan insisted that it was his right to use drugs and that no one could tell him what to do. He claimed that all the students used drugs, although Mrs. Tilton denied this. Mrs. Tilton warned him that drugs could eventually harm him, but nothing she said made any difference. Dan continued to be cooperative and do well in his classes, but was beginning to go downhill by the end of the year.

Despite his heavy use of drugs, Dan won the history prize in his junior year. As he walked across the stage to receive his award, the students booed him. Because of his involvement with drugs, they had no respect for him.

For some reason, this peer rejection turned Dan around. Since he cared about his fellow students and their feelings toward him, he stopped using drugs and was elected president of the student body in his senior year. According to some, he was the best student body president the school ever had. He went on to the local university, where he carried a double major and made the Dean's List each semester.

DISCUSSION QUESTIONS

1. Observe the groups that have been set up in your class. Can you see the reason for each type of grouping? Do you think it would be helpful to have additional groups? How might grouping be used more advantageously? If there are no groups now, can you see any reasons for forming them? If so, how would you do this?

2. Do you see any indications that students are discouraged by group placement? If so, how could you try to correct this situation?

3. Did you waste time today during the classes you taught? What did you spend time doing that wasn't really important to achieving your goals?

4. What special reports and records does your school require? What is your responsibility for keeping these records?

5. What is the school's grading system? Is there any provision for giving information to a student's parents about effort, attitude, or interest? Is it important for parents to know this information?

6. What purposes do bulletin boards serve? How often should you change them? What role might students play in the design and composition of bulletin boards?

7. Analyze the seating arrangements in your room. Could they be improved? If so, how?

8. Is your classroom highly structured or very flexible? What aspects of your classroom reflect structure or flexibility?

9. Can you recognize ways in which your mentoring teacher is integrating the curriculum? If so, how well are they working? If not, how could some subjects be integrated?

10. Observe your mentoring teacher carefully. How does she or he manage student behavior? Do the teacher's signals, warnings, nonverbal messages, or other subtle measures prevent discipline problems from arising? Which techniques seem most successful? Do all students respond the same way?

11. Develop a plan for helping your students acquire self-discipline. What reasonable responsibilities can you give them? Can you vary the responsibilities to meet the capabilities of each student? How can you check students' progress toward developing self-discipline?

4 Planning for Instruction

Case Study 4.1: Importance of Planning

*M*r. *Thomas is the mentoring teacher,* Miss Alwood is his student teacher, and Mrs. Marshall is the principal.

Mrs. Marshall: Miss Alwood, Mr. Thomas called in sick today. We have called a substitute, but she won't be here for a couple of hours. I know that you have been checking the roll and leading opening exercises for some time now. That shouldn't be a problem. And Mr. Thomas said that you were supposed to teach the science class today. You can switch the times for the science class and the reading class, and the substitute will be here in time to teach the reading. Will that be all right with you?

Miss Alwood: Well, I guess so, but I was planning to locate the materials for an experiment and run off some handouts for the science class while Mr. Thomas was teaching reading this morning. I guess I can postpone the experiment until tomorrow, though.

Mrs. Marshall: You mean that you waited until an hour before the lesson to locate your materials and make your handouts? What if you were unable to find what you needed here? What if the copier were broken?

Miss Alwood (staring at the floor): I didn't think about that. I just assumed that I would be able to find everything here because Mr. Thomas said he did that experiment last year with his class, and I know he has a big box of stuff for science experiments. I did bring a battery, because I thought his old one might have gone dead in a year.

Mrs. Marshall: How many other lessons did you have to prepare for today?

Miss Alwood: None. I don't take on another subject until next week.

Mrs. Marshall: What did you do after school yesterday?

Miss Alwood: I went shopping first. Then I went home, ate supper, and prepared a crossword puzzle for the class. After that, I watched some television. I was really tired from the day because the class was rowdy, so I just tried to relax.

Mrs. Marshall: Doesn't Mr. Thomas ask you to plan your lessons in advance?

Miss Alwood: Oh, yes. I gave him my plans for this whole week last Friday. He liked my experiment with electromagnets and having the students write a lab report. He said yesterday's lesson on magnetism got my unit off to a good start. We brainstormed about the topic, and I made a web of what they already knew about it on the board. The students all copied the web on their papers. We are going to add to it as they learn new things about the topic.

Mrs. Marshall: Was that your whole lesson?

Miss Alwood: Yes.

Mrs. Marshall: Did it take the whole science period?

Miss Alwood: Well, it took most of it for some of the students, but some of them copied the web really fast. I had to watch them, because they bothered the ones who were still working. Mr. Thomas suggested that I have something prepared for those "fast finishers" to do while the others finish. Today I had a crossword puzzle with terms related to magnetism all ready for them. I just needed to run it and the lab report forms off this morning.

Mrs. Marshall: I'm glad you are taking Mr. Thomas's suggestions seriously, but I think that you need to prepare for your lessons further in advance. Your written plan will be useless if you don't locate the needed materials.

1. When should the preparation for Miss Alwood's science lesson have taken place?
2. Did Miss Alwood make a good impression on Mrs. Marshall? Why or why not?
3. What does this situation tell you about the importance of time management?

REASONS FOR INSTRUCTIONAL PLANNING

Without planning for instruction, your teaching experiences are likely to turn into disasters. Planning organizes and directs your teaching efforts, and ensures that you cover all important aspects of a lesson, while avoiding overemphasis on isolated points that interest you but do not merit extensive coverage. Planning can save you from not having enough to do in a lesson, especially if you practice overplanning. (*Overplanning* means planning extra related and purposeful activities that you don't expect to have time for, but have ready in case the rest of the lesson progresses rapidly and time is available.) Chapter 8 contains some suggested filler, or sponge, activities. Planning can also help you avoid trying to cover too much material at one time. In reviewing the complexity of the concepts you plan to present in a lesson format, you may find you have selected more material than the students can readily absorb at once, and that certain complex concepts need much elaboration, rather than a hasty mention.

Good planning also enhances your poise and confidence, which will positively affect your class control. Since class control is a major problem for student teachers, this advantage alone should encourage planning.

Written plans allow you to consult your mentoring teacher and college or university supervisor about the likelihood of a successful teaching experience. Their valuable feedback may help you avert a teaching disaster brought on by your inexperience. Some mentoring teachers and college or university supervisors require written plans. If yours don't, we highly recommend that you do them anyway, for your personal benefit. It will pay off.

Schools currently emphasize teaching in accordance with standards set by a variety of professional organizations or by state organizations. Standards have been developed by the National Council of Teachers of English and the International Reading Association (1996), the National Council of Teachers of Mathematics (2000), the National Research Council (1998), the American Association for the Advancement of Science (1993), the National Geographic Society (1994), and the National Council for the Social Studies (1994). States have also gotten into the act. Clark and Wasley (1999) point out that the standards of the national subject–matter organizations have influenced these state standards. Being familiar with the curriculum standards of the state in which you are teaching and the professional organizations related to your subject area or areas will enhance your ability to plan lessons.

When you are actually assigned to teach, it is vitally important that you plan for instruction, whether or not you actually write down the plans. Your instructional plans should always relate directly to the course of study and build upon previous learning.

One good way to ease into your teaching experience is to plan a lesson jointly with your mentoring teacher, watch him or her teach the lesson in an early class, and then try it yourself in a later class. This arrangement allows you to see an experienced teacher move from plan to execution. Obviously, this procedure will only work in departmentalized settings where a teacher has several sections of the same course.

Initially you will probably be assigned responsibility for single, isolated lessons. In time, you will probably be assigned to teach entire units of instruction. These two planning tasks will be considered separately, in the order that you are likely to encounter them, even though lesson planning is obviously an integral part of unit planning.

Lesson Planning

Your lesson plans should be detailed enough that you or another qualified person can teach from them with ease, yet brief enough that they do not become cumbersome. More detailed plans are usually needed at the beginning of your student teaching experience than at the end or after you become a regular classroom teacher. Although more detail gives an inexperienced person greater confidence and makes the inclusion of all important material more likely, too much detail can inhibit flexibility in a lesson. Do not, for example, plan to get one particular answer from students and build all your subsequent plans on this answer, because it may not come. Plan to accommodate a variety of responses.

What belongs in a good lesson plan? Opinions vary, and each teacher generally has to create a planning scheme that fits his or her personality. Certain components appear almost universally; these components should be used in initial planning activities (see Figure 4–1).

When you write objectives for a specific lesson, be sure to study the overall unit objectives for the lesson, and check on previous instruction in that unit. Your chosen objectives should build upon previously taught material and lay the groundwork for future instruction, either by you or your mentoring teacher. Be specific in your objectives. Don't use a vague objective, such as "To help them understand verbs better"; instead, say "To help the students understand and apply the concept of subject-verb agreement" or, in more behavioral terms, "In 20 consecutive trials the student will demonstrate accurate use of subject-verb agreement," if you are looking for mastery learning.

FIGURE 4–1
Components of a Lesson Plan*

1. Subject

2. Grade

3. Date (not always essential)

4. Time (useful for secondary teachers who teach more than one section of a subject)

5. Objectives (be specific)

6. Standards addressed

7. Content to be covered (be specific)

8. Materials and equipment needed

9. Activities and procedures with time allocations (to keep you from running out of time in the middle of something)

10. Alternative activities (in case a piece of equipment won't work or you overestimated how long other activities would take)

11. Personal connections

12. Adjustments for individual needs

13. Method of evaluation (to determine if the students really learned the material)

14. Assignments (to provide practice on a taught skill, to prepare for a future lesson, or to achieve some very specific purpose)

15. Self-evaluation (Put this section in your written lesson plan, to be filled out after you teach the lesson.)

16. Supervisory feedback (Put this section in your written lesson plan, to be filled out after you have been critiqued by your mentoring teacher, your university supervisor, or both.)

* See Appendix B for sample lesson plans.

Because you are responsible for assisting students in meeting mandated standards, you should list the standards addressed by your lesson. These standards may have been set by a professional organization, your state, or your local school system.

In the content section of your plan, list the major concepts you intend to cover. Don't just write "Causes of the Civil War"; list specific causes. Consult resources other than the textbook when planning this part of the lesson.

On your list of materials, include everything you will need. For example, if you need a dry-erase marker, list it. This list can help you accumulate all necessary materials before the lesson begins, preventing the need to disrupt your lesson while searching for an appropriate marker.

In the activities and procedures section, you may wish to list questions you plan to raise, motivational techniques you plan to use, what you plan to do, and what you are going to ask the students to do. Consult your college or university methods textbooks when you plan this part of your lesson. Vary activities. Students become bored with lessons that require just one type

of response. Plan to have students do some combination of listening, watching, reading, speaking, and writing in each lesson. Develop background for the lesson before you begin the new material, and model for the students the skill or strategy you want them to acquire. When you model a skill or strategy for students, you demonstrate its use, including an oral explanation of your thought processes related to the activity.

Creating opportunities for students to make personal connections increases students' motivation and focus. You must know your students well to help them make these connections, and therefore make the learning more meaningful to them.

You also need to consider the individual needs of students. For example, make sure that the specifications of each student's IEP have been met. Don't focus only on struggling students, but also consider challenging the gifted students.

By estimating how much time each activity should take, you minimize the risk of finishing an hour lesson in 20 minutes or of getting only halfway through a 30-minute lesson before the time elapses. At first, of course, your time estimates may not be extremely accurate, but the very act of keeping up with them in each lesson helps you learn how to judge time needs better. A common problem for student teachers is finishing all the planned material early and being forced to improvise. This will not be a problem if you plan some good alternative activities to use in this situation, or if some other unforeseen difficulty occurs.

You should always consider how to determine whether or not your students have learned the lesson material. You can evaluate through oral or written questions, observation of students' performance, or some other means, but you must evaluate, because future lesson plans depend upon whether or not students have learned the material in the current lesson.

The assignments you give students for independent work should be carefully planned to meet a specific purpose. One assignment might be designed to offer further practice in a skill just taught in order to fix it in the students' minds. Another assignment might be designed to prepare the students for a future lesson. Any materials that students are assigned to read independently must be chosen carefully. Students will be unable to complete independent assignments in materials that are too difficult for them to read; for this reason, differentiated reading assignments may be necessary.

After teaching the lesson, you should evaluate your own effectiveness much as you evaluated lessons you observed others teach. When you recognize weaknesses, consider how you would teach the lesson differently if you repeated the lesson. Student teachers in departmentalized settings who are assigned to two sections of the same class may be able to try out their ideas for improvement later in the day. If they do, they must remember to evaluate the second presentation also. When you receive feedback from your mentoring teacher and your college or university supervisor about your lesson, compare their comments with your self-evaluation. If you noticed the same things they did, your evaluation skills are probably good. If they mention many things you missed, you may need to work at evaluating your performance more critically and objectively.

Complete the Lesson Plan Form in Activity 4.1 for a lesson you plan to teach this term. You can photocopy the blank form to use with other observations, either for your own benefit or at the request of your mentoring teacher or college or university supervisor. Although this is only one possible lesson plan form, completing it can help you determine important components for your lesson that need to be included on any form you might use for future lessons. Once you have presented the lesson specified in Activity 4.1, complete Activity 4.2 to help you analyze it.

FOR YOUR PORTFOLIO

INTASC Standards: 1, 5, 9
Include in your portfolio one completed lesson plan and an analysis of this lesson. Choose a lesson that shows some of your best accomplishments.

Thematic Unit Planning

After you have achieved some success at planning individual lessons, your mentoring teacher will probably move you into planning thematic units. Such planning involves developing coordinated sets of lessons built around central themes.

In elementary school, a thematic unit plan frequently cuts across disciplines and includes activities in language arts, mathematics, social studies, science, art, music, and other areas. A unit on the "Westward Movement" is an example. Although this unit basically has a social studies theme, the teacher can incorporate language arts instruction through reference reading, oral and written reports, and class discussions; mathematics instruction in figuring distances, calculating amounts of needed supplies and prices of supplies in those days to determine a journey's cost, and measuring ingredients for recipes of that era; science and health instruction through comparing disease remedies used then with those used today; art in illustrating modes of transportation, clothing, or other features of the times, in constructing dioramas and models, and in designing and making quilts; and music instruction through singing and playing songs of the time. When thematic units are thoroughly integrated across the curriculum, in a natural, holistic way, the approach is often referred to as *theme studies*. Because not all curricular areas will fit a particular theme study, do not force connections. Integration should be meaningful and natural.

Many middle-school units are also interdisciplinary thematic units and "explore topics that are grounded in real-life problems and experiences, such as survival or relationships" (Jenson & Kiley, 2000, p. 320). Secondary-level thematic units, especially in social studies and literature classes, may cut across disciplines, but this is not as common as at lower grade levels. Interdisciplinary instruction often takes place in schools that utilize block scheduling and team teaching.

Most thematic units at the secondary level and many at the elementary level are based upon major topics within single disciplines. A mathematics class, for example, may have a unit on measurement, incorporating a multitude of mathematical concepts and skills. You should review your methods textbooks for types of thematic units appropriate to your grade and/or discipline.

ACTIVITY 4.1 | *Lesson Plan Form*

Name: _____   Subject: _____

Grade level: _____   Date: _____   Time: _____

Objectives (Be specific.):

Standards addressed:

Content to be covered (Be specific.):

Materials and equipment needed (Indicate sources.):

Activities and procedures (Include time allocations.):
       Introductory activities:

       Developmental activities:

       Concluding activities:

Alternative activities—emergency fillers:

Personal connections:

Adjustments for individual needs:

Method of evaluation:

Assignments—homework or in-class supervised study:

Self-evaluation:

Supervisory feedback:

ACTIVITY 4.2 │ ***Personal Lesson Analysis Form***

Name: _____ Date: _____

Class: _____

Area 1 Did the students seem to grasp how the lesson was tied to previous learning? _____ Did the motivational activities seem to arouse students' interest? _____ Why do you think they did or did not accomplish their goal? _____

_____

_____

Area 2 Were the purpose and relevance of the lesson made clear to the students? _____ Why or why not? _____

_____

_____

How might they have been better clarified? _____

_____

_____

Area 3 Were your procedures effective for presenting the content? _____ Might some other procedures have been more effective? _____ Why do you think so? _____

_____

_____

Area 4 Were the lesson materials appropriate and effective? _____ Would other materials have been more effective? _____ Why do you think so? _____

_____

_____

Area 5 Was your teaching style effective with this particular group and for this particular lesson? _____ Why do you think so? _____

_____

_____

Area 6 Did you have adequate knowledge of the subject matter? _____ Was enough outside knowledge brought into the lesson? _____ If not, what else might have been included? _____

_____

_____

Was content effectively related to the students' lives? _____ If not, how might this have been accomplished? _____

_____

_____

Area 7   Were adequate provisions made for individual differences? _____ If so, how? _____ If not, what steps might have been taken to improve the situation? _____

_____

_____

Area 8   Were classroom management techniques appropriate and effective? _____ Why do you think so? _____

_____

_____

If they were inappropriate or ineffective, what techniques might have been better? _____

_____

_____

Area 9   Did your personal qualities advance the lesson effectively? _____ Why do you think so? _____

_____

_____

Might changes in this area be helpful to future lessons? _____ How? _____

_____

_____

Area 10   Was the conclusion of the lesson effective? _____ Why or why not? _____

_____

_____

If not, what might have been done to improve it? _____

_____

_____

Area 11   Were your evaluation techniques appropriate and effective? _____ Why do you think so? _____

_____

_____

If not, what techniques might have been better? _____

_____

_____

Area 12   Did your lesson adequately address the standards it was designed to address? _____ If not, how could you change it to get the desired results? _____

_____

_____

Interdisciplinary units across the curriculum require collaboration among several teachers in departmentalized settings. To take part in such a collaboration, offer suggestions for objectives, major concepts to be studied, materials, and methods for instruction and evaluation. Be open and supportive of the suggestions of others as well.

Different situations require different types of units; that is, there is no one form for all units. Different reference books promote different formats, some of which are harder and some easier to use in a particular situation. You should examine these options and pick the one that best fits your situation.

Despite the variations in form suggested for unit preparation, there are certain important considerations you should not overlook when preparing any unit. They are described next.

Make your unit plan fit into the class's overall course of study. If you are allowed to pick your own unit theme, examine the course of study and pick a theme that fits into the long-term plans for the class. Whether you pick the theme or your mentoring teacher does, check to see how your unit fits into the overall instructional plan. Find out from your mentoring teacher the prior learning upon which your unit can build. Check on the relationships between your unit and the previous and succeeding units. Decide what concepts you must include to ensure students' success in succeeding units.

Ask your mentoring teacher how much time is allowed for your unit, and make your plans conform to this allotment. You will probably not be able to include every aspect of your chosen topic within the given time frame. Therefore, you must decide, either independently or in conjunction with the students, which aspects to include.

Plan the daily scheduling for the unit. Although this should be flexible, failure to plan could cause difficulty in including the needed instruction.

Consider carefully the students who will be studying the unit in terms of their backgrounds of experience in relation to the theme, their general levels of achievement in school or in your subject area (or both), their levels of interest in the unit theme, their reading levels, their attitudes toward school and the subject area or areas involved, their study habits and ability to work independently or engage in group work, and their special talents. Plan all your activities with these characteristics in mind. It may be useful to write down a class profile, including all these characteristics, to refer to as you develop objectives, teaching methods, activities, and evaluation methods.

Collect ideas for the thematic unit from a variety of sources: students' textbooks, your college textbooks, professional journals, local resources (businesses and individuals), resource units on file in your school or college or university media center, and, of course, your mentoring teacher. Make lists of helpful books, periodicals, websites, audiovisual aids, and resource people for future reference. One caution is in order here: Do not lecture straight from your old college or university notes. Remember that your students are not yet ready for material of such difficulty. Use the college or university notes as background material, and work in information from them only as it is directly applicable and appropriate for your particular students.

Draft your objectives for the thematic unit according to the content you want to cover and the students with whom you will be working. You may wish to refer to your methods textbooks to refresh your memory on writing clear objectives. Include both cognitive and affective objectives when appropriate.

Organize the procedures section of your unit plan to include the unit introduction, the body of the unit, and culminating activities:

1. The unit introduction should connect the unit with prior learning or backgrounds of experience, determine the needs of the students and their strengths in this area of study (through pretests or informal discussions), and arouse interest in the topic and motivate students to study it. Methods and activities for this part of the unit should be of high interest; frequently, they should vary from the usual classroom routine. When a theme studies approach is used, the students often have much input in the choice of the theme. This results in a high level of motivation because of their sense of "ownership" of the topic.

2. The body of the unit should address the teaching of each objective, matching teaching procedures and student activities, including assignments, to objectives. Include evaluative measures as needed. With a theme studies approach, the students will have some choice of activities and assignments, once again promoting motivation.

3. The culminating activities for the unit should tie together all the previous learning. Culminating activities frequently include practical applications of the concepts acquired in the unit, interrelating the various concepts. Teachers and students may choose these activities together. Overall evaluative measures may be a part of the culminating activities.

Vary your planned activities. This will help keep the students' attention and can help your unit progress more smoothly, because certain activities suit certain types of learning better than others. Consider audiovisual aids, field trips, resource people, class discussions, library research activities, computer searches, simulations and dramatizations, construction activities, oral and written

After you have learned how to plan individual lessons, you may be asked to plan a unit.

reports, games, demonstrations, and creative applications. Be sure, however, that all activities relate directly to unit objectives.

CASE STUDY 4.2

Failure to Follow Through

Jerry Clement was planning a unit on law enforcement. Jerry's mentoring teacher, Mrs. Granger, knew an excellent resource person, Mr. McDonald, whom Jerry might use in the course of his unit. She told Jerry about Mr. McDonald and, to her surprise, discovered that Jerry was a friend of his. She strongly suggested that Jerry ask Mr. McDonald to come to the class and share his knowledge with the students. Jerry seemed to think this was a good idea, but he never actually contacted Mr. McDonald. At the end of the term, Jerry was surprised that his mentoring teacher rated him lower than he would have liked on use of community resources.

1. Do you believe that having a resource person speak to the class would have enhanced Jerry's unit? Why or why not?
2. If you had been Jerry, what would you have done if you decided that having Mr. McDonald would not add substantially to your unit?

Determine the different types of evaluation you intend to use during the course of the unit in order to be sure you haven't overrelied on a single type. Consider the use of formal and informal written tests, oral

FIGURE 4–2
Unit Plan Outline*

A. Topic and overall time allotment
B. Students' characteristics and backgrounds
C. Resources and materials
D. Unit objectives
E. Unit procedures
   1. Introduction
   2. Body
   3. Culminating activities
F. Evaluation

* See Appendix B for sample unit plans.

or performance tests, observation of students' performance in activities and discussions, evaluation of daily in-class and homework assignments, conferences with individual pupils, and portfolios of work, among other evaluation methods.

Estimate the time needed for the various instructional procedures and student activities, and make tentative decisions about daily coverage. Make adjustments if your plans do not fit the allotted time.

Consult your mentoring teacher about the plan you have constructed. If it meets with the teacher's approval, make detailed daily lesson plans based on your unit plan. Figure 4–2 shows a brief outline to use in unit planning. If you remember that a unit of work is a series of interrelated lessons clustered around a central theme, then you will probably plan a good unit. Poor units are characterized by lack of continuity and interrelatedness and by irrelevant activities.

Complete Activity 4.3 as you plan your first thematic unit. You may wish to photocopy this activity form and use it for other units as well.

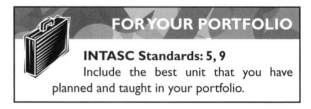

FOR YOUR PORTFOLIO

INTASC Standards: 5, 9
Include the best unit that you have planned and taught in your portfolio.

PLANNING FOR EVALUATION

You can check students' progress through various means—observation, informal techniques, and formal tests—as you teach. These evaluative activities will help you to decide whether or not learning is taking place.

ACTIVITY 4.3 | *Thematic Unit Planning Form*

Unit topic:

Major concepts to be covered:

Overall time allotment:

Daily scheduling plan:

Students' characteristics that need to be considered in teaching this unit:

List of resources and materials:

Unit objectives:

Unit procedures:

      Introduction:

      Body (list of lessons—*not* complete lesson plans, activities, and assignments):

      Culminating activities:

Evaluation:

Method of evaluation:

Assignments—homework or in-class supervised study:

Self-evaluation:

Supervisory feedback:

Teaching without evaluation is like taking a trip without checking the map to see that you are going in the right direction. Periodic assessment enables you to observe students' progress and then make adjustments in your instruction that enable students to achieve instructional goals.

Evaluation is an important component of any instructional plan, but it is not an easy task. You will want to know: How do I find out how well my students are learning? What kinds of tests should I give? How often should I give them? How difficult should the questions be? What happens if everyone fails, or if everyone gets a perfect score? What can I learn from the test results that will help me plan instruction? How can I measure different types of learning, and how can I be sure that my assessment techniques are appropriate for measuring each student's ability in various situations? You probably know some of the answers to these questions from courses in evaluation and measurement, from your own experiences as a student, and from observations of your mentoring teacher. In this section, you should find the answers to other questions.

CASE STUDY 4.3

Difficulty of Evaluation

Mr. Todd has been a student teacher in eighth grade for 4 weeks. During that time, he has discovered that evaluating students' progress is more difficult than he expected. Instead of simply averaging test scores, Mr. Todd finds that he should probably consider a number of other factors as well. Five students, in particular, puzzle Mr. Todd.

Amy is alert, interested, outgoing, and talkative. She always has her hand up to answer questions, even though she sometimes can't answer correctly. Despite her eagerness and enthusiasm during class, however, Amy makes very low grades on tests. Her written work is also below average for the class.

George appears bored during class, often gazes out the window, and seldom participates in class discussions. He makes average grades on tests. Mr. Todd notices, however, that George shows spurts of interest and creativity when the class works on special projects. He appears to be a natural leader during group work and can analyze and solve problems remarkably well.

Julie is a straight-A student. She rarely participates in class discussions and seems very nervous when called on to respond in class. Her homework is meticulous, but she never shows any interest in class activities other than what is required for getting good grades.

Barry is a careful, thorough worker. He pays close attention to details and conscientiously and systematically completes all assignments. He is never able to finish a test within the time limits, however, so his test scores are low.

Carol races through her work so that she can read her library books. She catches on quickly to new material and readily grasps difficult concepts. Her work is sloppy and careless, however, and she seldom turns in her homework. Her test scores are average.

1. From the information given, what do you believe are the learning strengths and weaknesses of each student?
2. For which students, if any, do you think test scores accurately reflect ability?
3. What factors should a teacher consider when evaluating students?
4. How can evaluation help a teacher plan appropriate instruction to meet individual needs?

Informal Evaluation Techniques

As a student teacher or practicum student, you will usually evaluate students' progress informally, although you may occasionally give a major examination covering a unit. You will gain the most useful information from day-to-day observations, samples of students' work, and short quizzes for checking students' understanding of the material you are presenting.

Observation. You have many opportunities to observe students in different situations, both academic (during class) and social (before and after class or during extracurricular activities). If you observe purposefully, perhaps by using the Observation Guide in Activity 4.4, you can determine a lot about how students learn, such as which students are self-motivated, easily distracted, uninterested, quick to learn, or capable of better work. You'll find that some possess leadership qualities while others prefer to be part of a group, and that some are naturally attentive and eager to learn while others appear bored and uninterested. As you systematically observe your students, you are acquiring information that will help you plan lessons and activities to meet the wide range of individual differences within any class.

Teacher-Made Quizzes. You need to consider certain factors when planning your testing program. After identifying the objectives and content to be covered in a test, make sure your test distributes the emphasis appropriately over the content. For example, if you spent most of your instructional time on identifying main ideas in novels, the greater part of the test should ask questions about main ideas in novels, not about interpreting the mood projected by the authors. After assigning relative importance to the topics for the test, you must decide what type of test items to use—for example, completion, short-answer, essay, true-false, matching, or multiple-choice. Completion, true-false, multiple-choice, and short-answer items are often used for short assessments, while essay items are best for major examinations that require students to organize and present a careful discussion.

A review quiz can be part of a lesson plan. The quiz may be oral, or it may be a short written one of perhaps three to five questions, limited to the material taught in the immediate lesson. The quiz should be varied, with true-false and short-answer items. The main purpose of such a quiz is to see what concepts each student has not grasped or perhaps has misunderstood. It may be marked by the students and then checked by you.

A longer test may be appropriate periodically. It may have 20 to 25 true-false, multiple-choice, and short-answer questions. Such a test should be duplicated, rather than written on the board or dictated.

A unit test covers a larger block of teaching and may require most of a class period to complete. You will want to have several parts, including short essay items. You should prepare a standard answer sheet before marking the test, so that you will be consistent in your grading.

Some teachers give midterms and final examinations to cover a half or whole semester of instruction. You can assign points proportionally to each part of the examination. The point values should reflect the importance of the material covered to the class objectives.

Completion items are often used to measure knowledge of names, dates, terms, and other simple associations. Choose only important concepts, and make sure only one response correctly completes the statement. Short-answer items are similar in format to completion items.

True-false items should cover only important content, not trivial items. Avoid the use of words, such as *all* and *never,* that may give clues to correct answers. Avoid negative statements, since students often misread these statements and therefore give wrong answers. To discourage guessing, students taking a true-false test should provide a reason for any item marked "false."

Matching items are often used to test knowledge of definitions or identification of objects presented graphically or pictorially. To help eliminate guessing on such items, present extra possible response items.

Multiple-choice items should be in the form of questions involving complete ideas. The four or five possible responses should be grammatically and logically consistent and similar in length, and correct responses should appear in different positions over the course of the test (for example, not consistently as the third choice or the last choice).

Essay items should be phrased carefully, specifically defining the expectations for each answer. Directions must be thorough and specific regarding the number of points or percentage weight assigned to each question. The answer key should contain the essential components of the answer, and you should score papers against these components.

Traditional types of test questions are not always suitable for evaluating certain types of knowledge. For example, it is better to judge a student's writing competence by evaluating actual writing samples than by asking objective questions about, for example, placement of commas and spelling of words. Also, when evaluating higher-order thinking skills, teachers should design open-ended test questions that allow students to give various solutions or interpretations.

Some guidelines for administering informal tests are:

1. Make sure that your test is based on the material you have taught.
2. Ask "fair" questions. Avoid using misleading, ambiguous questions or questions that relate to insignificant material.
3. Make sure that students have the materials they need for taking the test (sharpened pencils with erasers, enough paper, and so forth).
4. Give clear instructions, and make sure that students understand what they are to do. You may need to do an example with the students before they begin.
5. Be certain that students understand the purpose of the test.
6. Let students know your expectations regarding neatness and correct spelling and punctuation.
7. Space students so that they will not be tempted to cheat.
8. Walk quietly around the room while the students are taking the test, and make sure they are following directions.
9. Make sure that students understand your grading policy.
10. Make a scoring key on one copy of the test you are giving.
11. When grading papers, give students the benefit of the doubt, if there are two ways to interpret what they have said.
12. Return tests promptly, and go over them with the students so that they can learn from their mistakes.
13. Make sure that students understand the meanings of their scores in terms of letter grades and percentages of total grades.
14. Do not change a grade unless you have made an error in grading the test.

ACTIVITY 4.4 | *Observation Guide*

This observation guide will help you make systematic observations of students, which will help you plan learning experiences. You may wish to make copies of this observation guide for all your students, or you may prefer to make copies only for selected students.

Student's Name _____

Key:

_____ 1. Volunteers to answer questions posed to class   A—Always occurs

_____ 2. Listens carefully during class time; follows directions   B—Often occurs

_____ 3. Asks questions about what is not understood   C—Occasionally occurs

_____ 4. Completes homework assignments   D—Seldom occurs

_____ 5. Participates in voluntary projects   E—Never occurs

_____ 6. Likes to help others and share activities with them

_____ 7. Projects a good self-image

_____ 8. Attends regularly

_____ 9. Performs well on quizzes

_____ 10. Uses resource materials well

If all of your students made perfect or nearly perfect scores on the test, it means that either you taught very well, the students were very bright or studied very hard, the test was too easy, or some combination of these factors existed. If nearly all the students did poorly on the test, it may mean that they didn't understand the material, they didn't study, or the test was too difficult. If the problem seems to be that they didn't learn the material, you may need to reteach it. Your mentoring teacher can advise you on these matters.

FOR YOUR PORTFOLIO

INTASC Standards: 8, 9
Include in your portfolio one test that you have constructed. In a brief paragraph, indicate the purpose of this particular test and the results of its administration. In another paragraph, evaluate the effectiveness of the test for your purposes.

Rubrics.   Rubrics are essentially scoring guides that identify the characteristics of students' work at different levels of quality. For example, a rubric would list the characteristics of a high-quality paper or presentation; then it would list the characteristics of each succeeding lower level of quality. For example, a high-quality research paper might be identified as one in which the writer defines the topic in an exemplary fashion, presents an abundance of relevant information, includes information from several sources (possibly a designated number of sources) in a completely integrated fashion, presents thorough documentation, organizes the material well, and uses correct mechanics (syntax, spelling, etc.). A medium-quality paper might be one in which the writer defines the topic adequately, presents some relevant information, includes information from several sources with some attempt at integration, presents documentation that is minimally adequate, has a recognizable organizational pattern, and generally uses correct mechanics. Lower levels would be similarly described, allowing you to evaluate the research paper in a holistic manner.

If you give each characteristic in a scoring rubric (for example, definition of topic or presentation of relevant information) a numerical value (excellent = 5, very good = 4, average = 3, low = 2, very low = 1), analytic scoring can be achieved, and you can generate a numerical score by adding the ratings for all characteristics. Different characteristics may be weighted differently by multiplying each score by the percentage of the total score that you want it to represent.

Computer Applications to Testing.   Although computers can be useful in assessing students' progress, not all school systems have computers and software available for assessment and test analysis. If computers are available, you may assess the students' knowledge of skills by observing them as they complete class-related computer activities or by giving tests on the computer.

If you have access to a computer, you may use it for test construction and analysis of grades. Word processors facilitate test preparation, because even people who are not good typists can readily make corrections. Word-processing programs allow you to edit test questions and easily and efficiently move items from one section of the test to another. You can also use "authoring" software to assist your test construction and other computer programs to help you average grades, analyze the difficulty of individual test items, and keep records of students' scores.

Formal Tests

Most school systems only administer formal standardized tests once or twice a year, so you may not have an opportunity to give one to your students. Nevertheless, you should be able to interpret the scores and understand the place of formal tests in measuring students' progress.

Norms, averages of the test scores of students in the norming population, are ordinarily applied to formal or standardized tests. Group achievement tests show the teacher how the class, not an individual class member, is performing in comparison with other groups of students. The most important score, the class average, helps the teacher determine whether the class is

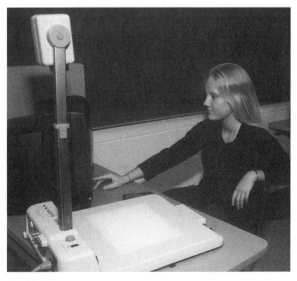

Computers are good tools for test construction.

performing about the same as, better than, or worse than students elsewhere.

Standardized tests report norms in several ways:

1. *Grade equivalents*—The grade level for which a given score is a real or estimated average. Scores are expressed in terms of grade and month of grade, such as 4.8 for fourth grade, eighth month.

2. *Percentile rank*—Ranking a test score based on its position within a group of 100 scores. The percentile rank of a score is the percentage of scores equal to or lower than the given score in some reference group.

3. *Stanine*—One of the steps in a nine-point scale of standard scores. The stanine scale has values from 1 to 9, with a mean (average) of 5.

Table 4–1 summarizes the types of tests that are appropriate for different assessment purposes.

Portfolio Assessment

Many educators believe that test scores alone do not accurately reflect what students can do. A popular alternative assessment technique is portfolio analysis. Portfolios are collections of varied, representative samples of students' work over a period of time or examples of the students' best work in specific areas. Although informal tests can be part of a portfolio, work samples—such as drafts of students' writing or videotapes or audiotapes of oral reading—are more likely to be present. The following items may be included: writing samples, project reports, lists of books read, tape recordings of oral reading, students' self-appraisals, semantic maps, checklists, illustrations, selected daily work, informal quizzes, teacher's notes on observations, literature logs (responses to reading), content area journals, pictures of project results, videotapes of presentations, multimedia presentations on disk, parents' comments, reflective analysis of portfolio contents, and a table of contents that shows the organization of the material.

At the secondary level, portfolios can be designed specifically for each subject. The following are examples of things that may be included in different areas.

- *Art*—Collages; prints; portraits; still lifes; sketches from rough draft to finished form; photographs of sculptures, weaving, and other three-dimensional pieces; printouts of personally designed websites; and analyses of various art processes students have used.
- *Science*—Progress reports on experiments, drawings (diagrams and charts), biographies of scientists, labeled earth samples, statistical data for projects, journals of direct observations of phenomena, videotapes of experiments or presentations, and multimedia presentations on disk.

TABLE 4–1 Guide for Selecting Tests	Purpose	Appropriate Types of Tests
	To check short-term progress	Short, objective written quizzes; oral questioning sessions; computer drill and practice
	To check depth of understanding of a subject	Thought-provoking essay questions
	To evaluate writing ability	Writing samples (evaluated using rubrics), essay questions, journals
	To assess problem-solving and thinking skills	Observation of performance, open-ended test questions
	To evaluate learning over an extended time period	Word-processed examinations with a variety of questions (such as essay, true-false, multiple-choice, and completion)
	To assess skill mastery	Short-answer or completion questions, computer practice
	To get a quick estimate of reading ability or level	Observation of oral reading performance and answers to oral comprehension questions
	To compare achievement with that of students across the nation	Standardized achievement tests

FIGURE 4–3
Key Concepts for Using Portfolio
Assessment

Portfolio inclusions relate to instructional goals.

Students engage in reflective and critical thinking as they select and review their work.

Both teacher and students select material for inclusion in portfolios.

Periodically, the teacher and students have conferences about portfolios, noting changes and progress, discovering insights, and seeking new directions for growth and learning.

Portfolios combine instruction and assessment by looking at the learning process as well as the product.

Portfolios are accessible to students at any time; they are working folders.

Students and teachers become partners in learning as they cooperatively assess students' work.

- *Composition*—Initial and all other drafts through publication of articles and stories, note cards, letters, poems, and essays.

If you decide to use portfolios, explain to the students what you are doing and why. Students need to understand that, instead of simply averaging test and daily work grades, you will be asking for their help in evaluating samples of their work. In cooperation with the students, establish guidelines for the types of material to include. In most cases, selections should relate to instructional goals and represent the students' work processes and best work; otherwise, portfolios can become stuffed with all sorts of materials that may have little value for analysis. Make sure that students date each piece of work so that you and they can see the progress they are making. Schedule periodic individual conferences with students to discuss their portfolio items and assess progress.

Although you may require students to include certain work samples, it is worthwhile to let them select most of their portfolio items. Deciding what to include and how to organize the contents requires students to use critical thinking skills, reflect on the merits of their work, and evaluate their progress. In fact, you may ask them to write on cards or large stick-on notes why they selected particular pieces to include. When they do this, they must justify their selections, and you will see what they value about their work.

You may want to place in students' folders some of your observations, such as anecdotal notes about their contributions during class discussions. You may also want to include checklists about such areas as their progress toward achieving literacy or their participa-

tion in a social studies unit. Some key ideas for using portfolios are given in Figure 4–3.

Portfolio assessment requires additional time and effort, but it keeps you informed about how and what your students are learning. Portfolios are also useful for conferences with parents because you can show examples of what students are doing in class. Additionally, portfolios provide you with supporting information when you fill out report cards. You may want to try portfolio assessment for just one 6-week period to see how it goes. (Activity 4.5 contains key concepts for using portfolio assessment.) If the system works well, you may want to continue using it. You and the students, along with your mentoring teacher, must decide what happens to the portfolios when you leave. Your mentoring teacher may want to keep them, pass them along to next year's teacher, give them to the students to keep, or send them home to parents.

DISCUSSION QUESTIONS

1. What are some different lesson plan forms you might use? What are advantages and disadvantages of each form?
2. Are units more effective in your teaching situation when they cut across disciplines or when they are chosen from content within a single discipline? Why do you think so? Is there a place for both types of units?
3. How would you modify the observation guide (Activity 4.4) to fit your particular class or classes?

4. What types of tests would be appropriate for the following situations?
   a. To see if a group of third graders can divide words into syllables
   b. To discover the reasoning powers of high school students in relation to foreign policy
   c. To assess the knowledge gained during a 6-week unit on plant life
   d. To find out how your class compares with the national average on mathematical computation
   e. To assess the creative writing abilities of students
   f. To check understanding of last night's homework assignment, which was to read part of a chapter from the textbook
5. How might test scores indicate which students are or are not working up to their ability?
6. How does evaluation enable a teacher to plan better instruction?
7. In the grade or subject you teach, what items would be appropriate to include in an assessment portfolio? How would you guide students in selecting which items to include?

ACTIVITY 4.5 | *Summary Sheet for Portfolio Assessment*

Complete this summary sheet for your conferences with your students. You will probably want to make enough photocopies of this page for all your students.

Grade: _____ Subject: _____ Date: _____

List of items in portfolio:

Student's assessment of portfolio items:

Teacher's assessment of portfolio items:

Conclusions and recommendations:

Student's signature _____

5

Integrating Language, Thinking, and Study Skills

Case Study 5.1: Making Sense of Text

Mr. Viera, a student teacher, had started teaching a unit on the Holocaust. He had involved his students in planning and implementing the unit by finding out what they already knew and what they wanted to know, by helping them to locate resources, and by discussing events during that time period. The students found several Holocaust-related books, and one student brought some sample identification cards from the Holocaust Memorial Museum in Washington, D.C. It was now time to turn to the textbook and ask students to read the chapter dealing with the Holocaust.

Despite Mr. Viera's careful introduction, many of the students had trouble comprehending the text. Some found it difficult, and others were completely confused.

Mr. Viera (attempting to clear up the problems): What can you do when you try to make sense out of what's in the textbook?

Beth: I just keep reading until I get to the end. I don't know what else to do.

Mr. Viera: But if you don't understand what you are reading, isn't there something you can do about it?

Juanita: Sometimes I go back and read the parts I don't understand over again slowly until I get it.

Mr. Viera: Good idea! Let's write some of your ideas on a chart so you can refer to them as you read. (He begins recording students' ideas.) Does anyone else do something while you're reading if you don't understand?

Clay: I sort of predict what I think is going to happen and then read on to see if I got it right.

Jamie: I try to put it in my own words. The textbook has big words, and I try to put it in easy words.

Mr. Viera: That's called paraphrasing, and it's a good strategy to use. We're going to have a test covering this chapter on Friday. What are some things you can do to help you study?

Carl: I like to write down the important names and dates so that I can remember them.

Steve: And sometimes I say things out loud to myself to help me concentrate.

Mr. Viera: These are good ideas. Anyone else?

Mateo: There's a glossary in the back of the book. I can look up words there if I don't know what they mean.

Veronica: The headings and subheadings help me get my thoughts straight. They sort of give the main idea of what's coming.

Carol: Sometimes I study with Betsy. She asks me questions and I ask her questions so we know if we understand it.

Mr. Viera: That works. There's something else that you should all do. We've talked about it before.

Jon: We can think about what we already learned about the Holocaust, like how we pretended to write our experiences in journals and how we acted out how the prisoners must have felt. And we can think about the books and pictures we found.

Mr. Viera: That's one of the most important things to do. Think about what you already know and use that knowledge as you read more about the subject. You've come up with a pretty good list, and we can add to it if we think of something else later. First, you need to know whether you understand it or not; then, if you don't understand, you need to find some strategies like the ones you just listed. When you read, always be sure you're getting the meaning. If the text isn't making sense to you, do something about it!

1. How was Mr. Viera's questioning useful for his students? Was he right to take time to discuss reading and study strategies?
2. Do you think all the students will begin to apply these strategies after this lesson? If not, what else could Mr. Viera do to make sure students use them?
3. What were some of the ideas he used during the presentation of the unit? Were these good teaching strategies?
4. What are some options that you have as the teacher if the text is indeed too difficult or confusing for the students to read?

RELATIONSHIPS AMONG LANGUAGE, THINKING, AND STUDY SKILLS

Language and thinking are intricately related. People use language to think; without using words and sentences, it is virtually impossible to think, and it is certainly impossible to express complex or abstract ideas. By improving skill in language use, teachers develop an important tool for higher-order thinking. Study skills, such as location and organization of information, retention, interpretation, and metacognition, involve the use of higher-order thinking skills and effective use of language. Study skills promote the effective learning of academic content. Therefore, all the areas discussed in this chapter promote effective learning.

LANGUAGE ARTS

Language skills are vital to your students' success in all curricular areas. The National Council of Teachers of English (NCTE) has identified six language arts that are important to students in functioning as productive members of today's society—listening, speaking, reading, writing, viewing, and visually representing. Elementary-grade teachers may have one or more special periods devoted to language arts instruction. Secondary English teachers should also include the language arts in their instruction. Simply focusing on language skills in a separate period is not sufficient for their complete assimilation, however. Language is used daily in all classes. A close reading of the Standards for the English Language Arts that were developed by NCTE and the International Reading Association (1996) reveals that all 12 of the standards relate to important skills for effective content area learning. Without emphasis on these skills throughout the day, students will not see their applicability to content area tasks.

Elementary teachers should help students apply language skills in every curricular area as the students read and view to complete assignments, give and listen to oral reports, participate in discussions, complete written assignments, and make visual presentations. Secondary teachers of content areas other than English should try to reinforce language skills as they are needed for specific assignments.

Reading Proficiency and School Assignments

Although students are expected to learn much content from their textbooks and other supplementary printed materials, the textbooks chosen for particular classes are often too difficult for many of the students to handle with ease. You must be aware of the difficulty of the materials and provide appropriate alternative materials for students who cannot handle the standard assignments.

You may adjust reading assignments for students who are unable to read the text or other assignments by providing those students with easier texts or materials that cover the same topics, or by writing explanations of key concepts at easier reading levels for their use.

Teachers should be prepared to help students apply their language skills as they read and complete written and oral assignments.

You or a good reader from the class may also record the assigned material so poor readers can listen to it as they "read" it. When students follow along in their books as they listen, they should pick up some of the key terms and add them to their sight vocabularies, making further assignments in this subject area easier to read. If you delegate the recording to students, check the materials before you release them for use by their classmates. Poorly prepared materials can do more harm than good. Using videos or other media, manipulatives, and activities such as creative dramatics and simulations also helps students who have difficulty in reading assignments.

To promote comprehension of assigned reading material, give students purposes for the reading. Purpose questions help students focus on important information and promote comprehension and retention of the material, but remember that good purposes will be of no value if assignments are too difficult for the students to handle. Another way to help students set purposes for reading is to ask them for predictions about what the material will say or to have them decide upon questions that they hope the material will answer for them.

You can also enhance reading comprehension in content materials by building background for reading material that you are about to assign. Class discussions, videotapes, pictures, websites, computer simulations, and class demonstrations can all provide background concepts that will make the reading assignment easier to understand. Introduction of new vocabulary terms related to the concepts at this point can help students acquire the information in the assignment more readily. This approach works because vocabulary terms are labels for the concepts that are presented, and knowing the proper labels makes discussing the concepts easier.

Writing Across the Curriculum

Writing is a useful skill in every curricular area. In English and language arts classes, students are taught how to write effectively, but in all classes writing is an effective technique for learning that you should take advantage of when you teach. Although you will focus on composition and mechanics of writing if you are an English teacher, you may also employ some writing assignments that are primarily designed to help students learn other things that you are teaching. If you teach another subject, you may occasionally ignore dangling participles and comma splices in favor of focusing exclusively on the student's message. Of course, if the message is obscured by poor mechanics, a teachable moment for this skill area exists. Students will not succeed in many future endeavors if their writing skills are not sufficient for clear communication.

Write Time for Kids is a commercial program for Grades K–8 designed to teach the writing process and nonfiction writing skills to students. High-interest articles from *Time for Kids* magazine are the vehicles for instruction. This research-based program is correlated to many state standards. The directed writing activities are similar to ones on standardized tests, and they help students prepare for test taking while reading meaningful material.

Another commercial program, the Write Source Handbooks and Language Series, also covers the writing process and many types of writing. There is *Write One* for first grade; *Write Away* for second grade; *Write on Track* for third grade; *Writers Express* for fourth through fifth grades; *Write Source 2000* for sixth through eighth grades; and *Writers Inc., School to Work*, and *Write for College* for high school.

Writing can be used as a tool for learning in different curricular areas if you have students write summaries of class lectures, which can sometimes be shared with the class and revised as needed; explanations of new concepts presented in the textbook or in class; descriptions of processes being studied; reactions to curricular material; and descriptions of applications for ideas presented in class. The following list shows some ways for students to apply writing skills in various areas of the curriculum.

- *Literature*—Writing imaginative newspaper accounts of happenings in a novel, sketches of major characters, or diary entries that a character might have written.
- *Science*—Recording the results of an experiment, composing an essay about the impact of a scientific discovery on society, tracing the development of an area of technology over a period of time, or writing research papers on scientific topics.
- *Social studies*—Producing imaginary letters from one historical character to another, writing reactions to a historical character's actions, writing explanations about the causes of historical events, or developing research papers on related topics.
- *Physical education*—Writing directions for a sports activity or an exercise, or writing about the benefits of an exercise program.
- *Art and music*—Writing descriptions of techniques or reactions to paintings, sculptures, and compositions.
- *Family living*—Writing case studies related to child-care techniques or nutritional practices, or writing about advantages and disadvantages of certain home-management practices.

Writing opportunities are available in every area, and writing activities can help students organize their knowledge, as well as clarify their feelings, about many topics. Having students write about their studies provides an opportunity for you to see each student's current level of understanding and allows you to plan instruction to correct misconceptions. These writing activities also make students more aware of what they already know and what they need to find out. Personal journals, which may be read by others only at the invitation of the students who produced them, may allow students to explore their feelings and clarify their personal beliefs.

Research papers are often assigned in many curricular areas. Students must learn to paraphrase and synthesize information from multiple sources. With the ease of copying and pasting information from Internet sites, teachers must diligently explain to students the importance of putting material into their own words to avoid plagiarism. Recently, multigenre reports have become popular with some teachers because they require students to transform the information found during their research into different genres, thereby applying interpretation of the material and creativity in its presentation, as well as avoiding direct copying from sources. Endnotes or rationale cards generally explain the purpose of each genre used to convey information about the subject. Although the main part of the report is different in appearance and style from a typical research paper, students provide a standard bibliography of sources from which the information was drawn (Allen, 2001; Moulton, 1999; Romano, 1995).

Consider possible writing activities as you plan each lesson. Think about possible benefits of each activity, and choose judiciously. These activities—if handled well—can offer dividends in initial learning and retention and may even improve attitudes toward the area of study. Sometimes English teachers and teachers from other disciplines work together to assign and grade research reports. If you share the same students with another teacher, you may want to try this type of collaboration. Complete Activity 5.1 to help you analyze your use of writing in your classes.

Literature Across the Curriculum

Literature is often relegated to English class, especially in secondary schools. Many teachers have found, however, that literature can also enrich other curricular areas. Integrating literature across the curriculum can be accomplished more easily in self-contained classroom situations than in departmentalized settings, but it can provide rewarding results for teachers in departmentalized settings if they work together as a team.

Social studies classes are a natural place to use literature to enrich the curriculum. Both fiction and nonfiction selections set in specific historical periods can make these times come alive for readers. Many stories in books, for example, are set during wars; and they can help students see, in a way that history textbooks cannot, how these wars affected the people's lives. Similarly, stories set in particular geographic regions can add to the understanding of material presented in a geography text. Some books can also clarify lifestyles and occupations for students. Biographies of important historical figures can make these people's contributions to civilization clearer, and books about people from diverse cultures can help students understand themselves and others better.

Literature can also help students in science classes understand scientific concepts and obtain insight into the lives of inventors and innovators. Finding out the painstaking experimentation behind many scientific discoveries can put textbook information in perspective. Reading books that focus upon a single aspect of science, such as the solar system, also can be helpful to students, since textbook material is often so condensed that its clarity suffers. A book on a single topic is able to elaborate on and flesh out spare textbook discussions. Books that contain experiments for the students to perform allow hands-on experiences that promote motivation and understanding of concepts. Many books for young children highlight the cycles of the seasons and life cycles of plants and animals. Many books focus on conservation and the environment.

Students in physical education classes may read books about the sports that they are playing or biographies of sports personalities. Both factual how-to-play books and fictional and factual sports stories can add interest and motivation to these classes.

Even in mathematics classes, literature can be useful. Books are available for young children that emphasize counting, concepts of numbers, telling time, understanding calendars, learning about measurements, and comprehending concepts of size. Older students may enjoy and learn from mathematical puzzle books, such as Martin Gardner's *The Unexpected Hanging and Other Mathematical Diversions* and *My Best Mathematical and Logic Puzzles.*

Applications of literature in English classes are numerous. Literature can be used to study genres, characterization, plots, settings, themes, and writing styles, as well as to promote literary appreciation, or it can serve as a stimulus for writing. Comparing and contrasting literature selections can help students understand genres, cultures, and points of view, among other things. Even though an English class without literature would be unthinkable, many uses of literature may not be included in English classes if the teacher fails to examine the many available possibilities. Activity 5.2 gives you a chance to assess your use of literature in the class or classes that you teach.

ACTIVITY 5.1 | *Writing Across the Curriculum*

Place a checkmark (✓) before the writing activities that you have used or intend to use in your class or classes. After you have tried each activity, place a plus (+) after the activity if it worked well or a minus (−) after the activity if it was not successful in meeting your goals.

_____ Summaries of class lectures _____

_____ Summaries of textbook readings _____

_____ Summaries of outside reading assignments _____

_____ Explanations of new concepts _____

_____ Descriptions of processes being studied _____

_____ Reactions to material presented in the texbook or in class _____

_____ Applications of ideas presented in class or in the textbook _____

_____ Newspaper accounts based on material read _____

_____ Character sketches of real or fictional characters _____

_____ Diary entries that real or fictional characters might have written _____

_____ Results of experiments _____

_____ Explanation of impact on society of a scientific discovery or political action _____

_____ Account of the development of an area of technology over a period of time _____

_____ Imaginary letters from one historical or fictional character to another _____

_____ Written reactions to the actions of one historical or fictional character _____

_____ Written explanations about the causes of historical events _____

_____ Written directions for a game or other activity _____

_____ Explanation of benefits of an exercise program or particular diet _____

_____ Written description of an artistic technique _____

_____ Written reactions to works of art _____

_____ Case studies _____

_____ Personal journals _____

_____ Other _____

_____ Please describe:

_____ Other _____

_____ Please describe:

_____ Other _____

_____ Please describe:

ACTIVITY 5.2 | *Literature Across the Curriculum*

List four literature selections related to a class or several classes that you are teaching. Note how the use of each of these selections could enrich the teaching of your class or classes.

1. Class:

SELECTION   USEFULNESS

2. Class:

SELECTION   USEFULNESS

3. Class:

SELECTION   USEFULNESS

4. Class:

SELECTION   USEFULNESS

FOCUS ON THINKING

To focus on thinking, teachers must give learners an opportunity to use their reasoning abilities. A constructionist position focuses on thinking to construct knowledge.

Constructivism

Constructivism means that learners construct their own knowledge instead of reproducing someone else's knowledge (Zahorik, 1995). They create understanding as they try to make sense of their experiences. For example, two students may interpret the same reading selection in different ways or view participating in the same event differently because of their varied prior experiences and attitudes. People's knowledge and understanding can also change over time as they learn more, have more experiences, and understand at deeper levels.

Constructivist teaching emphasizes thinking, understanding, and self-control over behavior. Many of the teaching strategies you have learned and will continue to use are likely to be constructivist, as are many of the ideas presented in this chapter. Some characteristics of constructivist teaching and their classroom applications appear in Figure 5–1.

Literal-Level Thinking Skills

You may associate school with literal-level thinking; that is, looking for directly stated facts. Your teachers' questions may have abounded with *who, what, where,* and *when* queries that could be located in the text in exact words. Whereas such thinking is a basis for higher-order thinking, it is not sufficient for the development of a properly educated citizenry. Higher-order thinking skills must be directly addressed in instruction, even though they are more difficult to teach than literal-level thinking skills.

Higher-Order Thinking Skills

The current educational interest in higher-order thinking skills is making many teachers aware of the need to help students learn how to think, not just recall information. Thought processes, including learning how to learn, are far more useful for dealing with life than is simple knowledge of facts. In and of themselves, facts have little value, but a person trained to use thinking skills can use facts to solve problems, make decisions, and generate new ideas. Knowledge-level skills, such as recognition and recall, are not included in this discussion.

Although you may occasionally want to do some puzzles or problem solving for specific purposes, you should usually integrate thinking skills with subjects across the curriculum instead of teaching them in isolation. Thinking skills then become a natural part of learning. Students not only learn information in each content area, but they also learn how to think about what they are learning.

FOR YOUR PORTFOLIO

INTASC Standards: 4, 9
Write a summary of the teaching practices that you plan to use. Begin with a statement of your philosophy about instruction.

FIGURE 5–1
Characteristics of Constructivist Teaching and Class Applications

Constructivism	Class Applications
Activate prior knowledge. Relate new knowledge to what is known.	Brainstorm what students know. Create timelines of events.
Focus on the whole, the "big picture." Identify major concepts, not fragments.	Demonstrate square dancing as a whole; don't focus on only one movement at a time.
"Scaffold," or provide support. Build on prior knowledge. Withdraw support gradually.	Model a skill by thinking aloud. Use manipulatives, models, explanations.
Understand concepts. Enable students to explore new content and share views.	Compare a book with its film. Hold debates, role-play, do simulations, make displays.
Use knowledge in authentic, interesting, holistic, long-term, and social ways.	Solve "real-world" problems. Create a quilt or totem based on family traditions.
Reflect on knowledge. Know what you know and how you know it (metacognition).	Write in journals. Do role playing and simulations. Teach someone what you know.

A Framework. Higher-order thinking skills can be organized in many ways, but the framework for thinking skills in this handbook is relatively simple. It looks like this:

Higher-Order Thinking Skills

Inferential thinking

    Making inferences

    Generalizing and drawing conclusions

    Observing relationships

Critical thinking

    Analysis

    Evaluation

Creative thinking

    Synthesis

    Fluency and flexibility

    Imagination and visualization

    Originality

Combinations of thinking skills

    Problem solving

    Decision making

Before looking at ways to implement instruction in thinking skills, you need to understand the meanings of some of these terms.

In *inferential thinking,* the learner must put together clues in order to understand information that is not directly stated, but is implied. *Generalizing* is the process of grasping an overall meaning or purpose from limited information, and *drawing conclusions* is making decisions based on evidence. *Observing relationships* is the ability to perceive similar or dissimilar features of ideas or objects. These relationships may be in the form of (a) *classifications* (systematic ways of categorizing), (b) *comparisons and contrasts* (awareness of similarities and differences), or (c) *cause and effect* (observance of the relationships between actions and their consequences).

Critical thinking is the process of interpreting, analyzing, or evaluating something. *Analysis* is the act of breaking down a whole into its parts and studying the relationships of the parts, and *evaluation* is the process of questioning and making judgments based on existing information.

Unlike inferential and critical thinking, which are reactions to existing ideas, *creative thinking* leads to the development of new and unusual ideas or products. *Synthesis,* like inventiveness, is the process of combining simple ideas or elements into larger concepts or products. In school, synthesis often occurs when students write stories or poems, collaborate on projects, find different solutions to problems, or express ideas or

emotions in art. *Fluency* is the ability to generate many ideas, and *flexibility* is the ability to create ideas that fit into many different systems or categories. *Imagination* and *visualization* both involve creating mental pictures or patterns of things that are not actually present, and *originality* is the ability to produce unique responses.

Some thinking processes, such as *problem solving* and *decision making,* are actually complex combinations of various types of thinking skills. Problem solving consists of several steps, including the following:

1. Identifying a problem
2. Obtaining information related to the problem
3. Forming hypotheses
4. Testing the hypotheses and forming a conclusion
5. Applying the solution and evaluating its effectiveness

Decision making is similar to problem solving, but it involves the following steps:

1. Identifying a goal
2. Collecting relevant data
3. Recognizing obstacles to reaching the goal
4. Identifying alternatives
5. Analyzing and ranking alternatives
6. Choosing the best alternative

You can integrate thinking skills with your teaching in every area of the curriculum from kindergarten through twelfth grade, but be aware that young children are limited in their ability to think abstractly. Not until the age of 10 or 11 are children able to deal successfully with abstract thought and concepts beyond their experiences. Therefore, in the lower grades you should teach the rudiments of various thinking skills by having the children manipulate concrete objects or apply these skills to what they already know and understand.

Middle school students are better prepared for learning higher-order thinking skills because many are now capable of abstract reasoning and can think outside the realm of personal experiences. By the time they reach high school, students are capable of analyzing situations in greater depth, creating more complex thoughts and products, solving problems logically, making rational decisions, and evaluating concepts more critically.

If you consider thinking skills to be a high priority in your teaching, you should establish a classroom climate conducive to developing them. To do this, you need to show respect for your students by accepting their ideas and treating their mistakes as natural parts of learning experiences. Listen to them, help them find alternatives, and show them that there may not be a single correct answer for every situation. Give them time to work through real problems, and provide opportunities to experiment with ideas and materials. Encourage your students by providing constructive feedback, and build their confidence by enabling them to succeed with simple tasks. Perhaps most important of all, learn to think and create along with them; let them occasionally see you struggle and make mistakes, then try again and eventually reach a conclusion.

To develop thinking skills in your instruction, structure activities, provide opportunities for student interaction, and ask questions that cause students to think critically and creatively. On the next several pages you will find sample activities for promoting thinking at different grade levels and in different content areas.

Inferential Thinking Activities. Two types of inferential thinking activities—classification and making inferences—are presented here with suggestions for using them. Try to think of other possibilities as you plan your lessons and units.

Classification. Classification means organizing items or concepts with similar features into categories. In classifying, you first scan the material to get a general impression, then select a characteristic common to more than one item, and finally group together items that share this feature. (Some items may fit logically into more than one category.) You repeat this process until all items are categorized. Classifying is based on making comparisons and is one of several ways to see relationships and make meaningful connections.

Children who start classifying at an early age might group concrete objects with common characteristics together, while slightly older children might categorize pictures that have been cut from magazines or catalogs. Still older students might classify words, concepts, literary works, or artistic masterpieces according to common features. At whatever level students are working, it is important for them to give reasons for their classifications. In order to clarify their thinking and justify their choices of categories, students need to explain the relationships they perceive.

Suppose you give an envelope containing pictures of the following items to a group of second graders and ask them to group the pictures that belong together. The children will probably consider many possibilities and find that some items could be placed in more than one category. Likely categories are given immediately following the items.

Items

set of drums	doll carriage
chalkboard	chair
television	CD player
cheese	recipe book
roller skates	computer
lawn mower	stove
harmonica	

Possible Classifications

Things with wheels—lawn mower, roller skates, doll carriage

Food-related items—cheese, stove, recipe book

Toys—doll carriage, set of drums, harmonica, roller skates, chalkboard

Household furnishings—stove, chair, television, CD player, computer

Electrical things—television, computer, CD player, stove

Music—set of drums, CD player, harmonica

Things for reading and writing—computer, recipe book, chalkboard

You can use classification skills as you teach subjects in any area of the curriculum. Some types of classification activities are:

- *Math*—Group objects, pictures, or line drawings by classifications of geometric shapes.
- *Science*—Classify animals according to various attributes.
- *Political science*—Categorize types of governments by salient features.
- *Music*—Classify musical recordings by such types as country, rock, classical, jazz, and gospel.
- *Art*—Classify works of art according to their historical periods or creators.
- *Literature*—Group literary works by genre, author, or theme.
- *Geography*—Classify cities by the countries where they are located.
- *History*—Make categories of great people through history (e.g., military leaders, philosophers, artists, heads of state, scientists, and religious leaders).

Making Inferences. Making inferences requires observing clues and using them to arrive at implied meanings. The thought processes involved are similar to those used in drawing conclusions, making predictions, and making generalizations. When you read a murder mystery, you look for clues in order to determine who did it. If you want to know if someone likes you, you watch for behavioral clues, such as a smile. Frequently, the information you need is not clearly given, so you have to "read between the lines" and then make reasonable assumptions as to the full meaning. Although making inferences is an important skill for critical reading and thinking, students often have a great deal of difficulty learning to use it.

One technique you can use when teaching inferences is the "grab bag" approach, in which you give a bag of objects to a group of students, perhaps objects that you have around your home. Students read the directions on the bag and create a story from the objects by making inferences about the objects' relationships to each other. You can use sets of pictures or sets of words and phrases, as well as sets of objects, to teach students to infer. An example follows.

Grab Bag Activity

Contents—An old wallet with three pennies, a "help wanted" ad asking for someone to deliver papers, a handwritten note that says "Do you know anybody who wants firewood for this winter?," and an ad from a catalog with a stereo system circled.

Directions—Someone has a problem. Can you figure out what the problem is from these clues?

Possible answer—A young person wants to earn money to buy a stereo system.

Students must understand how they made inferences from the clues in order to transfer this thinking skill to other learning tasks. Students need to use the same thought processes for making inferences with word clues in reading as they used for making inferences from objects. Having students underline word clues in reading selections is a good way to help them make inferences in their reading.

Critical Thinking Activities.   Critical thinking activities involve analyzing and evaluating information. Students need to consider the accuracy, timeliness, purpose, and appropriateness of information that they hear and read. Accuracy can be verified by checking other sources. Timeliness can often be determined by checking copyright dates. Deciding about appropriateness requires matching the information with the reader's purposes, for example, to inform, entertain, or persuade. Critical thinking must be applied to material viewed on television, videos, or the Internet, as well as print materials such as books, magazines, newspapers, advertising fliers or brochures, and pamphlets.

Persuasive material often includes *propaganda,* a form of persuasion intended to influence the audience through such techniques as exaggerations and emotional appeals. One way to develop critical thinking skills is teaching students to recognize propaganda. Both you and the students can enjoy this activity as you look for examples of propaganda, which are readily found in political promotions and product advertisements. If you are teaching during a political campaign, you can bring brochures and newspaper articles to class, or you can videotape messages by the candidates and play them during class. In order to choose the best candidate, students should critically analyze material for evidence of misleading statements, biased or one-sided reports, false assumptions, avoidance of issues, exaggerated statements, and emotional appeals.

Advertising contains a great deal of propaganda, and you can obtain samples from newspapers, magazines,

television, and the Internet. Some types of propaganda are name calling (using negative words to produce an undesirable effect), transfer (associating a worthy concept or desirable person with a product), testimonial (having a person endorse a product), plain folks (identifying with ordinary people), and bandwagon (trying to get people to accept something because everyone else does).

Suggested propaganda-detection activities that will help stimulate students to think critically include having the students:

1. Distinguish between advertisements that simply make emotional appeals and those that give information.

2. Find examples of propaganda techniques, and make displays of them.

3. Look for examples of exaggerations, emotional appeals, and other propaganda techniques for a type of product or service in which the students are particularly interested (e.g., CDs).

4. Compare ads for the same products, such as cereals or motorcycles, produced by different companies. Tell students to look for use of fact versus opinion, propaganda techniques, and emotional appeals.

Creative Thinking Activities.   For the following activities, students need to use creative thinking skills. Brainstorming requires students to think fluently as they generate many ideas and flexibly as they think of divergent ideas. Their responses to brainstorming situations are often unique. In simulation, role-playing, and creative dramatics, students use their imaginations to project themselves into situations that differ from their own experiences. These and other creative activities encourage children to use higher-order thinking skills.

Brainstorming.   Brainstorming helps develop creative thinking at any grade level. Students are given a real or imaginary problem and asked to think of as many ways as they can to solve it. You will probably have to direct the activity yourself the first time you try it, but later a student can lead it.

Here's one way to conduct brainstorming. First, identify a specific problem, one that is limited in scope. Then divide the class into groups. Appoint a recorder for each group to write down the ideas. Brainstorming sessions should be brief. You may want to ask students to meet again the following day for additional "afterthoughts" and to select those ideas that are worth following up.

Before they start brainstorming, students must understand how the session will be conducted. Have them think of as many ideas as they can, including wild ones. They should build on the ideas of others, combining and modifying what other students suggest.

Each student can offer only one idea each time he or she speaks, and only one person can speak at a time. Most important of all, there must be no criticism of any ideas during the session. Ask anyone who criticizes or ridicules someone's idea to leave the group, because such criticism destroys creative thinking.

Brainstorming can be used to solve real problems or simply to promote creative thinking. Here are suggested topics for both types of brainstorming sessions:

Real Problems

1. What are some things we can do to make our classroom more attractive?
2. How can we become more considerate of Jorge? (Conduct session on a day when Jorge, a student with a disability, is absent.)
3. How can we prevent a group of ninth-grade bullies from picking on the seventh graders?

Creative Thinking Exercises

1. What would happen if we learned to create energy from sand?
2. In what ways are a steam engine and a chain saw alike?
3. How many ways could you change a bicycle to make it more fun to ride?

Simulation. An interesting way to involve your students in real-life situations is through simulation activities. In simulations, a realistic situation is created in which students play various roles or act out scientific processes. It is "learning by doing." By acting out a situation, students come to understand what processes are involved and how problems are solved.

Although simulation offers many advantages over textbook learning, it has disadvantages, too. Most students are enthusiastic about participating in simulations, are motivated to learn about the roles they are playing, and use high-level communication skills and think creatively during the activities. They need freedom to move around and negotiate with each other to accomplish these tasks, though, so your classroom may become noisy and disorderly at times. Some students may remain on the fringe of the activity and not get the full benefit of the experience. In addition, the entire simulation can be a waste of time unless you direct the experience and the follow-up discussions skillfully.

Simulations can provide opportunities for students to learn by discovery and to apply their knowledge to actual situations. If you try simulations, you must locate an activity appropriate for the students' age level, the time available, and the lesson topic. You may want to use computer simulations or commercial board games that require students to think about what they are learning. Some classic computer simulations deal with flying an airplane, running a lemonade stand, investigating underwater ecology, and traveling on the Oregon Trail during pioneer days. Many more simulations are currently available, including online simulations. One called Westward HO! was inspired by the Oregon Trail program. Westward HO! involves collaboration on projects in a number of curricular areas in an integrated manner. The Westward HO! Simulation 5-week classroom project and online event was back in 2005 for its thirteenth year (Westward HO!, *www.cyberbee.com/wwho/*, 2005). A number of Oregon Trail sites are available on the Internet (Coffey, 1996). Because Internet sites change frequently, you may need to use a search engine such as Alta Vista to get an updated address.

Controversial issues are often the subjects of simulation activities. Conducting a political campaign followed by a mock election is an excellent way for students to understand political maneuvering and strategic campaigning, especially during an election year. Other simulations can deal with zoning decisions, profits and losses, and ecology, to name but a few examples. Students discover why people hold certain values and attitudes as they play out the roles they have assumed.

Creative Dramatics. Creative dramatics involves acting out a story or an event without a script or props. You can effectively use this method in the classroom for interpreting literature and reenacting episodes from history. Students can become totally involved in creative dramatics through thinking, speaking, listening, movement, and imagination. Therefore, they are more likely to understand and remember what they portray than if they were merely to read from a textbook or listen to a lecture.

The procedure for creative dramatics is fairly simple. All you need is space. The students should become totally familiar with a story or historical event, including its sequence of action and its characters' feelings. Sometimes students do additional research to learn more about the story. Then you choose students to play the parts. If there are not enough parts to go around, some parts can be invented (for example, extra members of a crowd or bystanders during a conversation involving only a few characters). The students improvise the dialogue as the story unfolds. After the play is over, help them evaluate the performance by asking them what was good about the presentation and what could be done to improve it. Usually, half the class participates while the other half is the audience, and then the play is performed again with students reversing roles.

Almost any historical event can be dramatized. Here are some good scenes to try:

A pioneer family's journey westward in a Conestoga wagon

The Boston Tea Party

Neil Armstrong and Buzz Aldrin in the first moon walks

Some stories are better suited to dramatization than others, and in some cases you will want to dramatize just one or two scenes from a story. Most folktales move quickly, involve conflict, and have strong characterizations. Scenes from Shakespeare's plays are also good sources for classroom creative dramatics. These are some other good selections, ranging from primary to secondary levels:

The Pied Piper of Hamelin by Robert Browning (New York: Scroll, 1970)

Stone Soup by Marcia Brown (New York: Scribner, 1947)

The Patchwork Quilt by Valerie Flournoy (New York: Dial, 1985)

Maniac Magee by Jerry Spinelli (New York: Little, Brown, 1991)

Anne Frank: The Diary of a Young Girl by Anne Frank (New York: Doubleday, 1967)

To Kill a Mockingbird by Harper Lee (Philadelphia: Lippincott, 1960)

The Glass Menagerie by Tennessee Williams (New York: Random House, 1945)

Role-Playing.   A student can assume the role of another person—that is, engage in *role-playing*—in order to understand the other's feelings and attitudes. Role-playing that involves solving problems is sometimes called *sociodrama*. Role-playing can develop communication skills and creative thinking processes and can clarify values.

In directing role-playing situations, you should observe certain guidelines. Encourage the players to speak distinctly and make their actions clear to the audience. Remind students who are not participating to be good listeners and not interrupt or carry on side conversations. When you choose students to play certain parts, assign roles that are unlike their own personalities; for instance, let a well-mannered student be a class bully.

Usually, in role-playing, two or more characters become involved in a conflict. There should be plenty of action and dialogue. The characters are led to a point where they must choose from among several possible courses of action. After students play the situation, you should discuss what took place and whether or not the problem was solved.

Role-playing helps students see emotional situations more objectively. In playing out a situation, they experience the emotions connected with it. Good subjects for role-playing include conflicts on the playground, misuse of drugs, disobedience, and peer relationships. You can develop role-playing situations from real life or create imaginary circumstances. Here is an example:

Nick doesn't do his share—Mrs. Miller's ninth-grade class, after studying different systems of government, is divided into groups to make presentations as a final project. All students in each group will receive the same grade. Janie, Roger, Mel, Sandy, and Nick are investigating socialism. They agree to research certain aspects of socialism and combine their information into a final report. The day before the presentation is due, all the students are ready except Nick. When they ask him to do his part, he says he has a job after school and doesn't have time. The other four students are concerned that their presentation will be incomplete because Nick hasn't done his assignment. What courses of action are open to the four students? What is the best way to resolve this problem?

Combinations of Thinking Skills.   Although students solve problems and make decisions every day, they seldom approach problem solving and decision making logically or systematically. Both processes require many different thinking skills. Examples of procedures and topics for each one appear in the following text.

Problem Solving.   When introducing problem solving to your class, start by having the students identify a real problem. Use the following example to help you understand the procedure.

Step 1: Identifying a Problem.   The children brainstorm several problems to solve, including ways to improve the food in the cafeteria, get better playground equipment, and eliminate homework on weekends. After some discussion, the students agree on a problem: how to take an end-of-year field trip, even though no funds are available for transportation. They decide they want to go to the Space Center, and they determine the approximate cost for hiring the school bus. The problem is that they need to find a way to get the money.

Step 2: Obtaining Information Related to the Problem.   Once again, the students brainstorm. This time they generate multiple ideas for getting money, including various ways of asking for it and earning it.

Step 3: Forming Hypotheses.   The students consider the advantages and disadvantages of each option and check with people in authority about the merits of each alternative. They list several possibilities, discuss the practicality of each one, and choose the three best ideas.

Step 4: Testing the Hypotheses and Forming a Conclusion.   The three best possibilities are (a) asking the principal to take the money from a special fund, (b) earning the money individually by doing chores at home, and (c) earning the money through a class project—writing a school newspaper and selling it. The students make inquiries about the special fund and find that it is only for schoolwide projects, and they also discover that several students' parents will not pay them for doing chores. The students check about the newspaper and find that, although they will have to pay for the paper, the school office will reproduce copies. They decide that if they can sell 350 copies for 40 cents each, they can cover the cost of the paper and have enough money for the trip. Therefore, they decide that writing a school paper is their best option.

Step 5: Applying the Solution and Evaluating Its Effectiveness.   The students begin writing the paper and advertising it. Because of their enthusiasm for the project, nearly everyone in the school wants a copy. When the paper is ready, the students sell 429 copies and have more than enough money for the trip. The solution was therefore satisfactory.

A similar process can be followed at almost any level and can be integrated into content areas. For primary grades you will want to use fairly simple problem situations with fewer options, such as rearranging the classroom to improve traffic patterns or finding ways to thank parent volunteers; in the upper grades, however, you will be able to deal with more complex situations.

You can use the following ideas for involving students in problem solving. Tell the students to:

1. Design an attractive display to fill a large empty space at the school entrance. (math, art)
2. Discover why plants die in the school library and correct the situation. (biology)
3. Survey the community to find volunteers and tutors. (social studies)
4. Find ways that the school can save money to alleviate the budget deficit. (math, business)
5. Determine the cause of uneven heat distribution in the school and research remedies. (physics)
6. Plan a physical fitness program for your school to raise students' fitness to an acceptable level. (physical education)

You can also use hypothetical problem-solving situations, such as the following:

1. As community leaders, develop a plan to reduce unemployment in the area. (social studies)
2. As engineers, find practical alternatives for energy sources. (science)
3. As food service managers, plan a month of school cafeteria menus with food that is nutritious, delicious, attractive, and affordable. (health, home economics, business, math)
4. As curriculum designers, develop an annotated list of recommended reading for specific grade levels. (English, reading)
5. As directors of a cultural center, plan a series of concerts with famous performers that will offer a wide variety of good music to the citizens. (music)

Decision Making.   Imagine that you have planned to work through the decision-making process, according to the steps given earlier, by helping your tenth-grade students decide on suitable careers. You might begin by discussing various career options and inviting a guidance counselor to answer questions about career opportunities. You could then let individual students find out about educational requirements, prospects for employment, prospects for advancement, salaries, job satisfaction, and other information for their chosen fields. The students should realistically assess their likelihood of success by examining such possible obstacles as financial resources, length of preparation time, access to specialized training, their current grade averages, geographical location, and parental support. They can find alternative ways of overcoming each potential obstacle.

Now imagine that Bob, one of your students, has chosen a business career and has identified some obstacles to reaching it, including lack of education and lack of financial resources. As he identifies alternatives, he considers overcoming financial problems by getting a scholarship, working part-time, or getting a loan. He can overcome his lack of education by going to college full-time or part-time, or by going to night school. In ranking his alternatives, he finds that the most practical solution for him is to go to college part-time, work part-time, and take out a small loan.

You might help Bob and the other students analyze their options more carefully by teaching them to make decision trees, a way of graphically organizing their alternatives. The students might list their alternatives and then place them on blank "trees" that you have given them, or they might want to create their own trees. Bob's tree might look something like the one in Figure 5–2.

Some ideas to use with your students follow. You can simplify or expand these ideas to serve different ages, and you can integrate them with various content areas.

1. Calculate the best forms of transporation (or the best routes) to take to reach various destinations. (math, geography)
2. Decide which car would be the best purchase for you or your parents. (math, social studies)
3. Identify the best form of energy to use for various specific purposes. (science)

FIGURE 5–2
Decision Tree

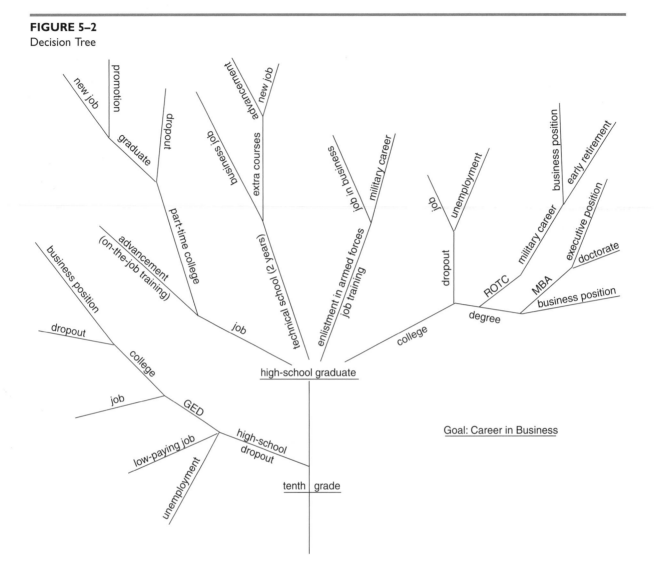

Goal: Career in Business

4. Decide on the best way to spend the $100 given to your class by the school. (math, social studies)
5. Justify the use of a specific language for worldwide communication. (language)

Complete Activity 5.3 to help you focus on your use of such activities.

Computer Applications. In some schools the computer is used to encourage creative thinking. For example, the computer allows art students to experiment with colors and shapes without fearing permanent errors, because change is easy. This situation promotes risk taking and problem solving and provides an environment for developing skills of divergent thinking, analysis, and criticism.

Videoconferencing has been used to connect students in Chicago, Los Angeles, and the Bronx for an environmental studies program. The students share information about pollution and recycling in their neighborhoods and then write scripts and plan an interactive theater production.

A New Jersey school has had students create inventions and then develop multimedia presentations about them. Such activities promote problem-solving skills (M. M. Smith, 1996). *Inspiration* and *Kidspiration* facilitate the making of concept webs for older and younger students, respectively.

ACTIVITY 5.3 | *Creative Thinking Activities*

Examine the following list of creative thinking activities. Place a checkmark (✓) by the ones you have used in your class. Place a plus (+) by the ones you intend to use. Under each activity you have used or intend to use, briefly explain how you applied or plan to apply it in your class or classes.

_____ Brainstorming

_____ Simulation

_____ Role-playing

_____ Creative dramatics

_____ Problem solving

_____ Decision making

_____ Computer applications

STUDY SKILLS

Students at all levels and in all disciplines need to master a set of basic study skills that will enhance their ability to learn from content area materials. It is, of course, beyond the scope of this book to teach you how to teach study skills; the purpose of this discussion is to make you aware of what the important study skills are, so that you can help your students acquire them. Don't assume that students have learned these skills simply because they have been previously exposed to them. Check to see—through pretests, oral questions, and observation of classroom performance—if the students have actually acquired them. Many students have been exposed to the skills, but the exposure has not "taken." Many of Mr. Viera's students in the opening vignette may need several experiences with reading and study strategies before they can apply them successfully.

CASE STUDY 5.2

Make No Assumptions

Ms. Jamison, the student teacher in a fifth-grade class, assigned each class member to write a report on a famous historical figure. Class members were initially to check encyclopedia accounts and then seek additional information. Ricky was asked to report on James Otis.

Ricky: Ms. Jamison, James Otis isn't in the encyclopedia. I checked all three sets.

Ms. Jamison (puzzled): I'm sure you just overlooked his name, Ricky. I know it's there.

Ricky: No, it's not. I'm sure.

Ms. Jamison (suddenly realizing what she should do): Let's go to the encyclopedia together, and you can show me how you looked for his name.

Ricky (walking toward the reference books): Okay. Oh! I can't show you now. All the J encyclopedias are being used.

Ms. Jamison: Why did you look under J?

Ricky: His name starts with a J.

Ms. Jamison: It's his first name that starts with a J. In the encyclopedia, people's names are alphabetized according to their last names. That's why you couldn't find James Otis in the J encyclopedia. You should have looked for Otis in the O encyclopedia. Nobody is using the O encyclopedia now. Why don't you try it while I watch?

Ricky (picking up the encyclopedia): Okay. Let's see. Here it is—Otis, James! Thank you, Ms. Jamison.

1. What assumption had Ms. Jamison made about the students' research skills when she assigned the lesson? Was it valid?

2. What might you do before making an assignment like this one, to avoid a similar situation in your class?

Location Skills

Starting with the problem posed by Ms. Jamison's class, you should first consider the study skill of locating information. To carry out many routine assignments in content classes, students must be able to locate information in trade books (nontextbook reading materials), textbooks, and reference books. They also must be able to locate materials in the media center and search electronic reference materials and Internet sites.

If students are to use trade books and textbooks to best advantage, you must ensure that they understand how to use prefaces and introductions, tables of contents, indexes, appendixes, glossaries, footnotes, and bibliographies. Many students do not even know the functions of these book parts; therefore, their chances of using them effectively to locate information are poor. Before some students can use indexes and glossaries effectively, they may need instruction in the prerequisite skill of alphabetizing. Most secondary students have mastered alphabetical order, which usually receives initial attention in first grade, but some will have difficulty with alphabetizing beyond the first letter of a word. For use of the glossary, they may also need instruction in using guide words and pronunciation keys, and in choosing the meaning that fits the context. Some students also need instruction in identifying key words under which to look when using the index or doing electronic searches. You need to assess the students' knowledge of the skills they need for using trade books and textbooks, as well as electronic sources, and offer information, instruction, and practice as necessary. Informal assessment will usually suffice. You can ask students to use each of the book parts and observe their performance, or you can ask them to explain the function of each part. Primary students will be concerned only with tables of contents and, by second or third grade, glossaries. Intermediate students should use all book parts, with the possible exception of the preface or introduction, and students in junior and senior high schools should use these parts as well. Students in classes with computers need to work with a variety of types of electronic searches.

Reference books call for a wide variety of skills. Knowledge of alphabetical order and the ability to use guide words are necessary with reference books, especially encyclopedias and dictionaries. Many secondary students still have trouble with guide words, although most have had repeated exposure to them since at least fourth grade. The ability to use cross references is particularly important for using an encyclopedia. Of course, students need to use the same skills with the dictionary that they need for a glossary, including the ability to use a pronunciation key and to choose the meaning that fits a particular context. To use printed encyclopedias, students must be able to determine which volume of a set contains the information they seek. (This is what Ricky could not do in Case Study 5.2.) Encyclopedia users must also be able to determine key words under which they can find related information. To use an atlas, students need to know how to interpret a map's legend and scale and how to locate directions on a map.

Reference books are often written at relatively high reading levels, considering the populations for which they are intended. Guard against assigning students to look up information in overly difficult reference books. Students will not learn from such assignments and are likely either to do nothing or to merely copy from the reference book without understanding. These responses will not result in the learning outcomes you anticipated.

To teach or review library skills, plan cooperatively with the librarian or media specialist, whose familiarity with the media center may have made him or her aware of potential uses you have overlooked. Consider this resource person, as all support personnel in the school, an ally in your teaching endeavor.

FOR YOUR PORTFOLIO

INTASC Standard: 10
Describe a way that you collaborated with the librarian or media specialist to provide resources or offer instruction.

Organizational Skills

Organizational skills are highly important to students working on reports for content area classes. These skills include outlining, summarizing, and organized note-taking. They are most easily taught in conjunction with an assignment on writing a report, since students can best see the need to learn them at such a time. These skills are usually not taught before the intermediate grades, but they ordinarily receive attention then. Even so, many secondary students have not mastered these skills, perhaps because they were never taught in a functional setting. If you are teaching above the primary level, you need to assess students' mastery of these skills and help the students acquire the skills if they have not yet done so. Primary teachers lay the groundwork for these skills, especially outlining, when they help students determine main

ideas and supporting details. They lay the groundwork for note-taking and summarizing by encouraging students to paraphrase what they have just read.

Retention

A major goal of content area learning is retention of subject matter. Teaching students how to study so that they will retain what they read is an important task: Here are some ways you can help students retain content. The codes indicate the appropriate levels: A = all levels, primary through secondary grades; I = intermediate grades; S = secondary grades.

1. Have class discussions covering all material you assign students to read. (A)
2. Encourage students to evaluate what they read. (A)
3. Give the students an opportunity to apply what they have read. (A)
4. Use audiovisual aids to illuminate concepts presented in the reading. (A)
5. Prepare students before they read by giving them background about the topic. (A)
6. Encourage students to picture in their minds what the author is trying to describe. (A)
7. Have students retell what they have read, in their own words, to you or a classmate soon after they finish reading. (A)
8. Always give students purposes for reading. Never just say, "Read pages 2 through 9 for tomorrow." Tell them what to look for as they read. (A)
9. Teach your students a study method, such as SQ3R (Robinson, 1961). (I, S)
10. Encourage students to analyze the author's organization. (I, S)
11. Have students take notes on the main points in the material. (I, S)
12. Have students write summaries of the material after they finish reading. (I, S)
13. Hold periodic classroom review sessions on material that has been read. (A)
14. Prepare study guides for students to use as they read the material. (I, S)
15. Have students use mnemonic devices. (I, S)
16. Give students immediate feedback on correctness of oral or written responses to the reading material. (A)
17. Encourage students to classify the ideas in their reading material. (A)

These techniques will bolster the students' retention.

Reading Rate

Another useful study skill your students must acquire is the ability to adjust reading rate to fit the purpose for reading and the type of material. Many students have never had help in developing flexibility of reading rates. As a result, they frequently read everything at the same rate. Some employ a painstakingly slow rate that is inappropriate for reading light fiction, for locating isolated facts, or for seeking only general themes. Others use a rapid rate that is inappropriate for reading mathematics statement problems, science experiments they must perform, or any type of intensive study material.

Make the students aware that good readers use many different reading rates and match the rates to the purposes for reading and the nature of the materials. Offer them opportunities to practice varying reading rates in the classroom; for example, have them scan for isolated details, skim for main ideas, and read slowly and carefully to solve a mathematics problem.

Interpreting Graphic Aids

The ability to interpret graphic aids in content materials is also vital. Students need to interpret maps, graphs, tables, and illustrations in their textbooks, or they will not gain all they should from the content. Students tend to skip graphic aids, perhaps because their teachers have never explained the informative nature of these aids, or because they have never been shown *how* to interpret them. We have already mentioned the skills necessary for reading maps. When reading graphs, students must be able to decide what is being compared, the units of measure involved, how to extract specific information from the graphs, and how to make overall generalizations based on the graphs. When reading tables, students must be able to decide what type of information is included, the meanings of the columns and rows, and how to extract specific facts. Illustrations such as diagrams present problems because of their abstract nature, distortion of reality, and oversimplification. Students may think that a realistic illustration is just a decorative feature, when it really conveys information.

To help students understand the purpose and construction of graphic aids, ask them to create their own. They can make diagrams to compare the settings or characters in stories, charts or tables to summarize key points for a report, or graphs to compare their scores on a series of weekly tests. By making their own graphic aids, students understand how these aids work and are likely to find it easier to interpret other graphic aids.

Metacognitive Skills

Metacognitive skills allow a person to monitor her or his intellectual functioning. They are important for the comprehension and retention of content material. Metacognition includes awareness of what you already know, knowledge of when you have achieved understanding of new information, and realization of how you accomplished the understanding. You can help your students learn to monitor their comprehension of material presented in your classes.

In order to exercise metacognitive skills, students must become active learners by setting goals for their learning tasks, planning ways to meet their goals, monitoring their success in meeting their goals, and remedying the situation when they fail to meet the goals. You can help them acquire techniques to do these things. Teaching them to relate new information to things that they already know, to preview material that they are about to read, to paraphrase ideas presented, to identify the organizational patterns in written materials, and to question themselves periodically will help them to monitor their comprehension effectively. In the opening vignette, Mr. Viera encouraged his students to brainstorm ways that helped them make sense of their reading.

Teach students to expect their reading assignments to make sense and, if they cannot make sense out of the material, to attempt to find out why. They may ask themselves whether the words in the material are unfamiliar, the sentence structure is confusing, or some other problem exists. After determining the specific problem area, they should decide what reading skills need to be applied (for example, use of context clues) and apply the skills. Some ways to remedy the situation when material has not been understood are to read on and try to use subsequent context to help make sense of the material, to reread the material, and to use the glossary or a dictionary to clarify pronunciations or meanings of words. You can help students learn to monitor their comprehension by modeling the monitoring skills for them. Take a content passage and read it aloud to them, pausing to tell them how you are checking your own comprehension internally at frequent points in the reading. Tell them what questions you are asking yourself about the material and how you can tell when you have found the answers. This technique is very powerful and effective, if used appropriately.

Study Habits

Your students may also have very poor study habits. They must learn that study should take place in an environment that is as distraction-free as possible (many may not have an entirely distraction-free place available), that they should gather their study tools (books, pens, pencils, paper) before they start to study, that they should budget their study time so that nothing is left out, and that they should set aside a time for study that they will not be constantly relinquishing to other activities. Those who do not have a good place to study at home should be encouraged to use school study periods as effectively as possible. Students who change classes should learn to gather all necessary study materials before they go to the study hall period, to have all homework assignments written down to take with them, and to concentrate on homework during the study period rather than visit with other students.

DISCUSSION QUESTIONS

1. Do you believe in a constructivist approach to teaching? What are your reasons?
2. What can you do when there are students in your content classes who cannot read the assigned textbook? Would different techniques be better in different situations? Why or why not?
3. Choose a chapter from a textbook that you are using with students. What are some ways you could build the students' background for reading this material?
4. How can you incorporate writing instruction into your classroom instruction?
5. What opportunities do the students in your class have for developing higher-order thinking skills? How do you and your mentoring teacher react to students' efforts to think critically and creatively?
6. What can you do to provide a classroom environment that is more conducive to higher-order thinking? Would you need to make any changes in the room arrangement, scheduling of class work, types of activities, or assignments?
7. What critical or creative thinking activities are you willing to try in your classroom? What problems can you foresee in doing them? How could you prevent or minimize these problems?
8. What would happen to our society if there were no creativity? How are knowledge and creativity related?
9. How can you help students develop metacognitive skills?
10. What is the most appropriate time to teach outlining, summarizing, and note-taking? Why do you think so? How would you begin?
11. How can you and the librarian or media specialist cooperate to ensure that students master important library skills?
12. How can inappropriate and inflexible reading rates inhibit students' learning? What can you do to change these habits?
13. What study methods might you use in your grade or discipline? Why would these methods be appropriate?
14. What kinds of graphic aids are most common in your content area or areas? How could you let students create their own graphic aids?

Case Study 6.1: Breakdown of a Lesson

Mr. Ray, a student teacher, is introducing a unit on Scandinavia in a middle-school social studies class by showing his students slides of the region. He has reserved the slides and projector, arranged the slides in the tray, positioned the projector and is ready to begin. Mrs. Colby is the mentoring teacher.

Mr. Ray: Everybody sit down and be quiet. We're going to see some slides.

Students (shuffling to their seats and mumbling): Wonder what they're about. Probably something boring.

Mr. Ray: Hey, you guys. Keep quiet. Okay. Ellen, turn out the lights, please. Here we go. (Mr. Ray turns on the projector, and the students settle down. He begins explaining each slide. Suddenly the screen goes blank. Mr. Ray stares at the projector and wonders what happened.)

Mrs. Colby: I believe the bulb has burned out. Do you have another one?

Mr. Ray: I don't think so. Let me look. (Pause while students start whispering, poking each other, and laughing.) I can't find one. Do you think they'd have one at the resource center?

Mrs. Colby: They probably do, but the media specialist is out today, and I doubt if the substitute would know where to find one.

Mr. Ray: Peter, would you go to the resource center for me and ask the substitute if she can find a slide projector bulb? (Peter starts off in search of a bulb. By now the students are talking again, and some are getting out of their seats. Carmelita trips over the projector cord and falls against the filing cabinet.)

Mr. Ray (speaking in an excited, almost angry tone): All of you get back in your seats! Be quiet! Peter should be back soon.

Students: Oh, look! Carmelita hurt her mouth!

Carmelita (holding her hand to her mouth): It hurts!

Mr. Ray glances helplessly at Mrs. Colby, starts to say something, and then stops.

Mrs. Colby (speaking calmly and turning the lights back on): All of you get back to your seats now. Get out your math books and work on your assignment for tomorrow. (Students do as she says.)

Mrs. Colby: Let me see your mouth, Carmelita. I believe it will be okay if you go to the restroom and put a cold, wet paper towel over it for a while. Kim, you go with her.

Peter (just returning to the room): She looked for a bulb but couldn't find one. She says we'd better wait and show the slides tomorrow when the media specialist will be back.

Mr. Ray: Thank you, Peter. Class, I guess you might as well keep working on your math, and we'll do social studies tomorrow when we can see the slides.

1. Did Mr. Ray succeed in introducing his unit on Scandinavia? Could he have introduced the unit anyway, even if he couldn't show the slides?

2. Did Mr. Ray ever make clear to the students his purpose in showing the slides? If the slides had been shown, do you think the students would have gained much from them? What could Mr. Ray have done to create interest in the slides and make sure the students learned all they could from them?

3. What could Mr. Ray have done to prevent the class from becoming unruly?

4. How could Carmelita's accident have been prevented? How might Mr. Ray have handled the incident?

5. What would you do to avoid making the same kinds of mistakes Mr. Ray made?

6. Is there anything you think Mr. Ray did correctly? If so, what?

CASE STUDY 6.2

Salvaging a Lesson

Mr. Carson, a student teacher, is introducing a unit on Africa in a middle-school social studies class by showing his students slides of the region. He has reserved the slides and projector from Miss Rios, the school's media specialist; arranged the slides in the tray; and positioned the projector. He is ready to begin.

Mr. Carson: This afternoon to begin our unit we are going to see some slides. The slides are of scenes from Africa. Africa is the second-largest continent and is made up of many different countries. As you watch the slides, I want you to notice the different kinds of land regions you can find in Africa. Also, pay attention to the natural resources that Africa has. Kim, will you please close the blinds? I believe we're ready to start. (Mr. Carson turns on the projector and begins discussing the slides, but suddenly the screen goes blank.)

Students: What happened?

Mr. Carson: I'm afraid the bulb has burned out. I tried to get a spare just in case, but there wasn't one. I'll try to get one by tomorrow.

Mike: Oh, good. No slides. Can we play a game?

Susan: Let's have free time.

Sally (jumping out of her seat): I think I know where there's an extra bulb. I'll go ask Miss Rios.

Mr. Carson: Thank you for the offer, Sally, but I've already checked with Miss Rios, and she doesn't have one. We'll have to do something else instead.

Anthony: I want to get my math homework done. Is it okay if I do that?

Mr. Carson: Wait a minute, everybody. We can still begin learning about Africa today even if we can't see the slides. We'll begin by finding Africa on the globe. Who can come up and show us where it is?

Sonya (raising her hand): I can see it from here. Let me show them.

Mr. Carson (after discussing the features of Africa on the globe and on a pull-down map): Africa has been in the news quite a bit lately, and I've been clipping some items from the newspapers. I'm going to divide you into groups of four and let each group take one clipping. I want you to read your clipping and select someone from your group to report to the class about the article. Select another person to point to the country or region in Africa that is mentioned in your article. You may use either the map or the globe. I will give you a few minutes to do this work in your groups, and then I will call on you to make your reports. Do you have any questions?

Jimmy: Who's going to be in my group?

Mr. Carson: I'll put you into groups just as soon as I'm sure you understand what to do.

Jake: What if we can't find our country on the map?

Mr. Carson: I'll help you. You may come up ahead of time to try to find it. Any other questions? (pause) I think we're ready to start now.

1. Suppose that Mr. Carson had not thought to use the map and globe and that he had not brought the clippings. What would have happened to his lesson?
2. What are some other ways that Mr. Carson might have introduced his unit without the slides?
3. At what point was Mr. Carson about to lose control of the class? How did he manage to retain control?

Compare and contrast the lessons of Mr. Ray and Mr. Carson according to the following criteria: preparation, class management, effectiveness of introducing a unit, and flexibility.

INTRODUCTION TO INSTRUCTIONAL RESOURCES

People learn best through experience. Much learning takes place through the vicarious (indirect) experiences of listening, reading, and viewing pictures and videos, but learning is likely to be more meaningful and lasting if it is supplemented with direct, concrete experiences.

Instructional resources are available in a wide variety of places. You can obtain audiovisual materials through the school, the public library, a college or university resource center, and local and state agencies. Industries, farms, and parks provide opportunities for field trips. People in various occupations or with interesting hobbies can also serve as resources.

You may wish to make games and activities for teaching specific skills. The community is rich in resources to use in constructing such materials. For example, many home decorating and home supply stores give away scraps of materials that can be used for various purposes in the classroom. Newspapers may be a source of newsprint for murals and posters, and restaurants may provide place mats that have educational themes. If you use your imagination, you will find ways to take advantage of the resources that abound in your school and community.

Many audiovisual media are used in a variety of ways in schools today. If you are going to use audiovisual media effectively, you need to know where to obtain them, when to make use of them, how to use them, why they can enhance your lessons, and which types are most appropriate for your purposes. This chapter primarily discusses instructional media and applications other than those related to computers. Although computers are currently high-interest delivery systems for classroom information and activities, other audiovisual media are used more frequently in the majority of classrooms. Chapter 7, Supporting the Curriculum Through Computer Resources, will cover computer media and applications in detail.

Selecting Audiovisual Media

When you meet with your mentoring teacher, discuss which units, skills, and activities you will be expected to teach. Decide what materials you want to use for these teaching areas, and then check on their availability. Some materials may have to be reserved or ordered well in advance of the time you actually plan to use them.

One of the first things you should do is become acquainted with the school librarian or media specialist and find out what resources are available in your school. Most school media centers have supplementary reading materials, newspapers and periodicals, reference books, maps and globes, files of photographs and slides, art prints, audiotapes, videotapes, transparencies, charts and posters, models and exhibits, computer software, and sometimes videodiscs.

After assessing the school media center's holdings, you may wish to explore other possibilities. One place to look for additional materials is the school system's central office or teachers' center, which may have a file of resource materials. Another source is the public or regional library. You may be able to order videotapes or obtain computer software from the State Department of Education. In addition, don't overlook your local college or university's resources.

Materials are also available from other places. The Public Documents Distribution Center (Pueblo, Colorado), various state departments and agencies, and businesses and industries will send you free or inexpensive materials. Locally, you can get maps and other printed materials from the Chamber of Commerce, banks, local industries, and the Department of Health.

If you still can't find what you need, you may want to make simple materials yourself, such as transparencies, slides, mounted pictures, or teaching games. Protect some of these materials by laminating them, covering them with clear contact paper, or placing them in laminated sheet protectors. A good way to begin a collection of teacher-made games and activities is by making some on the insides of file folders. Write the directions on the outside of each folder, and then label and organize these activities according to learning objectives. (See Figure 6–1 for an example of a teacher-made language arts game.)

There are a number of factors to consider in selecting audiovisual materials to use with a particular lesson. Be sure you do not decide to use them simply to impress your mentoring teacher, fill up instructional time, or entertain the students. Consider these criteria in choosing materials:

1. Relevance to the lesson—Make sure the audiovisual material actually helps carry out the lesson's objectives. The material should be the most appropriate medium for your purpose, making the necessary points in the clearest possible manner. It should stimulate discussion and lead the way to further study.

2. Appeal to students—Be sure the material is suitable for the students' age level and that it will hold their attention. Students should have sufficient background information to appreciate the presentation.

3. Quality of the materials—Check your materials to make sure they are well designed and of high technical quality. The material should be accurate, current, and in good taste.

4. Objectivity—Examine your material for bias, propaganda, and controversy. If there is bias, help your students to see the other point of view. Point out misconceptions that arise as a result of propaganda techniques. If the material is controversial, be sure that each side receives equal emphasis. Free materials are often available to classroom teachers for the purpose of advertising a product or advancing a particular point of view. Be cautious about using these materials.

5. Practical considerations—Be sure you know how to operate the equipment you need for presenting your material. Check in advance to see that both materials and equipment will be available when you need them. Allow enough time to introduce the lesson, present the audiovisual material, and follow it up. Allow extra time in case something goes wrong. Prepare a suitable place for your presentation. Follow the checklist in Activity 6.1 to help you use audiovisual materials efficiently.

Effective Use of Audiovisual Media

Audiovisual media have many uses: introduction and orientation to a new area of study, representation of events and processes, and individualized learning experiences. They can arouse students' interest and curiosity as you introduce a new topic. A display of brightly colored photographs of wild animals, a recording of Renaissance madrigals, or a time-lapse video of a flower opening can be a stimulus for learning. Since students frequently acquire ideas and information through television, an audiovisual presentation, such as a videotape or television program, can command their attention

FIGURE 6–1
Teacher-Made Language Arts Game

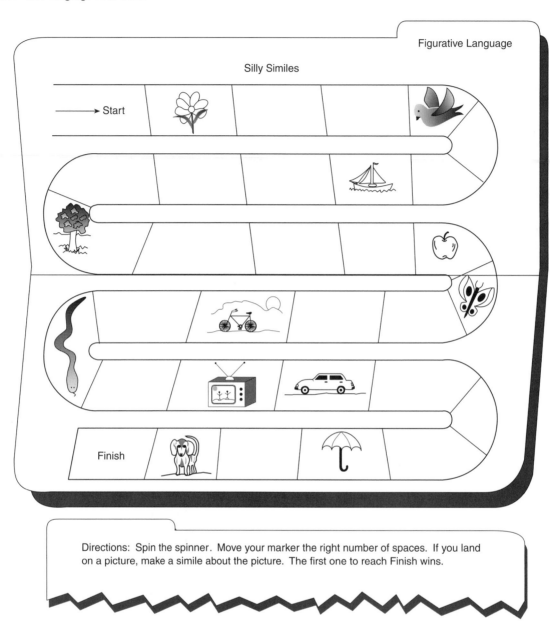

Directions: Spin the spinner. Move your marker the right number of spaces. If you land on a picture, make a simile about the picture. The first one to reach Finish wins.

more effectively than a textbook or lecture. In addition, because students have become accustomed to playing video games in arcades and on home game machines and computers, computer programs may excite interest not generated by other classroom presentations.

You can use certain types of audiovisual media to individualize instruction according to the learner's style or special needs. If the same information exists in different forms in the classroom, learners can choose the forms that best suit their ways of learning. For instance, a student who has great difficulty with reading can lis-ten to a tape about the African jungle. Another student who has trouble visualizing what is read might operate a video player and watch motion pictures of the jungle. A third student who is an excellent reader might prefer to read about the jungles of Africa in several reference books. Students with visual disabilities may need to use recordings or large-print materials. A student who learns best through active participation may gain information about the African jungle or any other habitat through a computer simulation. (See Chapter 7 for information on computer simulations.)

ACTIVITY 6.1 | *Checklist for Using Audiovisual Equipment*

PREPARATION

_____ Reserve or check out necessary materials and equipment.

_____ Preview material to make sure it is appropriate and in good condition.

_____ Prepare related materials for introduction or follow-up activities.

_____ If each student is to receive a copy of related materials, count the copies to make sure you have enough. Plan for efficient distribution.

_____ Arrange audience seats so that everyone can see.

_____ Consider the location of students with disabilities by placing those with visual or auditory difficulties near the front and providing places for students in wheelchairs.

_____ Check the room's temperature, ventilation, and lighting.

_____ Eliminate distractions as much as possible.

EQUIPMENT

_____ Practice operating equipment until you feel sure of yourself.

_____ Set equipment up in advance so that it is ready to use (check focus, position on screen, size of image, etc.).

_____ Have an extra bulb on hand, and know how to replace the old one.

_____ Get an extension cord or an adapter if you need one.

_____ Avoid having cords where the students will trip over them.

_____ Check the cleanliness of the lens and other vital parts of the equipment.

When you use audiovisual material, prepare your lesson carefully by previewing the material and reading the accompanying study guide or lesson plan, if one is available. If not, develop your own plan.

Create a feeling of readiness and anticipation among the students by raising questions and telling them what they can expect to learn. Relate the audiovisual material to what they are studying; make it a part of your overall instructional plan. Explain any unfamiliar terms or concepts that will be used.

During the presentation, observe the students' reactions. There may be some points they do not seem to understand or some parts that do not hold their interest. You may either interrupt the presentation or wait to address these matters during your follow-up discussion. Take notes of your observations so that you can recall anything that needs to be mentioned later.

The follow-up activities are based on the audiovisual presentation but are not limited to it. In fact, the presentation may primarily serve as a taking-off point. Follow-up activities may consist of lively discussions, the application of concepts to real situations, or experiments, projects, and reports. You can divide students into groups to pursue special interests and allow the projects to continue over an extended period of time. Students' participation in follow-up activities is essential for learning to take place.

Print Materials

Content area textbooks and basal readers (series of graded reading instructional books) can provide structure and sequence in the school curriculum. Although they may be the framework for learning experiences, they should never be considered as the total instructional program. You will want to use trade books and reference books to supplement textbook material. Magazines that focus on single topics of current interest can also be used for both informational and recreational reading. Collect leaflets and pamphlets on various topics, as well as pictures and photographs to mount and cover with laminating film or clear contact paper for use as resources.

Dry-Erase Boards or Chalkboards

Dry-erase boards or chalkboards are among the most familiar visual devices in the classroom. Both students and teachers can use these boards in a number of ways. As a change of pace, students may enjoy going to the board individually or in groups to do their work. For teachers, the board is readily available for recording information, writing seatwork and homework assignments, and teaching lessons.

These boards are good for listing the key vocabulary for a lesson and webbing the words when the students have read the material, heard the discussion of it, and therefore had an opportunity to grasp the connections among the terms. They are also good for recording the results of brainstorming that often takes place before reading and writing activities are begun.

Although you are accustomed to seeing the chalkboard or dry-erase board used in the classroom, you may not feel comfortable using it yourself. It is difficult to write a lot of material on the board while you are teaching, since you cannot watch the students when you are facing the board. If you have extensive material to put on the board, do it the night before or early in the morning, when you are not rushed. It is important to form your letters correctly and use correct spelling and syntax to provide a good writing model for the students to follow.

Writing legibly on a board is complicated by the need to write sentences in a reasonably straight, horizontal line. Some teachers line their boards to facilitate this feat. You can, however, learn to write horizontally by keeping the writing at eye level as you move from right to left. That will necessitate bending your knees to lower your eye level as you move to lower lines on the board. Practice can make this action fairly automatic.

Individual dry-erase or chalkboards in the hands of the students are excellent teaching aids. They allow every-student-response activities to be used. You may ask young students to draw a picture of something that starts with the same sound or letter as a word that you speak or write on the large board or to write the letter that begins a word that you pronounce. You may ask older students to write synonyms or antonyms for words, words that complete oral cloze statements, answers to math problems, names of states or capitals that answer social studies questions, chemical formulas, and a multitude of other short-answer responses. One secondary math teacher found the boards to be particularly good for having all of the students work a math problem simultaneously and show their work, after which one student was asked to copy his or her work on the larger board.

Models, Globes, and Maps

Models are three-dimensional replicas of actual objects that may be smaller (an airplane) or larger (the ear) than actual size. Models of the body help students to understand the skeletal, circulatory, muscular, digestive, reproductive, and excretory systems, for example.

Globes are models of the Earth, and maps are two-dimensional representations of the Earth's geographic and/or political features. Globes and maps can help students visualize geographic relationships and understand world affairs. Map jigsaw puzzles can be helpful learning devices for young children, whereas atlases are important learning tools for older students. Be sure that the globes and maps you use are current, because political boundaries, names of countries, and other features may change over time.

Math Manipulatives

Mathematics concepts are often learned most effectively when manipulative devices are used to help the students visualize the mathematical operations. Manipulatives can help students learn place value, fractions, addition, subtraction, and other basic concepts. Counters, color cubes, shape blocks, pattern blocks, linking pop cubes, sorting sets, place value charts, magnetic calendars, base-10 blocks, fraction pieces, dice, dominoes, rulers, measuring tapes, beakers, measuring cups, measuring spoons, calculator cash registers, geoboards, play money sets, learning clocks, thermometers, and playing cards can all be used as manipulatives in math lessons. As students do their own measuring, sorting, money changing, and other such activities, they see direct applications of the concepts being presented.

Audio Media

You should use audio media when sound is of primary importance for learning or appreciation. Recordings of folk songs, important historical speeches, or famous symphony concerts are especially useful. You might want to play recordings of town meetings or forums as a basis for discussions of controversial issues. In many schools, students learn foreign languages in language labs that use audio media for instructional purposes. Dramatizations, documentaries, poetry readings, and great moments from history are also particularly well suited to audio presentations.

The most common type of audio media in classrooms is the audiotape recorder. Audiotape recorders have many features that make them desirable for classroom use. Students can record themselves when they read orally or make speeches, play back the tapes to listen for errors, and make efforts to improve. You can record classroom activities such as dramatizations, interviews, panel discussions, or musical programs and play them back later. You can also record some stories or lessons for students to use individually or in groups at listening stations while you are working directly with other groups of students.

You may want to have your own audiotape recorder because so many good opportunities exist for using it during the school day. An audiotape recorder is fairly inexpensive, and tapes made in class can be erased and reused. Your school may have a tape library where you can find prerecorded tapes for various purposes.

Sometimes a radio can be a useful audio medium. It can provide immediate communication on national and international affairs through newscasts, although television is currently more likely to be used for this in most classrooms. Radios can also be used to listen to foreign language broadcasts.

Audiotapes of oral presentations by students are good artifacts for portfolios. They are particularly useful to show elementary students how they are improving in reading skill over time. They also work well for music class artifacts.

Individual dry-erase boards or chalkboards keep students actively involved in lessons.

Projected Still Pictures

Still pictures can be projected in classrooms with slide projectors, overhead projectors, multimedia projectors linked to computers, and smart whiteboards, which allow teachers to present files from their computers on the board and also write on the board with a marker, saving the information on the board in a computer file (Maddux, Johnson, & Willis, 2001; Solvie, 2004). Solvie (2004) found the digital whiteboards to be extremely helpful for early literacy instruction.

Slides can be selected and arranged to suit your purpose. After you assemble them, you can add a commentary tape with background sound effects; or, instead of using a prepared narrative, you may prefer to discuss the slides as you go, taking as much time with each slide as you wish. Remote-controlled projectors allow you to stand at the front of the class and point to details you want the students to notice.

The overhead projector is simple to operate, and it can be used to project images on a screen in a normally lighted classroom. You can easily create your own transparencies by writing with a grease pencil or transparency marking pen on a clear sheet of acetate, or by photocopying material that you wish to make into a transparency, using a copy machine designed to transfer your copy onto a transparency. Computer programs, such as *PowerPoint* (Microsoft) and *mPower* (Multimedia Design), also allow you to design transparencies easily. In addition, commercially prepared transparencies designed for your textbook or units can be helpful. Many publishers make such materials available.

If you make your own transparencies, check them before you use them with a class to ensure that they are readable from where students in that room arrangement will sit. You may find that the print must be larger than you originally envisioned. Carefully proofread your material to make sure you have no misspellings or typographical errors.

You have probably used overhead projectors in your teacher-preparation program, but, if you have never used one, attempt it during your student teaching. Practice using it by yourself before using it with your class. Remember three important points: (a) check the placement and focus of the projector before the lesson starts; (b) know how to place the transparencies so that the images on the screen are readable; and (c) identify items by pointing on the transparencies, not on the screen.

Visual presenters are more versatile than overhead projectors. They allow you to use either transparencies or regular printed pages. You can even display book pages that you are discussing on the visual presenter and show them on the screen. This allows analysis of pictures in the students' textbooks, as well as those in reference materials that you choose to present.

You can use smart whiteboards to project material from your computer onto the board, incorporate material that you write on the board, and save the modified version to a file for later viewing. Any type of computer file—word processing, spreadsheet, database, or graphics—can be presented in this manner (Maddux, Johnson, & Willis, 2001).

Video Recordings

Videotapes, CDs, DVDs, and videodiscs help you create interest in a unit, review and reinforce a subject, provide a vicarious experience, or initiate discussion. Many useful lessons and other types of programs can be found on these media, which are often available through the school system from the central office. For example, there are video presentations of Shakespearean plays and other literature selections. Hibbing and Rankin-Erickson (2003) showed struggling middle-school readers movies about content area topics to provide them with important background information to help them understand the printed material. Such movies can help students comprehend the settings, time frames, and language used in some content material and provide "memory pegs" for new information read in the texts.

Some video presentations are springboards for creative activities; others are straightforward presentations of subject matter through illustrated lectures. As processes are speeded up or slowed down on tape or disc, students can watch changes occur that would otherwise be unobservable.

Using videotape recorders, you can record television programs and play them back later, although you must be sure to observe the copyright laws. Prerecorded tapes are also available for most subject areas. For example, the National Geographic Society has a series of animal videos for grades pre-K to 4, called *Tales from the Wild.*

You can also record students' performances with videotape recorders and play those performances back for the students to see. Students can use these recordings for self-analysis. They are particularly useful in speech, drama, dance, and physical education classes. The recordings may also be used as visible evidence of improvement in these and other areas. For example, creative dramatic performances can be recorded over a period of time, and all the performances can be played back in a single viewing. The students can see how their actions and speech have changed over time.

Videotape recorders are easy to operate and can provide focused instruction for the whole class or targeted groups of students. Students can learn to use them and then assist in documenting class presentations or special programs.

Videodiscs, CDs, and DVDs provide video images and high-quality sound. They also allow random access to desired frames or video segments. This gives them an advantage over videotapes for some applications. Realize that you need to analyze educational videodiscs, CDs, and DVDs to make sure that they are not all "flash," without reliable, accurate, and well-organized information. You also must be sure that they are easy to navigate.

FOR YOUR PORTFOLIO

INTASC Standards: 4, 5, 9

Videotape or audiotape student presentations in a class that you teach. Include the videotape or audiotape in your portfolio with an explanation of how your lessons led to these presentations.

Television

"The National Council of Teachers of English and International Reading Association *Standards for the English Language Arts* (1996) mentions popular film and television as visual texts worthy of study in K–12 classrooms" (Morrell, 2002, pp. 74–75). Students "spend an average of six-and-a-half hours per day with all media" (Scharrer, 2002/2003, p. 357), so critical viewing skills are vitally important, even if television is not going to be used as a classroom learning tool. Learning that television programs have predictable structures, represent distinct genres, are designed to appeal to particular audiences, and must be critically analyzed for audience manipulation are important concepts. Some view it as "a bridge to more sophisticated print literacy" (Williams, 2003, p. 546). Contrary to the beliefs of some educators, some television viewing can help to meet instructional goals.

Two types of television programming are appropriate for instructional use: educational programming, much of which is on the Public Broadcasting System (PBS), and commercial programming that happens to cover areas of educational interest. Students may have access to either of these types of programming during the school day, depending upon scheduling considerations, or they may be assigned programs to watch at home, outside of school hours, with the understanding that these programs will be discussed in class later. PBS has programming that is pertinent to many different areas of the curriculum on a regular basis.

Whether or not you make use of instructional television will probably be determined by your mentoring teacher and the availability of a television set in your classroom. Unlike videotapes, CDs, and DVDs, live television programs cannot be previewed. Therefore, you must study the manual, if one is available, or at least read program listing explanations of program content to develop your lesson. When using a television program, turn on the set at least 15 minutes before the scheduled starting time to make sure it is operating correctly. Introduce vocabulary and concepts by writing them on the board or a transparency and discussing them, and thoroughly prepare your students for what they will see. When the program starts, encourage students to respond to the television program by participating actively in the lesson yourself. During the lesson, take notes on points to discuss later. Walk around among the students to make sure that they are actively involved in the lesson. After the program is over, don't reteach the lesson, but follow through with related activities.

St. Clair and Schwetz (2003) describe the use of the PBS show *Between the Lions* as a classroom tool for kindergarten and first-grade students. With its lion-family puppet cast, this show uses music, stories, and word play to assist children in learning about reading and encouraging them to enjoy reading.

If you assign regular television programs (e.g., documentaries, cultural programs, or a series of educational significance) for the students to watch at home during the evenings or on weekends, you should provide the students with specific objectives. Television guides are often available for teachers to use for these types of programs; sometimes they can be downloaded from the Internet. With the help of a guide, you can assign students to watch for certain points or ideas as they view the programs. The next class day, you should follow up with a discussion or other experiences related to the programs.

As previously mentioned, you may videotape television programs to view later. "Cable in the Classroom is a public-service initiative of the cable television industry. It is a joint project of local cable operators and national cable programmers to provide schools with free basic cable service and more than 540 hours of commercial-free educational television programming each month" (Cable in the Classroom Fact Sheet, 1999, p. 2). These programs have liberal copyright clearance, so they may be taped and used for educational purposes. Some allow unrestricted use, while others have time limits for use, but these may be as generous as 1 or 2 years. For example, teachers who taped C-SPAN's *American Presidents: Life Portraits* series in 1999 are unrestricted in the time that they can show it for educational purposes. Cable in the Classroom programs are available for many curricular areas. Look at *www.ciconline.org* for further information.

Newscasts are often pertinent to studies in secondary school social studies classes, and sometimes it is possible to anticipate the appropriateness of a newscast for a particular day, for example, the day of a space shuttle launch, election day or the day before or after an election, or the day of a presidential pronouncement. All-news channels or all-weather channels may be monitored during national events or disasters, such as some schools did during former president Ronald Reagan's funeral and during the hurricanes that produced destruction across several states. The History Channel and the Discovery Channel often announce appropriate programming in advance through publications. Any programming used in class must be chosen with care and must be appropriate for the grade level and class in which it is watched. Individual schools or school systems may have guidelines for use of such programs. Be sure you are aware of any regulations that are in place. For example, even if an R-rated movie is related to the subject matter, it would not be acceptable to show in most schools.

Calculators

Calculators are used extensively in mathematics classes to do time-consuming or complex calculations, thus leaving more time for the students to perform the cognitive processes necessary to solve problems. Calculators are also often useful in science classes when lab experiments require calculations.

COMMUNITY RESOURCES

The community in which your school is located offers many opportunities for purposeful learning experiences. Use of resource people and field trips provides links between the basic skills taught in the classroom and the application of these skills in the outside world. You may have limited community involvement while student teaching, but you can still utilize many resources if you begin early to explore the possibilities.

Resource People

A resource person can often attract students' attention more effectively than the classroom teacher can. Because of the resource person's direct experience with a topic, the presentation is usually more credible and more likely to make a lasting impression. Since you cannot be an expert in every field, other people can sometimes supplement your knowledge. A resource person can be especially effective at the beginning of a unit to create interest or near the end of a unit to reinforce and extend concepts.

The first step in using resource people is to consider who has expertise in the topics you plan to cover. Your personal friends may have hobbies or experiences that would make them valuable resource people. If you are student teaching in your hometown, you may already know people who could contribute to your unit. School personnel may also discuss their work experiences or offer special knowledge. Your university employs specialists in many fields who may be willing to work with you. People from varied cultural, ethnic, and religious backgrounds may be available to share their heritages. Businesses and industries, banks, protective service agencies, public utilities, and government agencies at all levels often have representatives who go into the schools to provide information.

Resource people can be identified through various approaches. Your school may have a volunteer services program or a file with the names of resource people and their areas of expertise. Your mentoring teacher or other school personnel may be able to recommend a suitable resource person for your subject. Senior citizens can be recruited from senior centers and religious and community organizations. You may also wish to survey your students to see if their parents or someone else they know can be helpful. A sample survey form is provided in Activity 6.2. Before you take a survey, be sure to get permission from school authorities.

After you select someone with the appropriate specialized knowledge, contact her or him concerning the proposed school visit. Tactfully discuss the type of presentation, the need to adjust to the students' level, and the amount of time available. Discuss the students' background knowledge, attention span, and probable questions. The visitor may prefer to lecture, show slides, demonstrate a process, or talk informally. Be sure she or he understands the purpose of the visit and how it relates to what you are teaching.

You must also prepare students for resource visitors. Involve them in the planning and have them make lists of questions prior to visits. Students can issue invitations, arrange for any special equipment, meet guests upon their arrival, introduce them, and assist them in their presentations. Students should be encouraged to show their appreciation at the time of the visit through oral means and later in the form of thank-you letters. As the teacher, you must relate the presentations of resource people to your units by preparing the students for visits and following them up with reinforcing activities.

Some business and civic leaders may not be willing to come to the school but will grant interviews to students who come to see them. The experience of conducting an interview is worthwhile; however, careful and detailed arrangements need to be made prior to the interview. School personnel must approve the interview. Consent must also be given by the prospective interviewee and by the parents of the students participating in the interview. The students should draw up questions in advance, practice note-taking skills, and learn proper conduct in handling an interview. They may be helped by role-playing an interview with the teacher or someone else before the actual interview takes place. After the interview, students need to organize their notes and write summaries of the information to share with their classmates.

Students at the secondary level can become involved with resource people by taking surveys. The students can identify an issue in which they are interested and design a simple questionnaire to give to people they know. Topics might include whether or not to build a new gymnasium, establish a teen center, or extend the city limits. Students can get additional information about their topics by searching through records and interviewing city employees. The students can summarize their findings and draw conclusions that might have implications for community action and then submit the results to the media for public dissemination.

Field Trips

A field trip is an organized class excursion for the purpose of obtaining information through direct observation. A child's earliest experiences with field trips usually consist of visits to places like a fire station. In the fall, classes may visit a pumpkin farm and learn about growing pumpkins that are purchased for pies, general harvest decorations, or jack-o'-lanterns, or they

may visit a tree farm that produces Christmas trees for the holiday season. Field trips to newspaper offices allow students to learn about how the reporters gather news and material for feature stories, how papers are put together, and how they are printed. Field trips to factories can help students learn how goods are produced and distributed. Community theaters often offer students special matinee shows that have age-appropriate themes and special group rates. Some classes take end-of-year trips to zoos or museums. Older students may "run" City Hall for one day of the year; each student is appointed to a position and assumes the responsibilities of the person who occupies the corresponding position in city government. Participating in field experiences during their school years gives students many opportunities to understand how their community operates and to broaden their knowledge of specific subjects. Acquaintance with different occupations can also give students direction in choosing careers.

Although a field trip can be a valuable learning experience, it requires a great deal of planning; otherwise, it can be a fiasco. Initial planning includes contacting the target location and setting up an appointment to see the appropriate people and operations. If students are not properly prepared for the experience, they may become disorderly and disruptive, get injured, destroy property, and generally damage relations between the school and the community. Unless you make careful preparations and develop background for

A resource person can often attract students' attention more than the classroom teacher can, and he or she is more likely to make a lasting impression.

ACTIVITY 6.2 | *Survey of Resource People*

Date _____

Student's name _____ Grade _____ Phone _____

Teacher's name _____ School _____

Address of student _____

Parent's name _____

Address (if different) _____

Are you willing to volunteer your help in your son's or daughter's classroom? _____

If so, what days and hours are most convenient? _____

Do you have any special knowledge, talents, or skills that you can share with the class? _____

If so, what are they? _____

_____

Perhaps you know someone who would be able to contribute something worthwhile to the school. If so, please fill in the information below. (Use other side for additional suggestions.)

Name _____ Phone _____

Address _____

Possible contribution _____

Thank you for your cooperation!

the experience, students may not see the reason for the trip, which will likely diminish its educational value. Appropriate follow-up activities after the field trip can help to solidify learning. Students can have small-group and class discussions about the trip, write about it, prepare oral or multimedia presentations about it, or add information gleaned from the trip to a class web page. The checklist in Activity 6.3 can help you plan a successful field trip.

Field trips present other problems as well. With school budgets tightening, many school districts no longer provide free bus transportation for field trips. In addition, increased liability and lawsuit concerns have made many teachers wary of the risk involved in taking students away from the school.

In self-contained classrooms, scheduling a field trip is usually fairly simple because only one teacher is involved. It is sometimes more difficult, however, to arrange trips in secondary schools, because of the short class periods in schools without block scheduling. Sometimes teachers of other subjects will cooperate to permit the absence of your students, but it may be necessary to plan trips at this level for after school or Saturdays.

Students who know what to expect are likely to learn more from a field trip than students who have no background information. The class should be involved in planning each trip. Even though you may have the idea in the back of your mind, you may want to let the students think the idea is theirs. For young children, a discussion about the subject and the proposed field trip may result in a set of questions on a language experience chart. These questions can be used as objectives for the trip. Older students can research the subject and develop individual lists of questions, which may ultimately result in written reports. Students of any age may be able to visit a related website in preparation for the trip.

Field trips are most valuable when they are an integral part of a total learning situation. You need to make adequate preparation and reinforce the educational value of the field trip with a variety of follow-up activities. These activities often spill over into many areas of the curriculum—social studies, science, reading, language arts, art, and music.

Field trips within walking distance of the school can provide students with new experiences. Businesses or recreational facilities, such as parks, near the school can be the focus of such trips. The students may want to consider why the business or recreational facility was located where it is, what the effect of this facility is on the community, and whether or not they personally see direct benefits from it. One elementary school is located near a business that makes ceramic items. The students walk to the business and receive a tour and sample items. Then they return to their classrooms to write about the tour and the business.

You may find an opportunity for taking a nearby field trip, or you may want to plan a computerized virtual trip. (See Chapter 7 for more on virtual field trips.) Talk it over with your mentoring teacher and then make it work!

DISCUSSION QUESTIONS

1. Should you use a free, current, interesting video from a company that uses the video to advertise its product? If you decide to use the video, what are some ways to handle the advertising message?

2. How can you use your community's resources? What people, places, or agencies are available that relate to your subjects? How can you find out?

3. What do you do if one student's parent offers to share information with your class that you feel is inappropriate? How can you avoid offending the parent and the student? Is there another way you could use the parent's services?

4. What is the policy regarding field trips in your school? Are they permitted? How is transportation arranged? What regulations are in effect? Would a field trip be a good learning experience for your students?

ACTIVITY 6.3 | ***Checklist for Field Trip***

1. _____ Permission to take a field trip has been granted by the school.

2. _____ Personnel at the destination have been contacted, and a time has been set for the visit.

3. _____ Transportation has been arranged.

4. _____ If you are using private cars, insurance and liability regulations have been checked.

5. _____ An adequate number of adults have agreed to accompany the students.

6. _____ Proper arrangements have been made regarding the facilities at the destination: restrooms, cafeteria, picnic tables, parking areas, size of observation areas.

7. _____ Lunch money and other fees have been collected (if applicable).

8. _____ Parental permission notes have been sent home.

9. _____ Parental permission notes have been returned.

10. _____ Students have been told how to behave and what to wear.

11. _____ Students have been told what to expect and have adequate background knowledge to understand what they will see.

12. _____ A list of questions has been prepared to set purposes for the visit.

13. _____ Tape recorders and notepads are available for recording specific information.

14. _____ Safety hazards, if any, have been noted and appropriate precautions taken.

15. _____ A first aid kit is available for emergencies.

16. _____ A signal (such as a whistle or raised arm) has been agreed upon for getting students' attention.

17. _____ Students have been paired and assigned buddies (if appropriate).

18. _____ Policy manual regarding field trips has been read, and policies have been followed.

Chapter 7

Supporting the Curriculum Through Computer Resources

Case Study 7.1: Making Use of Technology

Miss Dycus, a student teacher

in a seventh-grade English class, was assigned to a classroom that had just received two multimedia computers from the school's Parent Teacher Association. Mr. Tompkins, Miss Dycus's mentoring teacher, felt that two computers were not sufficient for curricular applications, so he had made computer time a reward for students who finished assignments early or received high scores on papers or exams.

When students went to the computers to claim their reward time, they almost always chose the *Flight Simulator* or *Game Empire* CD-ROMs. Miss Dycus felt that was a waste of a valuable instructional resource. She tried to remedy the situation, with her mentoring teacher's approval.

Miss Dycus: Mr. Tompkins, I'd like for the students to make more use of the computer resources for their English assignments. Would you mind if I changed the types of computer use when I take over class instruction?

Mr. Tompkins: No, I don't mind your experimentation, but I don't think you will get far with only two computers and 30 students in a class.

Miss Dycus: I thought I would demonstrate the use of the multimedia encyclopedia, the almanac, the dictionary, the thesaurus, and the atlas, and then assign short cooperative papers that would require students to use these resources to find information.

Mr. Tompkins: How can you demonstrate to the whole class at the same time?

Miss Dycus: I can check out from our university media center a device that connects to the computer to show images from the computer on a large screen.

Mr. Tompkins: But there are only two computers for 30 students. They won't get a chance to look up the information.

Miss Dycus: I'll put the students in groups of three. Each group will choose a topic from a list I provide. Then each group will plan what types of information to include in its paper, decide which reference sources they need to check for different purposes, and submit the list to me. I'll check to see if they have made reasonable choices and give them a priority number for computer use. Five groups can use each computer, taking turns, according to the priority schedule that I post.

Mr. Tompkins: What about the ones not using the computer?

Miss Dycus: Oh, they will be brainstorming about the topic, outlining the paper, composing the paper, and revising the drafts. I'll put some other reference books in a resource corner for them to use, and I'll expect them to make use of their textbooks, as well. Synthesizing the information from all these sources should be a good experience and should keep everyone purposefully engaged. After the initial computer searches have been completed, students will be allowed to access the dictionary and thesaurus CD-ROMs if the computers are available, but I'll have printed dictionaries and thesauruses available as well.

Mr. Tompkins: It sounds good, but the students may not apply themselves to the task. They may be distracted by the computer element.

Miss Dycus: I have an idea that would help avoid that. Groups that finish a handwritten final draft within the project time frame without causing undue disruption to others could get to use the word processor to do a final draft for display in the classroom. If they don't have good typing skills, I could let them use the *Typing Tutor* CD-ROM to brush up on these skills.

Mr. Tompkins: I'm willing to let you try, but it sounds complicated.

Miss Dycus announced the plan when she started teaching the class. Some of the students grumbled about losing their game-playing time, while others worried that using the computer would be too hard. But some were excited about getting to try something new. Most of the students were at least mildly interested after the CD-ROMs were demonstrated.

Since the students had previously done group work, the formation of the work groups and selection of topics went smoothly. At first some of the groups had trouble using the CD-ROMs. A Computer Club member was recruited from study hall to help students as they worked on the computers, which facilitated the process.

The whole process took longer than expected, however, and was not completed before Miss Dycus had to leave. Although the papers had all been successfully written, there was no time to word process them at the end.

Mr. Tompkins told Miss Dycus he would continue the process after she left and let the students do that step as well. He did express concern at how much class time the project had taken and said he was not sure he would do it again.

1. Did Miss Dycus have a workable idea for use in the class?
2. How could she have made the experience more effective?
3. Was the result worth the time involved?
4. Would you try it?

COMPUTERS FOR INSTRUCTION

Incorporating computers into an instructional program involves more than just putting students on computers and letting them learn from the experience. As Sefton-Green (2001) points out, students need to be taught to work with new media, because they will not spontaneously know how to use the media effectively and appropriately. Of course, before you can assist them in learning to use computers, you must have a good working understanding of their use yourself. In other words, you must be technologically literate in computer use, knowing how to use computer tools to increase academic performance in school subjects (Smolin & Lawless, 2003) and how to help students acquire essential technological literacy (Dugger, 2001). According to Riel and Fulton (2001), technology is a promising vehicle for building learning communities in which students work and learn from people at distant locations. It offers them "power tools" for creating and communicating ideas. Later in this chapter you will see that teachers must be ready to supply students with necessary support for such endeavors.

Other challenges exist as well. More decisions are necessary in choosing computer software than are needed in choosing most other instructional materials. For example, choosing an audiocassette to play is not likely to be a problem for teachers. However, choosing the correct software to use on a specific computer is more complicated.

These additional considerations are necessary when choosing computer software for use in your classes:

1. Make sure the software was designed for the type of computer you have in your class. For example, some software designed for PCs will not run on Macintosh computers, and the converse is also true. The documentation accompanying the software will identify compatible computers for the program.
2. Make sure the program is easy for your students to use. Some programs contain useful information but are not user-friendly—they are hard to use, because of missing or inadequate instructions about how to enter information, how to progress through the program by moving from screen to screen, how to exit from the program, how to adjust the program's rate of presentation or level of difficulty, or where to obtain assistance when problems arise. If the programs are hard for you to use because of poor design, they will probably be hard for some of your students. Therefore, you should try programs out before using them for a class, even if reviews indicate that they are just what you need. The reviewers may never have had a class like yours.
3. Make sure sufficient time is available for all the students to complete the lesson. If you only have access to a small number of computers, some very good programs may be impractical on a whole-class or large-group scale.
4. Check the program for sound effects, and decide if they will be disturbing to those in the class not working on the program at the moment. If you think they may be distracting, see if the sound can be turned down or even off. However, if you plan to turn the sound off, make sure the program is still effective without it. An alternative is to have students use the program with earphones. Try to take all possibilities into account.

Obviously, computers are the specific focus of computer literacy and computer programming classes. In addition to these classes, however, computers are used extensively in many schools for a variety of purposes. A school's computers may be located in individual classrooms, but sometimes are only available in a computer laboratory that has scheduled times for different classes or specific purposes.

Some teachers use drill-and-practice programs, tutorial programs, simulations, interactive literature programs, game programs, word processing programs, desktop publishing programs, electronic databases, electronic spreadsheets, electronic reference sources, Web development programs, e-mail programs, and Internet search programs as a part of their regular class instruction. They may be central to instruction or may be used for special situations, depending upon the equipment and software available.

Types of Computer Programs

Computer programs perform many functions in classrooms. Figure 7–1 shows some types of programs with which you should be familiar. *Drill-and-practice programs* do not teach new material; they simply offer practice on previously taught skills. Students are often provided with drill-and-practice programs on mathematics, language, reading, and other skills in order to free the teacher from the repetitive drill and allow her or him to work at instructing students who need extra explanation and attention.

Tutorial programs, in contrast, offer skill instruction and also generally include a practice component. Tutorial programs may be used for students who need extra instruction in a previously covered area, students who were absent when initial instruction occurred, or gifted students who are ready for more advanced instruction than the class as a whole.

Some specialized instructional software helps students move through the writing process, from generating ideas to producing the final product. Likewise, some networked software allows students to comment upon each other's writing in a kind of electronic peer

FIGURE 7–1
Types of Computer Programs

Drill-and-practice programs—Offer practice on skills that have been previously taught

Tutorial programs—Offer instruction (may have a practice component)

Simulation programs—Provide situations that simulate real life

Interactive literature programs—Allow students to interact by having the material read to them, letting them record themselves reading the material, and/or letting them click on words or items to get information or see animations

Game programs—Provide recreation or skill practice in game format

Word processing programs—Allow the user to produce and easily revise text (may have desktop publishing features also)

Desktop publishing programs—Designed to allow the mixing of text and graphics in a document

Database programs—Allow creation and/or searching of organized collections of information

Spreadsheet programs—Perform calculations on organized sets of numbers, according to formulas that the user enters

Presentation software—Allows the development of multimedia presentations that can be presented on the computer

Web development software—Aids in development of Web pages by converting text into HTML code

writing conference. Such software makes it possible for students to discuss literature online, and to discuss different aspects of each other's writing. In addition, some Internet sites allow students to post their work to be critiqued by others.

Simulations replicate important aspects of real-life situations on the computer. These interactive programs require critical reading and critical thinking decisions by the users and allow students to see the consequences of these decisions.

Fairly large numbers of science, health, and social studies simulations are available to offer students experiences that are not otherwise attainable for them. For example, simulations of chemistry experiments that use dangerous materials can provide learning experiences without danger; simulations of running businesses can help students learn economic principles without an actual outlay of money or a need for space and equipment; and simulations of ecosystems can allow students to view such phenomena as food chains without leaving the classroom. Some interdisciplinary simulations combine learning activities that relate to a number of curricular areas (Roe & Smith, 2005). *The Oregon Trail II* (MECC), a simulation that combines history, geography, reading, writing, health, science, and math, has been widely used in schools, but Bigelow (1997) warns that, although *The Oregon Trail II* program and its associated trail guide have good information about the geography of the area, ailments suffered by pioneers, treatments used by trav-

elers, and equipment and supplies, it has aspects that are "sexist, racist, culturally insensitive, and contemptuous of the earth" (p. 85). Bigelow points out that this program has white male characters with different motivations and responsibilities from the females and blacks on the journey, limiting the learning experience. He also does not believe that the program has the students react in a culturally sensitive way to the Native Americans they encounter on the journey. However, no one program is likely to cover every aspect of the situation being simulated, and it is not surprising that historical simulations do not take on modern attitudes toward ecological and cultural issues. Teachers should be aware of these program characteristics and help the students understand the characters from a historical perspective, as well as help them to relate the situation to the present. Use of multiple resources related to the topic, such as CDs, Internet sites, books, and videos, can help to clarify these concerns.

Interactive literature programs, which are available on CDs, allow students to have material read to them, to record and play back their own reading of the material, to click on words to get pronunciations and definitions, and to click on pictures to get animations or explanations.

Games provide recreation, but, if playing them successfully requires content knowledge, they may also reinforce classroom learning. Games are often used as a reward for successful completion of work as well as for enjoyable skill practice.

Production software of various types helps the user develop a product. Computers with *word processing software* can facilitate students' preparation of class assignments in creative writing, reports in content areas, or class or school newspapers or magazines. Word processing programs allow students to insert or delete material and move blocks of text easily. Many programs have spelling checkers and grammar checkers that help students find problems in their papers. These tools make it more likely that students will make corrections to their writing. Students may be familiar with spelling checkers, but younger students may not completely understand how they work, as is true in the Family Circus comic below.

Word processing programs can also be helpful to you in preparing study guides, review sheets, and tests and in writing letters to parents. For the benefit of both you and your students, learn about the word processing software available to you, and make use of it.

Desktop publishing programs are valuable resources for developing class newspapers, class magazines, and other publications. Students can enter text, scan in pictures, incorporate clip art, and perform other activities that allow them to produce attractive, creative, or functional writing selections. Many current word processing programs offer these functions, blurring the distinction that was previously made between desktop publishing programs and word processing programs.

Be careful that you are not fooled by fancy fonts, color graphics, and neat page layouts so that you fail to evaluate the content in student papers prepared on desktop publishing or sophisticated word processing programs. Students may have beautiful papers that are empty of ideas or filled with incorrect ones (Holland, 1996).

Kidspiration (Inspiration Software) and *Inspiration* (Inspiration Software) are computer programs for younger and older students, respectively, that allow them to create webs of stories or reports. They are good tools for brainstorming activities. *Timeliner* (Tom Snyder Productions) allows the creation of time lines and sequencing charts (May, 2003). These programs are useful in language, science, and social studies classes.

Computer databases are also an important part of instruction in many schools. A database is a "collection of related data organized to address the information needs of a variety of users" (Heide & Henderson, 1994, p. 154). The information within a database is filed under categories for easy access. A computer database can be electronically searched to locate information of interest. Many preexisting databases may be used in schools; as a matter of fact, classes equipped like the one in the opening vignette have numerous databases available on CDs and have a program for creating databases on the computer's hard drive. Some school libraries are putting their card catalogs on computer, producing very useful databases that can be searched by title, author, and subject.

Many useful online databases can be accessed by students in classrooms with Internet connections. Students can also create their own databases on topics of study. Doing so gives students experience in categorizing material. Students should know how to search existing databases and how to create their own databases for class projects. If your school has database software, become familiar with it so you can help your students use it effectively. If you use database software to record information about your students or units that you plan to teach, the effort of learning about it will be even more worthwhile for you.

In some classes, students may learn to use *spreadsheet programs*, electronic accounting pads that can automatically perform calculations such as addition and subtraction on rows and columns of numbers. Users can enter calculation formulas to perform mathematical operations on the data. When new data are entered into the spreadsheet, the program automatically recalculates the results. Such programs may be particularly useful in science and mathematics classes.

Use of Electronic References

With the advent of multimedia computers with CD drives, electronic reference materials have become much more common in schools. Electronic encyclopedias,

THE FAMILY CIRCUS   By Bil Keane

11-9
©2004 Bil Keane, Inc.
Dist. by King Features Synd.
www.familycircus.com

"We can get marks taken off our homework for misspelling. Could you run this through spell-check?"

© Reprinted with permission of King Features Syndicate.

dictionaries, thesauruses, atlases, and almanacs are among standard reference tools in many school libraries and some classrooms. Some of these resources have pictures, sound, and animation, in addition to printed text, and are searchable through the use of keywords and phrases, topics, and titles (Roe, 2000). Other electronic reference materials can be accessed on the Internet, if the classroom or library has an Internet connection. For example, the concise version (not the full version available on CD) of Microsoft Encarta is available free online at *www.encarta.msn.com* (Buchleitner, 1999). There, reference sources are available for different grade ranges, and they need to be chosen with the potential users in mind.

Students can use Internet searches and information on CDs, along with printed texts, such as reference books, to do research for content classes. Goldman (1997) described the *Whole Day, Whole Year* project in which middle school students used all of these materials to search for relevant information and took notes in field journals on their findings. Then they evaluated the material they found and produced written reports (Wade & Moje, 2000).

As a teacher, you can search the Internet to collect information for classroom use. For example, C-SPAN's American Presidents website (*www.american presidents.org*) has an in-depth look at each president. Teachers can download free guides to use with this material (Notebook, 1999). In addition, many PBS programs have teaching materials available on the PBS website (*www.pbs.org*; Sourcebook, 1999).

Students should learn how to use a Web browser, such as Internet Explorer or Netscape Navigator, to locate information on the Internet. They may use Uniform Resource Locators (URLs), which are the addresses of the Internet sites, by entering them in the browsers' dialogue windows, if they know the specific addresses. Once the users are at specific sites, the Web browsers allow them to click on icons or words to link to other sites, without actually having to enter the URLs for those sites. If they do not know the URL for a needed site, are not on a site that links to that site, or do not know if a site with the information that they seek actually exists, they need to use search engines, such as Yahooligans!, Ask Jeeves, Google, AltaVista, and Dogpile, that "check terms that a user enters into the computer against keywords found on Web pages indexed by the search service" (Roe, Stoodt-Hill, & Burns, 2004, p. 162). Different search engines use different search techniques and consequently may find different sites. Therefore, some are more likely to locate certain types of information than are others (Mossberg, 1998; Wildstrom, 1999). Yahooligans!, a search engine designed for use by children, is "filtered" for their use by editors who check the sites for potentially offensive material (Buchleitner, 1999).

Online research projects make possible worldwide student collaboration on common research activities. Many projects are available for classes at all levels and in a variety of subject areas. Students may collect data about water pollution in their respective areas, about temperature and weather patterns, or about some other topic of general interest to students in various courses. All students may contribute collected data to a common data bank, which may be analyzed in a variety of ways by the various classes. Results may be posted on a website designated for the project.

In classrooms with Internet connections or other wide-area networks, you can use e-mail to communicate with teachers all over the world and to consult experts in your field for advice. Students can also use e-mail to communicate with other students or resource people in remote locations. Keypal (computer pen pal) projects are frequent in the area of literature study, in which students correspond electronically with paired peers or mentors in university classes about literature selections that they are reading in common (Carico & Logan, 2004; Roe & Smith, 1997). Keypal activities can be designed for any area of the curriculum. Students may also hold e-mail exchanges with their teachers, thereby building personal and sustained connections between the students and teachers (Doherty & Mayer, 2003).

Carico and Logan (2004) expanded their WebPal Project between preservice teachers and eighth graders with the use of bulletin boards, in which the participants posted to anyone involved in the project, and Multi-user, Object-Oriented environments (MOOs), which are "real-time, online chats in which 2–3 pairs are placed together to discuss a book read in common" (p. 294). Carico and Logan believe that the MOOs have brought the participants "together as a community of learners" (p. 294) more effectively than the other two experiences. In the MOOs the students talk to explore ideas, not to answer questions posed by the teacher.

Some teachers have had success with moderated online literature discussions. However, students may need explicit modeling of good student-student interaction to make these discussions more effective. They need to learn to offer appropriate compliments to other students and also to respond to them critically but courteously (Love, 2002).

Electronic videoconferencing is a possibility if schools have the needed cameras and software. Videoconferences allow students to meet over the Internet with others who are visible to them on their computer monitors and heard through their speakers. Scientists, historians, book authors, and other experts can speak directly to students who are studying topics within their areas of specialization. Students can construct interview questions, conduct the electronic interview during the videoconference, take notes on the information provided, and write reports or give oral reports based on the results of the interview (Roe, Smith, & Burns, 2005). Maring (2002) has made use of videoconferencing in his Cyber Mentoring projects at Washington State University.

Virtual field trips are available at a number of websites. Students can visit art museums, archeological digs, Antarctica, and countless other sites that coordinate with curricular studies. (See the discussion of field trips for more information, and for ideas about preparing students for any kind of field trip.)

Students can design and implement home pages for their classes on the Internet using hypertext markup language (HTML), special software that is designed to produce HTML code for users without the users having to know the specific code (for example, *FrontPage,* which works well for secondary school students, or *Sarah's Page Web Builder,* designed for ages 9 and up). Many word processing programs (such as Microsoft™ Word) can convert text files to HTML files. Students can use these home pages to post creative writing, news stories, poetry, and art. They may also be used to present the results of class or group projects, making use of photographs taken with digital cameras, images scanned into the computer from print sources, and clip art available on the Internet or on CDs.

FOR YOUR PORTFOLIO

INTASC Standard: 6
Design a home page for your class. Download it to disk to use in your portfolio.

Expanding Computer Use

Leu (2002) describes an instructional framework called Internet Workshop which helps students learn new skills and strategies that new technologies of literacy require. "Internet Workshop (Leu & Leu, 2000) consists of an independent reading of information on the Internet around a topic and a location initially designated by the teacher; it concludes with a short workshop session where students can share and exchange ideas and strategies they discovered during their work on the Internet" (p. 467). In between there is an openended activity in which students use the site to accomplish curricular goals. The activity must be open-ended in order to allow students to bring different information to the Internet Workshop discussion. The activity can at first be teacher directed and later involve independent inquiry projects. There are many variations of Internet Workshop, and it can be used from kindergarten on up through the grades.

Labbo (2004) developed a technique called Author's Computer Chair, which is similar to Author's Chair, in which students sit in the chair and ask for feedback on aspects of their writing from their assembled classmates and teacher. In Author's Computer Chair, a student can ask for feedback and help on computer-related activities. Students may also use Author's Computer Chair to share their knowledge and expertise about computer use or show their classmates a finished computer project.

Obviously, computers can provide enrichment in school subjects for all students, offer challenges for bright students, and give special assistance for remedial and compensatory purposes. Computer programs in languages other than English can help enrich students' learning when the students speak English as a second language and when the students are being introduced to the languages of various countries and cultures. Language translation programs can take English text and translate it into another language and vice versa. Students with special needs can be helped by computer programs that offer such features as enlarged print, synthetic speech, Braille translation programs, special input devices, and even speech recognition. Martin (2003) found that her at-risk readers had increased motivation and confidence with the computer when computer use was demonstrated and the students read the material in teams of three, took notes, and discussed the material in the teams.

Computers can present greatly enlarged text to accommodate students with visual impairment.

They supported one another in using the technology and reading and discussing the material. A follow-up activity required the material to be used in a way that made the readers accountable for the information read from the computer screen.

WebQuests, inquiry-based, Web-based lessons that explore particular topics, can be applied to a variety of teaching situations. The development of a WebQuest typically follows a predefined format, including such parts as an *Introduction* section, *Task* specification, *Process* instructions, *Roles* explanation, *Conclusion* explanation, *Standards* identification, and *Evaluation* description. Students are usually assigned to a cooperative group to take on a different role to investigate the various facets of the topic. One key component of the WebQuest is Internet research. The tasks should relate to real-world concerns and be relevant to the students. The *Introduction* provides motivation and introduces the topic. The *Task* instructions specify the end result of the student efforts. The *Process* instructions give a step-by-step description of how students will complete the task and the resources needed. The *Roles* explanation offers a description of each student's responsibilities. The *Conclusion* explanation provides instructions for student reactions to investigations as related to different roles. The *Standards* identification shows alignment with curriculum performance outcomes. The *Evaluation* component describes the overall assessment that reflects student learning (Coiro, 2003; Dodge, 1997, 2004; March, 2000; Spires & Estes, 2002; Teclehaimanot & Lamb, 2004).

Computers can reinforce teaching that is not heavily dependent on textbooks and lectures. For example, computer labs can be an avenue to hands-on science and, in general, a constructivist approach to learning (Hancock & Betts, 1994).

PREPARING FOR COMPUTER APPLICATIONS

As a student teacher, you may find that computer applications are an important component in your assigned classes. Your mentoring teacher or the media specialist should orient you to the particular computers and peripheral devices used in your school. You may, for example, have to know how to attach a projection device to a computer to demonstrate a program for the entire class.

You should know how to run commercial computer programs and what the special keys on the computer keyboard mean. You also need to know that what to do if a student "crashes" a program (causes it to cease to operate).

You may also be introduced to the world of scanners, laser discs, digital cameras, modems, and Internet connections. If you don't already know how to do so, learn to use browsers, such as Lynx (a text-only browser) or Netscape Navigator or Microsoft's Internet Explorer (browsers with a graphical user interface), to locate information on the Internet. Previewing sites you may want to use for instruction and "bookmarking" them for use during classes is a good technique. Many sites offer lesson plans for teachers of different subject areas and grade levels. These plans can give you good ideas to use in your own classes. They often provide lists of appropriate Internet sites for your students, as well.

You should know how to construct multimedia presentations for your classes and how to guide your students in constructing such presentations, if your school has appropriate hardware and software. Programs such as *HyperStudio*, *mPower*, or *PowerPoint* can help you form presentations that involve text, sound, animation, and pictures to enliven your classes. Your students can learn how to construct such presentations as class projects. Today's multimedia technology—which allows, among other things, manipulation of images—can make separating reality and fiction harder for students; for example, a multimedia presentation consisting of a picture composed from parts of several other pictures may look like an authentic representation of an actual situation. Students need to realize that someone can construct such an image. They will understand this better if they are allowed to compose images themselves (Research/Center for Children and Technology, 1994).

> **FOR YOUR PORTFOLIO**
>
> **INTASC Standards: 6, 7**
> Prepare a multimedia presentation to teach a lesson to your students. Include a copy of the presentation in your portfolio.

Judging the students' multimedia projects will also be a challenge for you. Brunner (1996) has addressed this problem. Based upon her ideas, here are some questions you may ask about multimedia projects:

1. Can students explain the importance of their topic?
2. Did they plan their report section by section, using a storyboard, before they started?
3. Did they use a variety of appropriate sources for the presentation?
4. Did they document their sources?

5. Is the material organized well? Is it tied together effectively, and is it easy to access?
6. Is the text easy to read?
7. Can users easily navigate the report? Are there good conceptual links?
8. Can the students explain why they chose different images, sounds, animations, videos, or text to make their points and how each one relates to the others and to the overall theme?
9. Were their choices of media appropriate, or did they waste time with "fun" animations or "interesting" videos that did not enhance the information presented?

You should also know the proper way to handle and care for computer equipment and software. Recognize that dust, food, and drinks can be lethal to equipment. Therefore, put on equipment covers when computers are not in use, and enforce regulations about not eating and drinking in the vicinity of the computer.

Be sure to read the documentation for each program your students are using. This will enable you to help students run programs, enter answers properly, and understand error messages. Some programs can be adjusted to the particular student; for example, response time or number of items can be varied. Usually, the accompanying documentation tells the teacher how to make these adjustments.

Some tutorial and drill-and-practice programs provide you with an analysis of students' performances and may move the students through new instructional sequences without your direct intervention. Obviously, such programs give you valuable aid. If the programs you are using do not provide you with a performance record, you may wish to check the results on the screen before each student ends the program.

Students are unafraid of tackling computer applications. They can do some astonishing things with word processing, desktop publishing, database, and spreadsheet programs, as well as Internet publishing, if they are given the opportunity and support. Typing tutorials are available for students who lack keyboarding skills. Many programs make extensive use of a mouse, however, minimizing the need for keyboarding for some applications. For example, a group of seventh and eighth graders in Illinois were first taught HTML, image editing, design principles, and file management skills and then were assigned the task of creating a virtual 3-D walk-through of their new school building. With two iMacs with Apple's QTVR Authoring Studio, three digital cameras with tripods, and a set of blueprints for the school, the students collaboratively planned and implemented the project, which advanced both their technology and communication skills. The result was a real-world, meaningful project (Basden, 2001).

The field trip of the future may be the electronic field trip, in which students prepare for the experience with hands-on activities and videotaped programs to provide background, and then have an interactive teleconference with the experts (Scherer, 1994). As mentioned earlier, students can go on virtual tours to many places by accessing their websites. For example, the Lincoln Park Zoo site is located at *www.lpzoo.com* (Buchleitner, 1999). Even without teleconferences with the experts, teachers can make use of such sites by careful preparation of the children before the visit and appropriate follow-up activities.

Consider the activities that you might use with the computer. Then complete Activity 7.1.

AVOIDING HAZARDS

Several hazards may affect your instructional efforts when you have computer-savvy students. They include viewing of inappropriate sites by the students, using inaccurate information found on Internet sites that are not reliable, and e-cheating. You also may have to take steps to protect students' privacy when material is being posted to the Internet.

Student Viewing of Inappropriate Websites

When students use the Internet, they may visit sites that contain inappropriate content. Be ready to monitor computer use carefully when students have Internet connections available. Although some software exists to block children from viewing inappropriate sites, you cannot depend upon it completely because of the changing state of the Internet; also, many schools do not have such software installed. Have guidelines for students' use of Internet resources, and enforce them (McGillian, 1996). Circulate while students use the computers and take note of which sites are being accessed. You may want to bookmark appropriate sites for your class and restrict class use to these specified sites. Bookmarks also help younger students and those with learning difficulties to participate in learning from images on the Internet without having to perform complicated searches (Forbes, 2004). If the students are going to visit an art museum that has a website, for example, bookmark the website so students can visit it before they go; this will help them develop a list of the things they want to experience on the trip itself. If students are going to visit a water treatment plant that does not have its own website, they might first visit a website that discusses what happens at such a plant, allowing them to make a list of questions about the specific facility they plan to visit.

ACTIVITY 7.1 | *Computer Applications*

Check the computer activities that you believe will work well with your class. On the line beside each activity, add a notation about its specific applications.

Example: Word processing programs <u>Creative writing; Research paper</u>

_____ 1. Drill-and-practice programs _____

_____ 2. Tutorial programs _____

_____ 3. Simulation programs _____

_____ 4. Interactive literature programs _____

_____ 5. Game programs _____

_____ 6. Word processing programs _____

_____ 7. Desktop publishing programs _____

_____ 8. Electronic databases _____

_____ 9. Electronic spreadsheets _____

_____ 10. Electronic reference sources _____

_____ 11. Web development programs _____

_____ 12. E-mail programs _____

_____ 13. Internet search programs _____

_____ 14. Electronic field trips _____

_____ 15. WebQuests _____

_____ 16. Other _____

Students Using Unreliable Websites

Because anyone with a computer, production software, and Internet access can post a Web page, regardless of the accuracy of the material that they post, students must be led to reliable sites and helped to decide whether or not sites that they locate on their own are reliable. In order to choose websites that are acceptable for use with class instruction or for use in student reports, both teachers and students must carefully evaluate the sites that they visit. Figure 7–2 offers a set of questions and cautions to help you and your students evaluate websites.

E-Cheating

Students may find that using computers to produce reports not only makes writing and editing easier than it was when reports were handwritten, but it also facilitates cheating. Students can use a CD on the topic, an encyclopedia article on CD or on the Internet, or material from a Web page, and simply copy and paste the material, add a name and date, and turn it in without much involvement with the topic or much strenuous searching. More devious students may visit "paper mills" on the Web, which are websites that sell or give away papers on various topics often used for research papers. These papers may be collected from former students who produced them for classes, or they may be custom written by the site managers. Several sites offer the same set of papers, and most of the sites offer papers on high school topics. Some sites ask the user to submit a paper in order to access other available papers in the database. Some students turn in papers from these sites, only to discover that classmates have turned in the same papers, making the offense easy to detect. To avoid this problem, some students have friends e-mail them papers from previous assignments they have done. Even these documents may be recycled from another source, and teachers may recognize papers that they have graded before (McMurtry, 2001).

FIGURE 7–2
Evaluating Websites

When you are evaluating websites, you must consider the reliability of the sources of the material, accuracy of the content, clarity of the material presented, and purposes of the sites. Ask yourself the following questions when judging a website:

1. Can you determine who has developed the site? (If not, you may not want to place undue confidence in its contents.) If so, is the developer a reliable source for the information you are seeking? (A noted authority on the topic or an agency of the government would be considered reliable. Someone you have not heard of before may need to be investigated.)

2. Is there enough information given on the site developer that qualifications can be checked? (If not, be curious.)

3. Are sources provided for information displayed on the site, so the user can cross-check information? (If they are, this is a definite plus.)

4. Does any of the information conflict with reliable sources that you have consulted? (If some of the information is in question, all of it is suspect.)

5. Is the layout of the site busy and confusing, making information difficult to locate and evaluate? (Disorganization, particularly, is a bad sign.)

6. Is site navigation easy? (Sloppy navigational methods sometimes indicate a lack of attention to detail.)

7. Is the presented material grammatically correct, and is it free from errors in spelling and mechanics? (If it is not, the clarity is badly affected.)

8. Is the site free of advertising? (If not, look for possible bias of information presented, based on the advertising present.)

9. If currency of information is important, can you tell when the page was developed and last updated? (If not, be careful in accepting the information. If currency is not a factor—for example, for a Civil War site on which the material is not likely to become dated—this will not be a major concern.)

Source: Roe, Betty D. (2000). Using technology for content area literacy. In Shelley B. Wepner, William J. Valmont, and Richard Thurlow (Eds.), *Linking literacy and technology: A guide for K-8 classrooms.* Newark, DE: International Reading Association, 2000.

McMurtry (2001) suggests that teachers explain plagiarism and its consequences to the students. In addition, they should design specific writing assignments that will not match papers that are available from previous classes or on the Internet; for example, specifying topics, length, and number of sources. Teachers should also check out websites, electronic articles on CD and the Internet, and any personal or school database that may have previously submitted papers. If students are required to submit their papers electronically, the teachers can do keyword searches on their databases of archived papers to detect plagiarism from former students' papers. Some commercial plagiarism search services will compare students' papers to their databases of papers as well as to Internet databases and Web pages. These services provide reports on exact phrase matches with links to the pages that allow the teacher to check personally. In addition to McMurtry's suggestions, you as a teacher may require the paper to be written from an unusual perspective or in an unusual genre, for example, writing a paper on photosynthesis from the perspective of a plant or writing a paper on a labor strike as a letter to the editor of a local paper from a striking worker.

Protecting Students' Privacy

In general, student papers or projects posted on websites should only be identified by first names. No personal information, such as students' addresses or phone numbers, should ever be included. In addition, student photographs are not recommended. These restrictions may not be necessary, however, if the sites are password protected and limited to use by a particular class or set of classes or when the posting is to a local area network within the school. Parents should be informed of any posting of their children's names, images, or work, and parents' permission should be secured.

DISCUSSION QUESTIONS

1. Choose one of this book's references on computer use, read it, and answer this question: How can the ideas presented in this source help me in my teaching assignment?
2. What kinds of software can be used by students for multimedia presentations? What are the pros and cons of assigning multimedia presentations to students?
3. How can you help students avoid inappropriate websites? How would you vary your approach for different grade levels?
4. How can you use a student-developed Web page to advance your teaching objectives?
5. Choose one of the articles in this book's reference section that cites websites or software. After reading the article, how would you evaluate the instructional value of one of the programs or websites?
6. Name several websites that you have found to be useful in your teaching or preparation of lesson plans. How was each one useful?

8 Using Teaching and Assessment Strategies

Case Study 8.1: The Challenge of Teaching Students with Different Needs

Ralph is a ninth grader who reads at a fourth-grade level in Mrs. Kelsey's reading class. During the year, Mrs. Kelsey and Mr. Sunas, the intern, encouraged Ralph to read by finding him high-interest, low-readability materials and offering rewards for progress. Ralph did not respond and has shown no interest in reading. Mr. Sunas is determined to find some way to reach Ralph before the end of the year. This morning Ralph came to school unusually tired.

Mr. Sunas: What's the matter, Ralph? You seem so tired today. Did you have a rough weekend?

Ralph: We were out planting soybeans all weekend, Mr. Sunas. I'm beat.

Mr. Sunas: I don't know much about growing soybeans, Ralph. Tell me about it.

Ralph: There's a lot to it. I don't know where to begin. My folks've been raising soybeans a long time.

Mr. Sunas: Is that what you plan to do, too?

Ralph: You bet! That's why I'm just waiting until I can drop out of school. I want to get out and work with the soybeans and not just sit here all day doing nothing.

Mr. Sunas: How are you going to become a good soybean producer?

Ralph: I guess I'll just do what my dad and his folks have always done.

Mr. Sunas: But Ralph, the Agricultural Experiment Station is developing better ways of raising soybeans all the time. There's a lot to know about disease control, fertilizers, soil conservation, and marketing. I'll bring you some information about it.

Ralph: No, don't bother. I don't want to read about it.

Mr. Sunas (a few days later): I found some pamphlets on how to raise soybeans. I thought you might want to look at them.

Ralph: Maybe later. (Ralph yawns and looks bored.)

Mr. Sunas: Did you have any trouble with blister beetles last year? I hear they're supposed to be bad again this year.

Ralph: Yeah. They really gave us problems last year. (pause) Why? Does it say something about them in here?

Mr. Sunas: Yes. It tells you what to do to prevent having so many and how to control the ones you do have.

Ralph: No fooling? I bet my dad would really like to know about that.

Mr. Sunas: Why don't you read about it for the rest of the period? I'll help you with the words you don't know.

Ralph: Hey, here's a picture of one of the beetles. This is really neat. What's this say here, Mr. Sunas? I really need to know this stuff.

Florinda came to first grade already knowing how to read. At age 3, she was reading highway advertising, and at age 4, she was picking words out of the storybooks her father read to her. At age 5, she could read simple books by herself. Mrs. Cho, Florinda's teacher, had 29 first-grade students. Mrs. Cho realized that Florinda knew how to read, but she didn't think she could afford the time to work with Florinda on a different level. Florinda was placed in a regular reading group with the first graders who were not yet reading and later in a beginning readers' group.

Florinda (one morning before school starts): Look, Mrs. Cho, this is the book my daddy read me last night— and I can read it all by myself.

Mrs. Cho: That's fine, Florinda. It is a good book. Now put it away. It will be time for reading group soon.

Florinda: But Mrs. Cho, those stories in reading group are too easy. They're no fun to read.

Mrs. Cho: I'm sorry, Florinda, but you'll just have to read what the other boys and girls are reading. I don't have time to listen to you read your books.

Florinda: Well, okay.

Mrs. Cho (observing Florinda reading her book during class time later that morning): Florinda, you need to do your worksheets.

Florinda: But I don't want to do them.

Mrs. Cho: Give me your book, Florinda. Do your work like the other students.

1. What motivational techniques were mentioned in the vignette about Ralph? Which one seemed to be successful? Why do you think it worked?
2. Was Ralph internally motivated? If so, why didn't he respond positively to the school situation? How are both intrinsic (internal) motivation and extrinsic (external) motivation a part of the story about Ralph?
3. Does Ralph's interest in the blister beetle mean that he is now motivated to learn? How could his interest be extended until it becomes intrinsic motivation?
4. How could Ralph's interest in soybeans be used to increase his achievement in other areas, such as math and science?
5. What was Mrs. Cho doing to Florinda's intrinsic motivation? What might happen to Florinda as a result of her teacher's attitude? How could Mrs. Cho have encouraged Florinda's interest in reading?
6. How did these two teachers differ in dealing with their students' needs and interests?

HELPING ALL STUDENTS LEARN

INTASC Standard #4 states that "the teacher understands and uses a variety of instructional strategies to encourage students' development of critical thinking, problem solving, and performance skills" (INTASC, 1992, p. 20). Whereas previous chapters discussed the development of lesson plans, classroom management, and instructional resources available to you as a professional educator, this chapter focuses on teaching and assessment strategies. It presents many different approaches to teaching and ideas for ways to actively engage students and help them learn effectively.

INTASC Standard #8 describes a teacher as one who "understands and uses formal and informal assessment strategies to evaluate and ensure the continuous intellectual, social and physical development of the learner" (INTASC, 1992, p. 29). This chapter describes a number of formal and informal assessment methods that can measure the amount of student learning as a result of your teaching. Student teaching is a good time to experiment with new ideas and find out what works for you.

When students successfully use a strategy to learn a skill, they select and use it automatically. For this to occur, a number of strategies must be modeled and demonstrated. Students must have practice selecting the appropriate strategy for the specific skill. This practice should take place in a variety of settings and with the teacher's guidance. The selection of strategies to be taught should be based upon the student's developmental level. Chapman and King (2003) suggest the following guidelines for selecting specific strategies for particular lessons:

1. Consider the skill or concept to be taught in the lesson.
2. Consider the assessment method to be used with the lesson.
3. Consider the instructional needs of the students.
4. Consider the organization of the lesson plan delivery (whole-class, individual, partner, or small group).
5. Consider the assessment of the student's use of the strategy.

Remember that you cannot teach your students all there is to know. What is important is that, through your teaching, you help students discover how to learn, provide them with strategies for solving problems, and teach them to think for themselves. Using a constructivist approach to teaching and learning, you can help students actively build knowledge, rather than just passively receiving it. Students use their past experiences and personal purposes to construct the meaning of their lessons, while you facilitate their learning by helping them connect the instructional material to their interests and prior experiences. In other words, you will try to build bridges between the new and the known. You will ask students to take part in authentic, purposeful learning experiences that connect with their own lives, thereby creating connections that are both cognitive and personal (Henson, 2004).

Since most teachers are responsible for assessing student learning, you will need to gather information from multiple sources, both formal and informal. During student teaching you will follow your mentoring teacher's grading system and assessment methods. However, you will be expected to administer and construct some assessment tools of your own. You may also be responsible for communicating assessment results to families and caregivers.

STUDENT-CENTERED LEARNING

Students at all levels are able to make some decisions about their learning. If given such opportunities, they are likely to improve their problem-solving, critical thinking, and language skills. In addition, they will be more motivated to learn because they are actively involved.

Most students have a sense of wonder and are naturally curious. Inquiry learning allows them to identify interesting topics and pursue them in depth. Students eagerly explore self-chosen subjects by collecting information, conducting research, and presenting their findings. They might investigate such topics as why dinosaurs became extinct, how birds migrate vast distances, or the benefits of alternative energy sources. Inquiry learning can occur at any grade level and across the curriculum. Howes, Hamilton, and Zaskoda (2003) successfully worked collaboratively to implement an interdisciplinary unit that linked literature, science, and technology for 22 middle-school students. The students were involved in a minicourse that required them to make observations of their environment (home and school), analyze their findings, and post their conclusions to a website. Findings from the project included high-quality student-generated questions, large amounts of cooperation and collaboration among the participants, and connections among disciplines noted by the students.

Listening to what children want to know and designing your lessons to enable them to find out should become part of your teaching. Although your lesson plans during student teaching are often mandated by the curriculum or your mentoring teacher, try to give students opportunities for inquiry learning.

Student-centered learning does not mean that you should abandon all plans and preparations; after all, you have knowledge and experience that can help students learn. It does mean, however, that you should find opportunities to let students grow in their ability to direct their own learning. The term *negotiated learning* means that you, with your expertise, and the students, with their increasing ability to assume responsibility, work together to plan, direct, and assess learning experiences (see Activity 8.1).

An example of negotiated learning is the theme cycle, a way of integrating the curriculum. Together, students and teacher select a topic for study. The teacher offers choices based on the curriculum for that grade level, and the students select the topic of greatest interest to them. For example, if the curriculum mandates the study of states within the United States, the students might choose Hawaii. Instead of providing the plan for the unit and related resources, the teacher asks students such questions as:

What do we already know?

What do we want to find out?

Where can we find resources?

How can we organize the class to get the information we need?

What are some ways to present the findings of individuals or groups to the rest of the class?

What time frame should we establish?

At the end, how should we evaluate what we learned?

Kerr, Makuluni, and Nieves (2000) and Hicks, Montequin, and Hicks (2000) describe a research project that involved parents, children, and teachers in investigating questions of interest. Research groups were based on the children's interests. Teachers helped students refine the research questions. Data-collection methods included reading from traditional print materials, using computer resources, conducting direct interviews, and doing experiments. This student-centered project allowed participants to learn about research procedures, as well as their topics of interest.

Through such problem-solving and decision-making activities, students not only learn content, but also discover ways to work independently and cooperatively. They may complete much of the work in cooperative learning groups, in which there is positive interdependence as well as individual responsibility for learning. It would be a mistake to assume that all students are ready for negotiated learning, because some may never have had opportunities to make choices and decisions at school. Cooperative teacher-student planning and decision making work best if the teacher makes careful preparations and follows guidelines such as these:

1. Create a learning environment that enables students to make reasonable choices, take risks, assume responsibilities, and use their imaginations.

2. Act as a facilitator, not a director, of learning, and be ready to serve as a resource person as needed.
3. Begin with small tasks, building gradually to larger tasks as you observe that the students are ready.
4. Involve each student as much as possible, and encourage each one to take a leadership role at some time.
5. Be sure that students perceive their activities as meaningful and important.
6. Before involving the students, be well prepared yourself: know the subject, available resources, and desirable outcomes.
7. Be accepting of students' attempts, intervening only when requested or as necessary.
8. Participate with the students in evaluating the final product.

Beginning in kindergarten, children can make choices, lead "show-and-tell" activities, work with partners, and so forth. As children mature, they can assume more complex roles in classroom planning and decision making. Grade level alone, however, does not indicate students' preparation for directing their own learning; their prior experiences, personalities, and social interactions, as well as the teacher's attitude toward student-centered learning, are also important considerations. In the following list, you will find some possibilities for negotiated activities.

Student-Centered Learning Activities

1. Determine what learning strategies to use (e.g., brainstorming, demonstrating, sharing, interviewing, using reference materials, etc.).
2. Identify reasonable time frames for projects, allowing for flexibility.
3. Decide what forms final products will take.
4. Lead activities, workshops, and games.
5. Direct independent studies with input from the teacher and students.
6. Set daily schedules and rules for behavior.
7. Participate in projects, such as making videos, writing computer programs, and conducting science experiments.
8. Be responsible for establishing and managing learning centers.
9. Participate in record keeping and evaluation.
10. Provide peer assistance.
11. Create bulletin boards, displays, multimedia resources, or visuals for the classroom.
12. Choose topics for investigation.

Remember that even when you turn a great deal of the responsibility over to the students, your guidance and support are needed for successful student-centered learning. Bomer (1998) believes that teachers should not be afraid to teach. He says that some teachers use vague language with students when giving directions because they think they cannot have a teaching agenda in "student-centered classrooms" without the children's permission. According to Bomer, "It would be useful for teachers . . . to say what they mean when giving students directions. Even though we do want students to be active and intentional, we also want to affect what they're doing, often to turn them in completely new directions" (p. 17). He sees the teacher's place in the classroom as not authoritarian, but still authoritative.

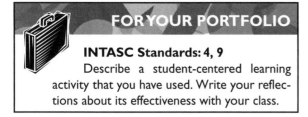

FOR YOUR PORTFOLIO

INTASC Standards: 4, 9
Describe a student-centered learning activity that you have used. Write your reflections about its effectiveness with your class.

MOTIVATION

One of your greatest challenges as a teacher is motivating your students. All learning is motivated in one way or another. Highly motivated pupils almost teach themselves in their eagerness to learn. In contrast, poorly motivated students are unlikely to learn much of anything, no matter how well you teach.

Intrinsic Versus Extrinsic Motivation

Motivation comes both from the student's inner self and from external forces. Internal or intrinsic motivation arises out of a student's needs, personality, attitudes, and values. Internally motivated students may be driven by the need to be popular, the desire to excel, the quest for information, or the fear of failure. Intrinsic motivation is generally long-lasting; it drives an individual toward her or his goals. Successful experiences tend to increase a student's internal drives, but repeated failures may eventually destroy inner motivation.

Intrinsic motivation is part of a student's basic personality and changes very slowly, if at all. This means that, as a student teacher, you will probably have little opportunity to change students' underlying motivational patterns in the short time you will work with them. By stimulating their curiosity and building on their interests, however, you can lay the foundation for lasting internal changes.

External or extrinsic motivation originates in the learning environment and causes the student to want to do certain things. As the teacher, you may want to employ various types of external motivation to modify students' behavior. Be aware, however, that this type of motivation is usually short-term and may disappear when the student reaches the immediate goal.

You can use incentives as extrinsic motivators to make students work or behave better. Generally, rewards are more effective incentives than punishments. Useful positive incentives include free time, extended recess periods, recognition on the classroom bulletin board or website, and prizes or awards. Students can also be motivated by earning good grades and seeing their names on the honor roll.

Keep in mind that external incentives are artificial ways of getting students to try harder and should never become the major reason for doing schoolwork. Otherwise, students will value the reward more than the learning. Most learning tasks don't require incentives. Students should develop self-discipline to get their work done. If you decide to use incentives, learn which types work best for your students, and then use them sparingly and only for short periods of time.

Be careful about giving awards or prizes as incentives for top achievers. These students are usually internally motivated anyway, and poor achievers become even more frustrated when competing against them. One way to overcome this problem is by having students compete against their own records instead of trying to be the best in the class. For instance, students can keep charts of their daily or weekly grades and try to show improvement. Another way to avoid the problem is to have one group or class compete against another group or class. Students work together to win a reward, and all students have a chance to win. Recognition can also be given for increased effort and for improvement in attitude.

Helping Students Set Goals

All your students need approval, acceptance, and achievement. Most of them also have special interests, such as taking care of a new puppy or rebuilding a car engine. These needs and interests become the bases for setting goals. If you can develop a relationship between students' goals and your instructional program, the students will be motivated to learn. That is what Mr. Sunas tried to do with Ralph in this chapter's opening vignette.

You can set goals for your students, but if you expect them to work toward those goals, they must accept the goals as their own. Students should see that your instructional goals will help them achieve something they want; otherwise, they will not be motivated to do their best work.

One eighth-grade teacher was frustrated because, even though her students could pass tests on the correct use of English, they used poor grammar as soon as they were outside the classroom. She realized they

ACTIVITY 8.1 | *Student-Centered Learning Activity Sheet—Plan for Negotiated Learning*

Date:

Type of activity:

Teacher's involvement:

Students' involvement:

Assessment of activity:

Recommendations for improving students' responsibilities and decision making:

didn't see any point in speaking Standard English. One day she asked them, "Can you think of any reasons for needing to speak correct English?" Finally, one student said, "Well, I guess so. I plan to earn money next summer by selling books. If I don't speak right, people may not buy books from me." Another student said, "When I go to church, sometimes they call on me to say a prayer. I get embarrassed in front of the preacher if I make a mistake in English."

Using students' interests to establish goals is a good way to motivate them. You can learn about students' interests by taking a simple written or oral survey. You may have a problem if the interests in your class vary widely, but students' interests tend to cluster around a few general topics. Once you identify these topics, you can begin to relate instructional objectives to them. If you find this procedure difficult, build on the students' interests until you make a connection with what you need to teach. For instance, if several students are interested in race cars, let them: (a) read books about race cars, (b) solve math problems that involve race cars, (c) do research reports on the history of race cars, and (d) investigate the construction of race cars. Common interests, such as holidays or community and school events, also make good focal points for setting instructional goals.

Students must also view goals as reasonable and attainable. Unreasonably long assignments will only frustrate them and discourage most of them from trying. If you want to assign work that will take a period of time to complete, break the work down into small steps. For instance, research reports or research presentations can be broken down like this: (a) select a topic, (b) read about it in different sources and take notes, (c) organize the report or presentation (web or outline), (d) make a rough draft, and (e) write the final report or give the presentation. Goals do not seem so difficult to reach when they become a series of small, related tasks.

Motivational Strategies

You may want to use some of these specific suggestions for motivating students.

1. Keep records of progress made, books reviewed, or tasks completed, so that students can see what they have accomplished.
2. Encourage students to identify their own problems; then help them solve the problems creatively.
3. Arouse their curiosity. Vary teaching strategies so that students will be eager to see what you do next.
4. Humor requires a special kind of intelligence. Work in some riddles and jokes and you will keep the students interested and challenged.
5. Vary the types of activities. Follow a quiet study session with a song or physical activity.
6. Be enthusiastic. Enthusiasm is contagious, and your students will catch it.

7. Create failure-proof situations for struggling learners and poorly motivated students. Offer challenges to highly motivated students.
8. Use educational games, concrete objects, and multimedia resources to create interest.
9. Write brief messages to students when you return their papers, instead of assigning only a letter grade.
10. Videotape a special presentation, debate, panel discussion, or activity.
11. Set up a mailbox, communications bulletin board, or electronic chat room for each class so that you and the students can exchange messages.
12. Use a popular song (choose carefully!) as a basis for a lesson in language arts. Look for new vocabulary words, synonyms, antonyms, rhyming words, alliteration, and special meanings.
13. Instead of the textbook, teach from a newspaper. It can be used for any content area.
14. In a foreign language class, translate the school menu each day from English to the foreign language, or play "Password" in the foreign language.
15. Encourage science students to prepare projects for competitions, such as science fairs.
16. Compute averages, figure percentages, and make graphs in math class from data the students collect. Sample topics include height of students, size of rooms, students on the honor roll, and male and female faculty members.
17. Let students set up and carry out experiments in science class. Be sure the students can explain what is happening and why.
18. In social studies class, assign different groups of students to present daily news broadcasts.

Now do activity 8.2.

RELATING INSTRUCTION TO STUDENTS' BACKGROUNDS

Schema theory is a term in education that may sound technical and theoretical, but actually is very simple in meaning and application. Essentially, your schema for a particular idea or thing is a combination of your knowledge, experiences, and impressions related to it. For instance, your schema for teacher includes memories of teachers you have had, information from your education classes about what teachers should do and be, and your own thoughts based on experiences in which you were the teacher. It may also include sensory impressions, such as the ache of hurting feet. Your schema for teacher should be rich and full, because of your association with the teaching profession, but your schema for paleontologist or philatelist may be limited or nonexistent.

A student's schemata (plural of schema), or clusters of information about various topics, are important factors in determining how well that student learns the material you are presenting. Students with many well-developed schemata bring a great deal of knowledge and understanding to the learning situation and are likely to absorb related information readily. However, students with poorly developed schemata will generally have difficulty understanding new concepts. In other words, they cannot relate new learning to old when they have little prior knowledge or understanding of a subject.

If students lack relevant schemata for a unit you are teaching, they will have trouble understanding your presentations, the textbook, or other instructional materials. Therefore, assess the knowledge the students already have of the topic and then, if necessary, provide additional experiences to fill in gaps before proceeding with the lesson or unit.

You can determine your students' prior knowledge about a subject by listing key vocabulary words on the board and asking the students what they know about each term. Through this exercise, they will reveal both their current knowledge and the gaps in it.

The K-W-L approach uses a similar technique in its initial step (Ogle, 1986, 1989). In this approach, the students chart "What I Know," "What I Want to Know," and "What I Learned" about the topic of the reading material. In the K step, the students list everything that they think they already know about the topic, activating their schemata; in the W step, they list the additional things they want to find out from the reading, setting authentic purposes for the reading; in the L step, they list the things they learned from the reading, filling in gaps in their prior knowledge and correcting misconceptions that they may have had originally. Figure 8–1 shows a blank K-W-L chart.

Another technique used to assess prior knowledge is semantic mapping. With this technique, the teacher puts the main topic in the center of the board and has students provide information that can be clustered around the main topic. In Figure 8–2, the main topic is farms, and related clusters are farm buildings, farm animals, farm work, and crops. Students who contribute answers such as these evidently have some background knowledge of farms, and you will not need to provide much additional information. However, you will need to enrich the backgrounds of students who could tell you little or nothing about farms. A semantic map such as Figure 8–2 not only checks prior knowledge, but also serves as a good introduction or overview for a unit.

If you discover that your students have very little prior knowledge of a topic, you may wish to provide vicarious or direct experiences for them. In the example of farms, you might take your class to a dairy farm,

have a farmer visit the class, view a video about farms, read stories and show pictures of farms, or do some other activity that would help students understand the concept of *farm*.

In any situation, you should try to relate new knowledge to what students already understand by making meaningful connections. For instance, you might point out how one concept is similar to or different from another by comparing a familiar concept, such as football, with another sport, such as rugby. As students build bridges of meaning between new concepts and old, they expand their schemata and establish a base of knowledge for acquiring new ideas.

INDIVIDUAL DIFFERENCES THAT AFFECT STUDENTS' LEARNING

Not all students learn in the same way. Just as you probably learn better in some situations than in others, students also have preferred ways of learning. Each person develops a set of strategies for acquiring information that remains fairly constant throughout life. You can improve the effectiveness of your teaching by understanding how each student learns best and using that knowledge to individualize instruction whenever possible.

In terms of cognitive factors that affect learning, some students are analytical learners and learn best by examining details and studying each element of a situation; others are global or holistic learners who look at large chunks of information. Analytical students are likely to learn better with instruction in discrete basic skills, whereas global or holistic learners may learn better by first considering an entire problem or reading selection and then breaking it down into smaller elements.

Affective factors, such as a student's sociability, willingness to take risks, sense of responsibility, and motivation, may help you choose appropriate motivational strategies and provide suitable opportunities for group or individual work.

Students also vary widely in their preference for such physiological or environmental factors as level of classroom lighting, time of day when they learn best, need to snack and move about while working, classroom noise level, and classroom temperature (Dunn & Dunn, 1987). Although you cannot always consider all these variables for each student when establishing your learning environment, you can provide a variety of learning situations and sometimes give choices for working conditions.

According to Howard Gardner's theory of multiple intelligences, all of us possess at least eight distinct intelligences (Gardner, 1983; Nicholson-Nelson, 1998).

ACTIVITY 8.2 | *Motivational Strategies*

Read the following list of motivational strategies, taken from the list in the text, and mark those you have tried. Put a checkmark (✓) beside those that have worked well and the letter "X" beside those that have been ineffective.

1._____ Keep progress records.

2._____ Encourage students to participate in solving their problems.

3._____ Arouse curiosity. Use variety in your lessons.

4._____ Add humor—jokes and riddles.

5._____ Alternate quiet and active periods.

6._____ Let students use manipulatives and media for independent learning.

7._____ Be enthusiastic.

8._____ Challenge motivated students and guarantee success for slow learners.

9._____ Write messages on papers you return to students.

10._____ Videotape special events.

11._____ Exchange messages with students.

12._____ Teach with popular songs.

13._____ Teach with a newspaper.

14._____ Use foreign language lessons for authentic purposes.

15._____ Let family and consumer science students prepare special meals.

16._____ Make math lessons meaningful by using real data.

17._____ Let students conduct science experiments.

18._____ Ask students to present daily newscasts.

FIGURE 8–1
K-W-L Chart

What I Know	What I Want to Know	What I Learned

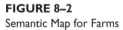

FIGURE 8–2
Semantic Map for Farms

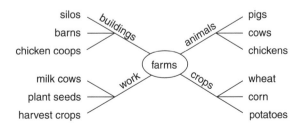

We are stronger in some and weaker in others, but all intelligences can be cultivated. These intelligences are as follows:

1. *Verbal-linguistic*: spoken or written language
2. *Logical-mathematical*: scientific thinking, reasoning, deductive thinking, numbers, and abstract patterns
3. *Visual-spatial*: visualizing objects and creating mental images
4. *Bodily-kinesthetic*: physical movement, bodily motion
5. *Musical-rhythmic*: sensitivity to rhythm, recognition of tonal patterns
6. *Interpersonal*: person-to-person relationships and communication
7. *Intrapersonal*: inner states of being, self-reflection, spirituality
8. *Naturalist*: understanding the nature of living things

Because students have many different areas of strength, your lessons should incorporate a variety of intelligences so that all your students can be successful. Often when planning instructional programs in school, we tend to emphasize linguistic and logical-mathematical intelligences more than the others, so students whose strengths lie in other areas may not be able to demonstrate their understanding. Figure 8–3 shows an example of how you can plan a theme study that uses a variety of intelligences. After you have examined this figure, complete Activity 8.3.

FOR YOUR PORTFOLIO

INTASC Standards: 2, 3, 7
Describe a lesson that you taught in which the students used three or more intelligences. You may want to refer to Activity 8.3.

CLASSROOM TECHNIQUES

Many techniques are available for helping students learn. As a student teacher, you should experiment to find out which techniques work best for you. Then complete Activity 8.4.

Lecture

"Good morning, class. Today our topic is . . . ." And so the familiar lecture technique begins. The teacher does the telling, and the students listen.

Lectures can be divided into two types: formal and informal. You can probably recall some of your college professors who delivered highly structured, carefully worded, inflexible, uninterrupted lectures. The formal lecture is generally inappropriate for public school teaching. However, informal lectures are often effective for conveying information. An informal lecture is usually brief and often involves use of audiovisual materials or a multimedia presentation along with minimal student participation.

Lecturing is often the most direct and efficient way to convey a message. Lectures are particularly appropriate for history and literature classes and can also be used to explain science experiments. Brief, informal lectures can provide background information when you introduce a new topic or summarize what has happened during a learning experience.

When you prepare to lecture, keep certain points in mind. Remember that younger students developmentally have short attention spans and cannot listen very long. Even older students probably won't want to listen for more than about 20 minutes without a change of pace. Get to know your students well enough so that you can adapt your lectures to their interests and needs and relate the lectures to their background experiences. Then prepare and organize your material carefully so you can make a concise, easy-to-understand presentation.

Delivery makes the difference between a boring and a stimulating lecture. Keep your voice pitched low, use expression, and make sure every student can hear you. Maintain eye contact, and occasionally interject a student's name if that student's attention appears to be drifting away from you. Speak in Standard English, and use vocabulary the students understand.

You can use several techniques to hold students' interest as you lecture. Begin by making sure that students remove all unnecessary items from their desktops so that they will not be distracted. Introduce your topic in such a way that you arouse curiosity and activate the students' prior knowledge, making it possible for the students to construct knowledge by joining the new information with previously known material. Use audiovisual materials, multimedia presentations, or demonstrations to supplement the lecture. Emphasize major points by writing them on the board or visually displaying them, and, when appropriate, encourage middle-level and secondary students to take notes. Occasionally ask a question to get students involved and to check on how well they are listening to your presentation.

Although a lecture is often a quick way to transmit information, it has many dangers. It does not encourage much student creativity or problem solving, nor does it enable students to practice applying the knowledge that is being passed along to them. During this one-way communication process, many teachers get carried away with their own speech-making while students sit passively.

FIGURE 8–3
Theme Study Using Multiple Intelligences

Theme Study: Ways Our Community Has Changed over the Past Century

Verbal-linguistic

Examine old records (e.g., courthouse documents, newspapers).

Make a scrapbook of your community's historical events.

Read historical books written about your region.

Logical-mathematical

Compare weather charts. Is the climate changing?

Create a time line that identifies major events.

Compare lifestyles of people over the last century (e.g., dress, food consumption, work habits, travel).

Compare population figures. How much has the community grown in population?

Compare areas included. How much has the community expanded in area covered?

Visual-spatial

Find and display old postcards and photographs.

Locate early maps. What roads have been built, paved, widened, or extended? How have road patterns changed?

Create sketches of what you think your community looked like 100 years ago.

Bodily-kinesthetic

Re-create a corner of your classroom to resemble a classroom from a century ago. Collect artifacts from attics.

Dramatize opening exercises and lessons from early school days.

Make a model of how the downtown area looked a century ago.

Musical-rhythmic

Compare old hymnals with today's. What changes are there?

Create a musical history (may be a rap or story told in rhythm).

Learn folk songs that people sang long ago.

Interpersonal

Interview elderly people in your community. Take good notes.

Work in groups to conduct research about your community.

As a member of a team, plan ways to present information.

Intrapersonal

Reflect on whether you would prefer living in your community today or in the "good old days." Record your thoughts.

Set personal goals for how you might improve your community.

Keep a journal on what you like about your community.

Naturalist

Locate and identify trees that may be 100 years old.

Make a scrapbook of pressed leaves and flowers.

Discussion

Guided discussion, another teacher-centered technique, affords greater opportunities for students to participate than does a lecture. Students can exchange ideas and consider the pros and cons of issues. Guided discussion is a natural and informal way for students to communicate their thoughts.

Engaging students in guided discussions helps them achieve many worthwhile goals. They learn to see different points of view and to keep their minds open. They begin to think critically about important issues and question whatever they are told or see in print. They develop speaking and listening skills by reacting to what their classmates say. They also develop tolerance for other people's ideas when they hear different opinions expressed.

If you want to conduct a guided discussion in your class, first decide whether you want a whole-class discussion or several small-group discussions. In the latter case, you will need to divide your class into three or four groups and appoint a leader for each group. Move from one group to the next, checking to see that students are making relevant comments. After small-group discussion, each leader can summarize the group's ideas for the rest of the class. Students who are afraid to speak out in front of the entire class are usually willing to participate in small-group discussions.

In a whole-class discussion, you have several responsibilities as the discussion leader. Choose a topic familiar to your students so they can discuss it appropriately. Create a supportive atmosphere where students are not afraid to say what is on their minds, but control the discussion so that it doesn't deteriorate into pointless conversation. Encourage widespread participation by asking questions directed toward students of different ability levels. Conclude the discussion by summarizing the points that were made and suggesting a solution that seems acceptable to most of the class.

A good discussion topic for secondary science students might be "What sources of energy should we pursue for future development?" Possible answers include solar, nuclear, geothermal, synthetic fuel, wind, and biological sources. You could consider these sources in terms of their cost to develop, the length of time before they would be available for independent use, their impact on the environment, and their safety. The whole class could consider these issues, or you could divide the class into groups, with each group discussing one source and drawing conclusions about its feasibility.

During a guided discussion or another type of lesson, students may raise questions you cannot answer. Rather than take a chance and give a wrong answer, admit that you don't know the answer. Then, depending on the situation, you can look the point up in a reference source immediately, tell the students you will try to find the answer, or suggest that they assist you in researching the answer and discuss it in class the next day. Although you should know your lesson, no one knows all of the answers all of the time.

Panel discussions and debates are variations of the discussion approach. In panel discussions, students locate information on a specific topic in advance and discuss it in front of the class. One student usually serves as chairperson and directs the discussion. Debates call for two teams of students to present opposing sides of a topic, obeying the rules for presenting arguments and rebuttals. With both procedures, make sure the participants understand the ground rules and are well prepared. At the conclusion of the activity, ask the rest of the class to respond to the presentation.

Demonstration

Another teacher-centered instructional activity is the demonstration, in which students learn by watching as well as by listening. You can use demonstrations in every part of the curriculum and at any age level. In the elementary grades, you might need to show some children how to form cursive letters or how to dribble a basketball. At the secondary level, you can demonstrate how to mix oil paints in art class. If you teach science classes, you will have many opportunities to demonstrate scientific processes by performing experiments yourself or helping students set them up.

Demonstrations create a feeling of anticipation in students. They welcome the change from routine lessons and give their full attention to what you are doing. To demonstrate a decision-making and risk-taking process, such as writing a poem or critiquing a piece of writing, you may want to perform the process in front of the students without prior preparation, so that they can view your mental struggles and decisions as you "think aloud" about it. This type of demonstration can be threatening for you, but very effective for the students.

Make sure your demonstration clearly relates to your objectives. Try to keep it simple and to the point—it's a mistake to try to teach too many concepts in a single demonstration. If your demonstration could cause injury, be sure to take safety precautions, and then practice it several times until you are confident that nothing will go wrong.

You are now ready to present the demonstration to your class. Collect all the materials you need, and provide a good viewing area for the students. Prepare them for what you will be doing so that they will know what to expect. During the demonstration, ask questions or point out what is taking place. Afterward, review what happened and why it occurred as it did. If something went wrong, ask the students if they can tell you why.

ACTIVITY 8.3 | *Lesson Using Multiple Intelligences*

Design a lesson that enables students to use at least three intelligences. For example, if your goal is to help students understand story sequence, you might read them "*Little Red Riding Hood*" (lesson focus). Then you might ask them to act out the story with attention to the order of events (interpersonal-social intelligence used as students meet in a group to plan their enactment and bodily-kinesthetic intelligence used as they act out the story), retell the story in sequence (verbal-linguistic intelligence used), and make a drawing of Little Red Riding Hood's route through the forest, beginning with her departure from home and ending with her arrival at Grandmother's house (visual-spatial intelligence used). You may make this kind of lesson for any subject area.

Write each type of intelligence involved in your lesson in the spaces provided. Then describe the activity that illustrates that type of intelligence.

Subject: _____ *Grade level(s):* _____

Goal: _____

Lesson focus: _____

Intelligence: _____

Activity: _____

_____

_____

Intelligence: _____

Activity: _____

_____

_____

Intelligence: _____

Activity: _____

_____

_____

ACTIVITY 8.4 | **_Classroom Techniques_**

In order to meet the diverse needs and interests of the students in your class, you should use a variety of teaching strategies. Listed below are several classroom techniques that you might try. For each technique you attempt, write a statement about its effectiveness.

Lecture:

Discussion:

Demonstration:

Guided study activities—supervised study:

Guided study activities—drill:

Guided study activities—review:

Guided study activities—project:

Homework:

Questioning:

Programmed instruction:

Case method:

Can you think of other teaching strategies to use? If so, what are they?

Reflect on the methods that you have used and identify the most effective ones. Why do you think these methods work best? What methods will you want to learn to use better? Which ones might you want to discard?

A demonstration creates interest in learning new concepts.

Guided Study Activities

By offering students opportunities to study class material while you are available to guide and monitor their efforts, you can help students overcome some of the hurdles to learning that they may face if left to their own devices.

Supervised Study

As the teacher, you may want to supervise occasional study sessions in which students are responsible for mastering assigned content. Create reasonable assignments that all students can complete successfully if they apply themselves to the task. To do so, you may have to individualize some assignments according to students' different instructional levels. You should walk around among the students while they study, stopping occasionally to answer questions, offer suggestions, and head them in the right direction. Your guidance during a supervised study session can help students learn to use study time efficiently when they are on their own.

Supervised study during class time is a useful teaching technique if you are introducing a new subject or type of assignment. Your role is to offer encouragement and make sure students are getting off to a good start. If possible, have the assignment require the use of resources in the classroom, school library, or media center.

Because of its limitations, however, you should use this approach infrequently. It can easily become boring and routine and may seem unrelated to real-life situations.

Drill.   Remember: 9 times 2 is 18, 9 times 3 is 27, 9 times 4 is 36. On and on, over and over. This is known as drill, or organized practice. You may wonder if it is really necessary. Why do we do it?

Drill can be a valuable instructional technique if it is based on solid understanding of a concept. It provides practice through repetition to the point of overlearning and automaticity. In such areas as math, spelling, grammar, and motor development, repeated practice, or rote rehearsal, is helpful for mastering skills or processes. Once a particular skill or process is practiced to the point of being automatic, the brain is freed to focus on more complex processes.

Although drill and practice can be boring, there are ways to keep it from becoming tedious. Think up games for practicing skills. Keep a drill period short—don't go beyond the time when it ceases to hold the students' attention. Vary the amount and kind of drill according to students' needs. Make sure students see the reason, or a real-life application, for complete mastery of the concept or task. Let students keep individual charts to record their progress. Intersperse drill with other types of instruction to avoid monotony.

Review.   Review is similar to drill, since it is based on previously learned concepts and makes use of recall. While drill simply provides practice in skills, however, review explores students' attitudes, understandings, and appreciations. Review is essentially a group process that extends initial learning by bringing out relationships and applications of the topic. Use review before tests and whenever you want to pull together the major concepts you have been teaching.

Projects.   Another type of guided study activity is use of projects. In this approach, students have more

Baby Blues Partnership © Reprinted with permission of King Features Syndicate.

freedom to direct their own work and can become more actively involved in the learning process. Projects may be completed by individual students or by groups of students. Regardless, each student should be responsible for completing the tasks, as is not the case in the above Baby Blues comic.

When projects are group assignments, several groups usually work simultaneously on different but related tasks. Groups may conduct research, construct models, or solve problems, and then present reports to the class. Your role as the teacher is to provide focus and to support, encourage, and assist the groups as they complete their projects. Quite often, course content is not covered as thoroughly in this approach, so you will need to fill in the gaps with other techniques.

Computer technology is often involved in project-based learning. CD-ROMs or DVD-ROMs are available with information for the different subject areas. WebQuests can provide effective inquiry-based research modules for students at all grade levels. In addition, the Internet has many sites that contain much pertinent information; there are even coordinated global Internet projects in some areas of interest.

Homework

"Can't tonight. I've got tons of homework to do." Sound familiar? Educators disagree about the value of homework. Research reports indicate, however, that achievement increases when students conscientiously do regularly assigned homework (Bennett, 1986). Homework is most effective when it relates to and goes beyond what students are learning in the classroom. Also, teachers should carefully prepare the assignments, thoroughly explain them, give reasons for doing them in terms of enhanced learning, and promptly return them with comments.

To keep your assignments from becoming boring and meaningless, vary the type of homework that you give. There are two major types of homework: (a) practice and preparation and (b) extension activities.

Practice and preparation homework includes most independent activities. It can allow you to provide extra practice for students who need it and to give assignments that are compatible with the needs of different students. However, it is often difficult to manage such individualized assignments. Extension activities often involve group work such as making maps, conducting surveys, doing long-term science experiments, and working on community projects. Use a combination of these types of homework so that students don't always have to work math problems or answer questions from the text. Instead, occasionally allow the students to investigate, discover, interview, work on projects, work with computer programs, and solve problems dealing with real-life situations.

Remember that some students have little time or opportunity to do homework. They may have jobs or after-school activities. The student's home may be so crowded and have such poor study facilities that doing homework is impossible. Furthermore, there may not be anyone at home for students to turn to for assistance or clarification.

Questioning

You can use questioning with almost any type of lesson, including an informal lecture, a discussion, a demonstration, a recitation, discovery, and inquiry. Questioning sessions should generally offer students time for thoughtful, reflective responses. Students benefit more from recitations that allow time to consider the implictions of higher-order questions.

Suppose you want to try your skill at leading a questioning session. How would you start? First, choose a topic that your students already know something about, that is important and interesting to them, and that is within their level of understanding. Get their attention before you begin, and then ask your questions clearly. Ask students each question only once, so that they will know they must listen carefully. Once the session begins, keep to the subject. Include all the students in the questioning, even those who don't volunteer.

One way of ensuring that all students participate is to use the every-pupil-response technique. In this approach, you ask questions that all pupils can answer at the same time by indicating one of two or more choices. You may read a list of statements and ask students to put their thumbs up if they agree, down if they disagree, and to the side if they aren't sure. Students can use individual dry-erase boards or chalkboards to answer questions as they are posed. Alternatively, you can make cardboard strips with "yes" or "true" on one end and "no" or "false" on the other end for each student to hold up in response to questions or statements. Other applications for cardboard strips include the following:

1. "Long" and "short" to indicate the vowel sound
2. Two strips with "add," "subtract," "multiply," or "divide" to show the appropriate mathematical process
3. "Fact" or "opinion" to indicate the dependability of a statement
4. "Vertebrate" or "invertebrate" to indicate the type of animal
5. "Acid" or "base" for the appropriate chemical property
6. "Deciduous" or "evergreen" to indicate the type of tree
7. "Before" or "after" to show the place of an event in history

Although this technique requires students to participate and can offer a fast-paced review, it does not allow for creative responses. You may want to follow up the initial question with "why" or "tell me how you know" questions, encouraging analytical thinking.

To help you ask good questions, write down in advance some questions designed to achieve certain purposes. Phrase them simply and clearly so students will know exactly what you want. Don't be afraid to include a questiion for which you don't know the answer—you and the students can seek it together. As the session progresses, you may find yourself discarding your prepared list and asking spontaneous questions that arise from students' responses. If so, avoid asking only literal-level, detail questions.

The types of questions you ask determine what kind of thinking your students will learn to do. Include diverse types of questions that stress higher-level thinking and, in most cases, avoid questions with only "yes" or "no" answers. Table 8–1 lists purposes for various types of questions and words or phrases to use to begin appropriate questions that meet these purposes. Activity 8.5 helps you become aware of the kinds of questions you ask.

Asking questions is only half of the process; the other half is obtaining responses. Give your students plenty of time to answer—at least 3 seconds. "Wait time" encourages more students to think through the question and consider the answer. Don't rush on after an answer has been given; leave the door open for other students to express their views. Extend a thought by asking "Are you sure?" and "How do you know?" Be willing to accept reasonable answers even if they don't agree with your preconceptions.

In your questioning session, let students ask questions of you and each other. Set an accepting, noncritical classroom atmosphere in which honest questions,

---

TABLE 8–1
Questions and How to Begin Them

Purpose	Questions
If you want to:	Ask questions that begin with:
Assess knowledge	Define, Describe, Tell, List, Who, When, Where, Identify
Check understanding	Compare, Contrast, Explain the relationships, How do you know
Help analyze problems	How, Why, What procedures, What causes, What steps in the process
Lead students to explore values	Why do you feel, What is important, Why do you prefer
Promote creative thinking	How else, What if, Just suppose, Create a new, Design an original
Help evaluate situations	Judge the following, Select, Evaluate the result, Rate as to good or bad
Show how to apply knowledge	Demonstrate, Show how to solve, Construct, Use the information to

no matter how silly they seem, are welcome. If students ask you something you don't know, encourage them to join you in finding the answer. A really productive questioning session involves a lively exchange of ideas in an effort to reach a logical and satisfying conclusion.

You can use questions to promote convergent or divergent thinking. When things converge, they come to a point. When they diverge, they go off in many directions. A convergent question is narrowly focused and usually has a single correct answer; for example, "Who was the first president of the United States?" Convergent questions primarily check knowledge of facts, but do not help students think creatively or critically.

Divergent questions, in contrast, challenge students to think of many possible solutions. These questions are the type used in reflective thinking or discovery inquiry. A good divergent question is "How many ways can we think of to help make our community more attractive?" You may want to begin a questioning session with divergent questions, then move toward more convergent questions as students approach a decision or reach a conclusion.

FOR YOUR PORTFOLIO

INTASC Standard: 4
Include a copy of Activity 8.5 in your portfolio to demonstrate your use of questioning.

Deductive and Inductive Teaching

You should also be familiar with deductive and inductive teaching. Both types are useful, but many teachers depend heavily on deductive teaching. Many of your teachers probably told you rules and even made you memorize them; then you applied them. The following text contains an example of a deductive lesson on syllabication.

Deductive Lesson: Syllabication

Say: "Today we are going to learn a new rule for dividing words into syllables. The rule states that whenever a word has two consonants with a vowel on either side, you divide the word between the two consonants. Here is an example. In the word *comfort*, we divide the word between the m and the *f*. Now I want you to divide the words on this handout into syllables." (See Figure 8–4 for a sample template.)

Say: "When you finish, be sure you can say the rule that tells you how to divide these words into syllables."

Inductive teaching, which calls for an inquiring mind and leads students to make their own discoveries, is based on the use of examples. By asking students questions about the examples or helping them form

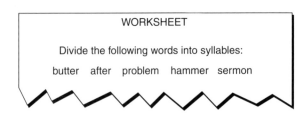

FIGURE 8–4
Sample Syllabication Template

> WORKSHEET
>
> Divide the following words into syllables:
>
> butter   after   problem   hammer   sermon

their own questions, you can guide them toward a solution. The discovery inquiry approach challenges students to think for themselves and pull together clues for discovering the answers. Students internalize what they discover for themselves; it becomes a part of them, and they aren't likely to forget it. An example of an inductive lesson follows. By using your ingenuity, you will be able to come up with other examples of inductive lessons that are pertinent for your class.

Inductive Lesson: Syllabication

Say: "Sometimes we need to divide words into syllables. How do we know where to divide them? Look at these examples on the board."

but/ter af/ter prob/lem ham/mer ser/mon

"How many syllables are in each word?"

"What do you think the slash mark means?"

"What do you notice about the position of the slash mark in each word in relation to consonants and vowels?"

"Does it make any difference whether the two consonants in the middle of the word are alike or different?"

"State a rule that tells where to divide words into syllables. Using this rule, where would you divide these words into syllables?"

suppose   sister   content   channel   blunder

Programmed Instruction

Programmed instruction is implemented through many types and combinations of media, but most commonly through workbooks or computers. Programs are either linear on branching. Linear programs consist of a series of small steps used to develop a skill or concept, with frequent provisions for the student's responses. These easy-to-use programs provide good practice in areas such as spelling and word recognition, math problems, and literal translations of foreign words.

Branching programs are much more complex. Students answer multiple-choice questions, and each answer determines what question they see next. If the student answers incorrectly, he or she leaves the main line of the program and is branched to a track where the concept is retaught. When the student is able to

ACTIVITY 8.5 | **Types of Questions**

Record one of your discussion or question-answer lessons. Play the tape and write down the questions you asked. Listen for the opening words of each question, and identify the purpose for the type of question you asked (see Table 8–1). Count the number of questions for each category and fill in the second column for each of the purposes listed below.

PURPOSE	NUMBER OF QUESTIONS
1. Assess knowledge	
2. Check understanding	
3. Help analyze problems	
4. Lead students to explore values	
5. Promote creative thinking	
6. Help evaluate situations	
7. Show how to apply knowledge	

Look at the number of questions for each purpose and find out what purposes you are meeting with the questions you ask. Consider whether you are selecting your questions to meet just one or two purposes or covering a wide variety of purposes. Are there any types of questions you should add? Do your types of questions relate to your instructional goals? Write a statement about your use of questions and any changes you might make.

answer the questions on the branched track correctly, he or she returns to the main line to continue the work. With branching programs, a student selects answers and moves to the next steps on the basis of his or her answers.

If you plan to use computer programs for practicing skills, evaluate the software carefully in order to choose user-friendly programs that give clear directions. The software you select should offer students practice on skills related to classwork at appropriate difficulty levels. Programs should be interesting enough to sustain attention, and they should provide immediate feedback.

The effectiveness of programmed instruction depends on how you use it. Don't expect programmed instruction to be the total instructional program; it should be used along with other learning activities. While students are engaged in programmed learning, you need to check their progress and help them with any difficulties they may be having.

The Case Studies Method

The case studies method is suitable for teaching students to analyze real-life situations. Case studies allow students to extend and apply information from their textbooks. To discuss the issues in each case, the students also must pull together knowledge from different subject areas. The case method encourages them to think critically and acquaints them with problem-solving techniques.

Cases are built around problem situations. They describe actual problems and supply facts related to the situations. Some cases may be open-ended, with no solution given; others may be closed, with one solution or several alternative solutions. The incident case, a short, three- to five-paragraph description of a situation, is more appropriate for young students than the more complex case studies used at the college level. Some of the case studies in this book could be used as incident cases in your college class or seminar. The case method is appropriate for almost any subject area, but is particularly effective for history, economics, sociology, psychology, and business courses.

If you want to try the case method with your students, first select a fairly simple situation that will interest them, such as the development of a well-known fast-food franchise or the promotion of a famous rock star. Then learn all you can about the subject. Draw up a set of questions that will lead students to define the problem, analyze different aspects of it, reach one or more possible solutions, and evaluate the possible consequences of their conclusions. Start with a simple case that can be completed in one class period, then work up to a more complicated case that could last for several days.

As the teacher, you must play an active role in presenting and developing a case. Lively discussion is the key to learning through this method. You must be knowledgeable about all aspects of the subject so that you can answer questions students might ask about the case. After students arrive at a tentative solution, you may need to offer alternative proposals to stimulate further critical analysis of the problem. You should guide the class in making a decision based on facts rather than personal prejudices or hunches. Finally, you will need to help the students evaluate their decision and look at its long-range implications.

ASSESSMENT OF STUDENT LEARNING

The assessment of student learning is essential in the development and implementation of an instructional plan. You should select instructional resources and the specific teaching strategies based upon your knowledge of each individual student's strengths and needed growth areas. Effective teachers use both formal and informal assessment methods to identify the instructional needs of their students. They use multiple measures to guide their instructional decisions and evaluate the growth of their students' learning.

Formal Assessment

Formal assessment methods include standardized tests, or published assessments, that are developed by experts in their field and have a specific set of criteria for administration, scoring, and interpretation.

You may have limited involvement in the students' formal assessment as a student teacher. However, you may have some proctoring responsibility during the administration of norm-referenced tests, often administered for the purpose of collecting achievement data and comparing groups to a normed population. You may also have an opportunity to review the results of norm-referenced testing for the students with whom you are working.

You should also review any results from criterion-referenced testing. Criterion-referenced tests, which may be published or teacher-made, indicate what a student is able to do according to an established list of expectations or standards. These tests are extremely helpful for teachers when planning an instructional program designed to meet these expectations or standards.

Alternative Assessment

As an educator, you should not rely on only one form of assessment to guide your instructional decisions. You must continuously gather assessment data and make decisions based upon that data. While some data may result from a scheduled, carefully administered formal assessment, many of your decisions will be based upon more informal approaches.

As discussed in Chapter 4, educators can observe students in many different situations. Just as other information can be used for instructional planning, observation can provide important assessment data. Effective teachers rely on their abilities to assess students through observation (Meyerson & Kulesza, 2002). They recognize behavior patterns and provide appropriate interventions when evidence is presented. As a student teacher, you should strive to refine your observation skills. You should spend some dedicated time carefully observing the interaction of students with each other and with your mentoring teacher.

Anecdotal records, written documentation of specific incidents, are flexible and useful for collecting assessment information. They may be kept for individual students, groups of students, or even an entire class.

The following are some informal assessment methods used by teachers to collect assessment data:

Teacher-made Tests of Specific Content Knowledge. These tests are constructed by the teacher to determine understanding of a concept or mastery of a specific skill.

Cloze Procedure. Cloze procedure is an instructional and assessment strategy used to determine student comprehension and use of context clues.

Rubric. Introduced in Chapter 4, a rubric is a scoring guide that outlines specific criteria according to varying levels of proficiency and can be used to collect valuable assessment information on student performance. A well-constructed rubric serves as a guide for students when attempting an assignment or task. Teachers should provide a rubric when the assignment is made so that it can provide a guide for performance expectations. Students may participate in constructing rubrics when a proposed unit is discussed or a new unit of study is introduced.

Student Conferences and Interviews. Carefully conducted interviews and conferences can help the teacher gain insights into the reasoning behind a student's decision or action.

Informal Reading Inventory. Typically, an Informal Reading Inventory (IRI) is a published collection of graded passages used to determine the following levels:

Independent level: A level of reading difficulty where a reader can read fluently with few or no miscues.

Instructional level: A level of reading difficulty where a reader reads fluently and with comprehension, with assistance.

Frustration level: A level of reading difficulty where the reader is unable to decode nor read the text with understanding.

Running Record. A running record is an account of a student's reading performance. The recording of the miscues (deviations from the print) is similar to the process used in an IRI.

DISCUSSION QUESTIONS

1. How can you more actively involve your students in your lessons? What kinds of responsibilities can they assume?
2. Are you motivated to be a good teacher? What motivates you to do your best? Is your motivation primarily intrinsic or extrinsic? Explain your answer.
3. Select a student in your class who appears to be unmotivated. What are some ways you might try to motivate her or him? Looking back through this chapter, can you find some strategies that might work with this student?
4. How would you assign homework so that it relates to what you are studying but doesn't involve the use of textbooks? Can you design it so that it requires problem solving or creative thinking?
5. Select a goal that you and your students would like to achieve. From Table 8–1, find the purpose that most closely relates to that goal. Can you compose a set of questions appropriate for reaching your goal?
6. Why are schemata important for understanding topics presented in school? What schemata are directly related to the next unit you plan to teach? How will you enrich the experiences of students who may be deficient in their knowledge of essential concepts?
7. What are some teaching and assessment strategies you might use to accommodate students' individual differences?
8. What are some lessons in which you could use the every-pupil-response technique for answering

questions? How would you implement this technique?

9. What kinds of homework could you assign that would extend learning through group work on long-term projects? How would such assignments benefit the students?

10. What is your response to Schifter's article, "A Constructivist Perspective on Teaching and Learning Mathematics," cited in this book's references? Would this approach to teaching mathematics be a good one for you to try? Why or why not?

9

Investigating
Legal Issues

Case Study 9.1: Suspected Child Abuse

*M*iss Cooper notices that Debbie appears listless and distracted in class and sometimes is bruised. She is concerned about Debbie and wants to help.

Miss Cooper (trying to gain Debbie's confidence): Debbie, tell me what you like to do when school is out.

Debbie: Nothing.

Miss Cooper: Where do you live?

Debbie: Over by the cannery.

Miss Cooper: You must do some things for fun.

Debbie: Nope.

Miss Cooper (2 weeks later, still patiently trying to bring Debbie out of her shell): Debbie, you really look nice today.

Debbie: Yeah. My cousin gave me this new shirt.

Miss Cooper: I think you could be a really good student in class, but sometimes you look so sleepy. What time do you go to bed?

Debbie: About midnight, sometimes later.

Miss Cooper: Couldn't you try to get to bed earlier than that? I'll bet you could really do well if you got enough sleep.

Debbie: I can't ever get to sleep before then.

Miss Cooper: Why? Surely you can go to bed earlier than that.

Debbie: I don't want to talk about it.

Miss Cooper (after another 2 weeks): Debbie, have you tried to get to bed any earlier? You know, it would really help you. You fell asleep during English today.

Debbie: I know. I really want to, but I just can't.

Miss Cooper: Why don't you tell me about it?

Debbie (sighing and looking doubtful): Will you promise you won't tell anybody? Anybody at all?

Miss Cooper: I promise. I won't ever tell anybody.

Debbie: Well, see, it's like this. My dad comes home; then he starts drinking. He's okay at first, but then he starts getting real loud and mean. Then he starts beating on me and my mom. We try to get away from him, but he's too strong. There ain't nothing we can do about it. Now don't tell anybody, because that'll only make it worse.

Miss Cooper, concerned after this disclosure, decides to tell Debbie's story to the principal. He shares her concern and realizes that this is probably a case of wife and child abuse. The principal notifies officials at the Department of Human Services at once, and they agree to investigate the matter. Miss Cooper is now worried that Debbie will know she told them and asks them to be discreet.

Debbie (one week later, with dark bruises on her arms and a bruise under her left eye): I thought I could trust you not to tell. I should've known better. All you teachers are just alike. You sent the welfare person out, and she asked my dad a bunch of questions. He figured I'd been blabbing, so he really laid into me and my mom last night. Now it's worse than ever. I wish I'd never told you!

1. Do you think Miss Cooper did the right thing? Are there laws about reporting suspected child abuse?
2. Should Miss Cooper have consulted the principal before she promised not to tell Debbie's story?
3. Is there anything Miss Cooper can do now to restore Debbie's trust? How might she try to do this?
4. Do you believe it is ever right to share a student's confidences with someone else after you promise not to tell? If so, under what circumstances?
5. What would you have done in a similar situation?

Throughout your student teaching and practicum experiences, your mentoring teachers and university supervisors have guided you in ethical and legal matters. As you become a licensed, professional educator, however, you will need to rely on your own knowledge of ethics and school law. You may wonder: Am I allowed to express my own political opinions when I teach? Can I do anything I want to do in my free time? Should I talk about my students with other teachers? What should I do if I suspect that a student in my class is using drugs or being abused?

PROFESSIONAL ETHICS AND LEGAL STATUS

Ethical Responsibilities to Students

Each student is entitled to your courtesy and consideration, regardless of her or his physical appearance, socioeconomic status, or ethnic origin. Even though it is easier to establish rapport with some students than others, you must be impartial in the way you treat your students. Never embarrass or humiliate those students who may not measure up to your expectations.

Your students should feel free to express their opinions and different points of view in the classroom. You should never impose your religious or political views on students, and you must always attempt to present both sides of controversial issues.

If students confide in you, they expect you to keep their secrets. It is unethical to take advantage of the information they share with you, or to embarrass them by revealing their information to other people. At times, however, the information they confide in you may present you with a moral dilemma. For example, they may be concealing information sought by law enforcement officials, or they may need psychological help you cannot provide. In these cases, as in the case of Debbie and Miss Cooper, you should discuss the information with someone in authority who will respect the student's confidence and know what to do.

You may overhear teachers talking, particularly in the faculty lounge, about some of their students. It is unethical for you to openly and informally discuss a student's character, personality, appearance, or behavior in a disparaging way. Such conversations violate students' rights to privacy, and you should avoid them.

Students also have the right to confidentiality in the grades they receive. You shouldn't post grades or read them aloud unless you use some identification other than the students' names. When you return papers, make sure that only the student receiving the paper can see the grade. Be aware of the importance of the comments you record in a student's cumulative record. The comments should be of an academic nature and not be informal or personal opinions.

Ethical Responsibilities to the Profession

Be proud to enter the teaching profession, and act appropriately. Present yourself in such a way that your students and colleagues will respect you. Try to get along with your colleagues, and show respect for individuals in authority, even if you don't always agree with them.

Your classroom should be one where students are comfortable and free to express their opinions.

Awareness of Legal Issues

Student teachers and professionally licensed educators must be aware of legal issues related to education. Complete the anticipation guide (Activity 9.1) on page 209 before reading the following section on legal issues.

Rights, Responsibilities, and Liabilities as an Educator

You must know and understand your legal rights, responsibilities, and liabilities as an educator. Since local and state laws differ and change frequently, be sure to find out what your legal status is in the school system where you will be teaching (see Activity 9.2).

If a serious problem arises, document the evidence as soon as possible. Record the time, date, and place; the names of those involved; and a brief account of the event. Be objective and accurate in your report, and avoid personal opinions and judgments. Such evidence is useful for later reference and in some cases may be used as court evidence.

Suspected Child Abuse. Laws in most states specifically direct school personnel to report suspected child abuse. Since many cases of abuse involve school-aged children, educators can play a key role in identifying and reporting students who have been abused. Learn to recognize these signs of possible child abuse:

1. Physical abuse: lacerations, missing teeth, fractures, rope burns, cigarette burns, bruises
2. Neglect: constant fatigue, excessive hunger, uncleanliness, body odor
3. Sexual abuse: difficulty in walking or sitting, torn or stained underclothes
4. Emotional maltreatment: low self-concept, behavioral extremes, frequent temper tantrums, demands for affection

Not every child who exhibits one of these characteristics has been abused, but a combination of these factors, frequent recurrence of injuries, or serious behavioral maladjustment may justify your suspicion. If you suspect that a student is being abused, contact a school authority—perhaps the guidance counselor, school nurse, or principal—who may interview the student in a relaxed, nonthreatening manner. The interview should be conducted privately, and the school authority should assure the student that the conversation will be confidential unless it becomes necessary to contact an agency for help. If further action is necessary, school authorities will then follow appropriate procedures for reporting the situation.

You can offer support to abused students in your classroom in a number of ways. Be understanding and patient with them. Be a model of behavior for them to follow so that they realize there are better ways to deal with frustrations and disappointments than physical violence. Focus on their strengths, and find ways for them to experience success. Praise them whenever there is cause. Be sensitive to their problems and willing to listen if they need to talk about their feelings.

Negligence. School personnel act "in loco parentis" or in place of the parent and, therefore, are responsible for the safety, well-being, and protection of students while they are in the school environment. When an accident or injury occurs to a student, you may be held liable if you are in charge and negligence, or extreme carelessness, can be proven. To protect yourself, report any accident and notify legal caretakers or families as soon as possible. In determining negligence, a court of law considers whether or not the person in charge exercised reasonable care and acted sensibly. If, for example, an accident occurs while you are out of the classroom on a day when you are responsible for the class, you could be found negligent if your presence most likely would have prevented the accident.

Accidents are likely to occur when unusual events are taking place. Physical education and vocational teachers must take special care to establish safe environments, warn students of known hazards, and provide adequate supervision. When the class goes on a field trip, each student should return a signed parental permission form that shows the date, destination, and type of transportation. Discuss the alternatives if permission forms are not returned with your school administration and make arrangements for these students to stay at school during the event if that is the alternative option. Do not accept phone calls instead of signed notes, because you will not have a written record of permission.

Avoid transporting students in your personal vehicle. If there is an accident and you are found negligent, you could be sued. If student transportation must be provided, be sure to make the proper arrangements through the school or school system and secure the services of an appropriately licensed bus driver.

Discipline.   Decisions of the U.S. Supreme Court have held that corporal punishment does not violate the Eighth Amendment, which bars cruel and unusual punishment. The Court supported the teacher's right to use corporal punishment even over parental objections. Although corporal punishment has been banned in nearly half of the states and in some local districts, other school systems permit it. As a licensed teacher, use it only as a last resort, however, after other disciplinary measures have failed. As a practicum or student teacher, you shouldn't use it at all.

The Supreme Court has established certain due process procedures for administering corporal punishment.

1. Corporal punishment should rarely be used for a first offense.
2. Students should know what types of misconduct could lead to corporal punishment.
3. A school official should be present as a witness when someone administers corporal punishment.
4. The student should be informed in front of the witness of the reasons for the punishment.
5. The disciplinarian should inform the student's parents of the reason for administering corporal punishment, if requested to do so (Connors, 1979).

Corporal punishment may take forms other than spanking or striking a student. It is sometimes interpreted as any action that could cause a student physical or emotional damage. Other forms of discipline can also result in legal action. For example, courts generally oppose a decision to punish all the students for the misbehavior of one when the culprit cannot be identified. Such mass discipline punishes the innocent as well as the guilty.

In addition, court cases indicate that teachers cannot lower grades as a penalty for misconduct. Grades should reflect academic performance, not behavior. Recent court cases also found that school districts could not reduce grades for absences due to suspension, or deny students the opportunity to make up final examinations because they were suspended (Hobbs, 1992).

The Individuals with Disabilities Education Act (IDEA) has significantly affected services to all students with disabilities in public schools and specifically impacts the implementation of disciplinary actions involving a student with special needs. If a misbehavior relates to a student's disability, you can't punish the student for the misbehavior.

Search and Seizure.   Courts have generally ruled in favor of allowing school officials to conduct searches and seizures. Searches consist of looking for illegal goods; seizures involve confiscating illegal goods.

Some items commonly prohibited in schools are drugs and drug paraphernalia, weapons such as knives and guns, and obscene materials.

The Fourth Amendment to the Constitution gives individuals freedom from unreasonable searches and seizures. In weighing this freedom against a safe and drug-free school environment, however, the courts usually rule in favor of the schools. Searches and seizures are increasing as drug use and violence in schools become greater problems.

If you suspect that a student possesses something illegal and the evidence warrants an investigation, you should ask a school official to search the student's locker. Do not conduct the search yourself, and do not search a student's body or clothing for suspected harmful items. It may even be necessary to include law enforcement officials in any search procedure.

You may find that your students are bringing items to school that distract their attention and interfere with instruction, such as cellular phones or handheld video games. You have a right to remove these things from them, but you must return them to the students at the end of a period of time or to parents or caregivers whom you ask to come to school for them.

Physical Intervention.   Physical intervention generally takes one of three forms: protecting yourself against a student who threatens bodily harm (self-defense), preventing one student from physically injuring another, and stopping a student from destroying school property. If a student is injured as a result of any of these actions, the courts will generally support you if you use "reasonable force." However, if you act out of anger and lose your temper, you may apply unreasonable force and eventually lose a court case. Whenever possible, avoid a physical confrontation, but if you must intervene, avoid excessive force when dealing with a physically aggressive student.

Consider any threats made against you for their potential danger. For example, a student to whom you have given a bad grade may say, "I'm going to kill you!" Although this is likely to have been said without true intent in a moment of anger or frustration, you need to consider threats to you or your personal property seriously and report them to the proper authorities.

First Aid and Medication.   The best guideline for a practicum or student teacher to follow in administering first aid is to act only in case of emergency, such as choking or bleeding. Whenever there is an injury, notify someone in the school, such as the school nurse (if there is one), another teacher, or the principal. Try to make the student as comfortable as possible, but avoid treating an injury unless absolutely necessary.

ACTIVITY 9.1 | *Anticipation Guide for Legal Issues*

Please respond YES or NO to each of the following questions:

_____ 1. Legally, may an educator be expected to foresee sources of potential danger to a student?

_____ 2. Legally, may an educator be responsible for what happens to a student on a class field trip even though a note has been signed by a parent/caregiver excusing liability?

_____ 3. Legally, may an educator refuse to allow a student use of the library for 3 days after the student created a disturbance there?

_____ 4. Legally, may an educator refuse to allow a student to take a math test after the student misbehaved in the cafeteria?

_____ 5. Legally, may an educator search all students in a class to find a missing necklace?

_____ 6. Legally, may an educator search a student seen leaving a classroom at about the same time a theft occurred?

_____ 7. Legally, may an educator give an aspirin to a student who is complaining of a headache?

_____ 8. Legally, may an educator refuse to assist an injured student?

_____ 9. Legally, may an educator encourage the class to say a prayer before lunch in a public school?

_____ 10. Legally, may an educator insist a student, against his or her religious beliefs, say the Pledge of Allegiance to the flag of the United States of America?

_____ 11. Legally, may an educator be held responsible for what he or she writes in student cumulative records?

_____ 12. Legally, may an educator choose not to implement an instructional modification outlined on the student's Individualized Educational Plan (IEP)?

Source: Adapted from Dr. Thomas Reddick and Dr. Larry Peach, Tennessee Technological University.

ACTIVITY 9.2 | **Legal Status of Teachers**

Because states differ in their laws, and because new legal decisions are made from time to time, it is important for you to know your legal rights and responsibilities. Check the law on the following issues and write a brief statement about each.

Child abuse (responsibility for reporting and to whom to report):

Negligence (use of permission notes, extent of responsibility):

Discipline (status on corporal punishment):

Individuals with Disabilities Education Act (IDEA) (involvement in preparing an IEP):

Liability insurance (availability, coverage, cost):

Self-defense (reporting procedures, what is considered "excessive force"):

First aid and medication (when to act, administering medication):

Copyright laws (photocopying rights, "fair use"):

Private lives of teachers (rights and responsibilities):

Academic freedom (censorship; prayer and other religious issues):

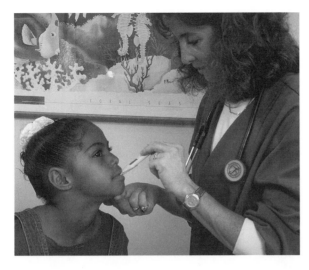

Never administer medication to a student. Always notify the school nurse or designated individual to dispense prescribed medication.

Some students must take prescription medication under certain conditions, but you should not administer the medication. Don't give students aspirin or cough drops either, because they could be harmful to some students. If a student needs an insulin shot during the school day, the school nurse or the child's parent or caregiver should give the injection.

Freedom of Expression. "Congress shall make no law respecting an establishment of religion, or prohibiting the free exercise thereof; or abridging the freedom of speech, or of the press; or the right of the people peaceably to assemble, and to petition the government for a redress of grievances" (First Amendment, United States Constitution).

A great deal of controversy has arisen over recent interpretations of the First Amendment. Many court cases have dealt with censorship of materials and subjects for instruction, as well as with school prayer and Bible reading. The issues of morality, politics, racism, and religion form the basis of most censorship incidents. Find out about your school's policy on controversial materials and if there are procedures to follow when a book or instructional materials are contested.

Teachers sometimes face the dilemma of either using uncontroversial and generally acceptable materials or using materials relevant to living in contemporary society that may offend some citizens of the community. When you deal with controversial issues, you risk confrontations with families and public criticism. Teachers who use books or instructional materials or teach subjects that have been specifically forbidden by the board of education may be dismissed. Consider these questions in determining whether or not to use controversial materials in your classroom:

1. Is the material you plan to use appropriate for the maturity and age of the students?
2. Is there a valid educational reason for using the material?
3. Is there any policy established by the board of education to prohibit use of the material?

In *Abington Township School District v. Schempp* (1963), the U.S. Supreme Court ruled that some school prayer and Bible reading violated the constitutional provision for separation of church and state. Because of different interpretations of the law, some schools ban all school prayer, whereas other schools permit silent periods of meditation or voluntary school prayer.

Students are also entitled to certain freedoms, as long as they don't disrupt class activities, infringe on the rights of others, or endanger others. Speech outside the classroom is generally protected, but students may be punished for offensive or lewd speech. If you are an advisor to a student publication, you may restrain the publication of some materials if you believe the materials may seriously disrupt instruction or violate the rights of others. Recent court cases have dealt with students' appearance, including restrictions on hair length and clothing associated with gang membership.

Disability Legislation

Recent laws have been designed to ensure that individuals with disabilities are provided with a free, appropriate public education. The Individuals with Disabilities Education Act (IDEA) is a federal statute that provides funding to provide services for individuals, ages 3 to 21, in a least restrictive environment (LRE). As an educator, you must know about the implications of IDEA. In addition, you should also be aware of the Americans with Disabilities Act (ADA) of 1990 and Section 504 of the Rehabilitation Act. Both the ADA and Section 504 protect the civil rights of individuals with disabilities and discourage discrimination (Karten, 2005).

As a student with a disability is identified and appropriate instructional needs are outlined, all educators are responsible for implementing the individual education plan (IEP). As a student teacher, you may have the opportunity to participate in an IEP team meeting. Even though you may not have participated as an IEP team member, you should be aware of any instructional modifications or accommodations that should be made as outlined on an IEP. If there are students with disabilities in your setting during student teaching, be sure to collaborate with your mentoring teacher to provide the appropriate services for the students.

No Child Left Behind Act (NCLB). The 2002 reauthorization of the Elementary and Secondary

Education Act (ESEA) has had a profound influence on schools. According to the NCLB legislation, by 2005–2006, all schools must provide evidence of adequate yearly progress (AYP) in reading and math. In addition, all schools must provide evidence that all teachers are "highly qualified." Schools that do not meet the requirements outlined by the NCLB legislation will have specified sanctions levied against them.

Copyright Laws. The U.S. Copyright Act contains certain provisions for photocopying material. You need to know what you can copy and how many copies you can make without violating the copyright law. Some magazines and journals state their photocopying policies on the title page of each issue. When reproduction of certain material is clearly prohibited, you may still write to the publisher for permission to use the material.

Several guidelines exist for determining if material can be photocopied under the "fair use" policy. Generally, "fair use" is observed when photocopying material has no effect on its demand. For instance, you can make a copy of an article or selection, but you can make multiple copies of only a very small portion of a work. You are not permitted to copy consumable materials, such as workbook pages and standarized tests, unless permission is granted by the publishers. You cannot reproduce substantial parts of materials for public performances, including sheet music and plays. If a work is out of print or unavailable, however, the policy of "fair use" generally allows you to photocopy it.

Liability Insurance. Teacher education candidates at the preservice level and professionally licensed educators need liability insurance. Liability insurance is available through several sources, including professional organizations such as the National Education Association (NEA). Liability insurance will not prevent you from becoming involved in legal disputes but it can provide you the confidence that you have appropriate support and representation if a legal action is taken and you are involved.

FOR YOUR PORTFOLIO

INTASC Standard: 9
Reflecting on your own educational experiences, describe an incident related to a legal issue. Critique how the incident was handled and perhaps suggest alternatives for dealing with it.

DISCUSSION QUESTIONS

1. Role-play what you should do if you join the teachers in the faculty lounge and hear them discussing one of your students in a way you feel is unfair to him or her. Should you get up quietly and leave, sit there quietly and not enter into the discussion, speak out and defend the student, or mention that you think it is wrong to talk about students that way?

2. Do you believe the school is responsible for providing education in values, sex, morality, and religion? If so, how should these matters be handled? What would your approach be? Discuss this issue in small groups.

3. Compare the following answers with your responses to the Activity 9.1 Anticipation Guide:

1. YES.	7. NO.
2. YES.	8. NO.
3. YES.	9. NO.
4. NO.	10. NO.
5. NO.	11. YES.
6. YES.	12. NO.

Chapter

10 Becoming a Professional Educator

Case Study 10.1: Professional Growth

Carmen and Mike, both student teachers at Jefferson School, walk together to the parking lot after school.

Mike: Have you observed in any other classrooms yet?

Carmen: Yes, I observed Miss Page and Mrs. Lansing. I guess I chose them because they were both my teachers when I went to school here.

Mike: I've observed both of them, too—what a contrast! Mrs. Lansing seemed to be using all the latest ideas of best practices we learned about, but Miss Page's class seemed to be dull and uninteresting. When I was in Mrs. Lansing's room, her students were playing a simulation game on appreciating cultural diversity, but when I observed Miss Page, her students were simply looking up the definitions of 10 vocabulary words and copying them directly from the dictionary.

Carmen: I noticed the same thing. Miss Page taught her class exactly the way she did when she was my teacher years ago, but I hardly recognized Mrs. Lansing's class. Students were working in cooperative groups, with some using computers to find information for research papers. I mentioned to her something about how things had changed, and she said, "You never stop learning how to be a better teacher." She has gone back to the university and earned a master's degree since I was her student, and she still takes occasional classes. She also showed me several professional journals she subscribes to. She said they have wonderful teaching ideas in them.

Mike: Miss Page made a disparaging comment about college courses when I had my conference with her. I don't think she's done any advanced work at the university.

Carmen: I don't either. I also doubt that she gets many journals, and I heard her mention to another teacher that she wasn't going to waste her money on useless professional organizations.

Mike: My university supervisor said it's possible to get 20 years of experience in 20 years or to get 1 year of experience 20 times. It looks as if he was right.

Carmen: It really does. I want to make sure I get a new year's experience for every year I teach. I guess that means taking more college courses and getting involved in professional organizations.

1. Did Mike and Carmen learn something from their observations besides teaching techniques? If so, what was it?
2. Do you agree with Carmen's analysis of the situation? Why or why not?

REFLECTIVE PRACTITIONER

The Interstate New Teacher Assessment & Support Consortium (INTASC) outlines 10 expectations for new teachers in their suggested core standards. Standard #9 describes a new teacher as "a reflective practitioner who continually evaluates the effects of his/her choices and actions on others and who actively seeks out opportunities to grow professionally" (Interstate New Teacher Assessment & Support Consortium, 1992, p. 31). This specific standard addresses each individual educator's responsibility for becoming engaged in ongoing self-assessment and professional growth. It further emphasizes that even beginning educators should seek out professional resources and colleagues in efforts to share new ideas and experiences. Beginning educators should reflect and revise practice based upon a commitment to continued professional growth. Being recognized as a professional implies a high level of skill and carries with it an expectation for high standards. Indeed, striving to be recognized as a professional is a worthy goal for all educators.

EMPLOYMENT

After you complete your student teaching, you need to search for employment and consider your continued professional growth. In this section, we will discuss employment—finding a potential position, developing résumés, getting letters of reference, and handling interviews.

How to Find a Position

One of the best sources for locating a position is the college or university career services office; it should have a complete and current placement file. This office probably provides placement files to employers who request credentials, arranges on-campus interviews with school systems, provides current listings of job opportunities, and makes job-search resources available.

You will also find a career library in the career services or placement office, with Web-based resources and additional materials such as brochures and applications; directories of community service organizations; encyclopedias of associations; CD-ROMs, DVD-ROMs, or tapes on interviewing; information on writing résumés; overseas teaching literature; and the AAEE Job Search Handbook. The AAEE Job Search Handbook provides a wealth of information, including articles on such topics as interviewing and writing résumés, a list of U.S. State Teacher Certification Offices, and advertisements of openings. Some private employment agencies specialize in placing teachers, and job vacancies are often advertised at professional meetings or on websites. If you have contacts among teachers or school administrators, they may be able to help you locate vacancies or suggest locations where teachers are needed. At employment fairs you can have interviews with a number of prospective employers who represent schools in various geographic areas. If you are unsuccessful in obtaining a regular teaching position, apply for a substitute teaching position. An effective substitute often gets a full-time position when an opening occurs.

Developing a Résumé

When you apply for a teaching position, you need a résumé and a cover letter. You should also send a thank-you letter to each interviewer and to anyone else who helps you obtain a job.

Résumé. A résumé is a brief statement about your abilities and experiences to help a prospective employer assess your potential for success in a school system. The résumé can serve as a general introduction to accompany your application. The résumé should be confined to one page, if at all possible, and it should tell at a glance what a prospective employer needs to know. Many employers prefer concise, bulleted information instead of paragraph-style descriptions. You may want to use a word processing program that has a résumé format. Here are some general tips for writing a résumé.

- Keep computer graphics simple. Use nondecorative typefaces and a font size of 10 to 14 points.
- Use standard-sized white paper, printed on one side only. Make sure it is immaculately clean (no smudges or fingerprints).
- Be consistent in the format and style you use.
- Organize the information logically.
- Place your name, address, and phone number at the top of the page.
- State your objective.
- Provide information about your education.
- List experience in reverse chronological order.
- Check carefully for correct grammar and spelling.

Activity 10.1 will help you see what should be included in your résumé. Figure 10–1 is a sample résumé showing an acceptable format and what data to provide; you can modify it according to your specific experiences and qualifications.

Writing a Thank-You Letter

Show appreciation for your interview by sending a warm and personal thank-you letter to your prospective employer shortly after the interview. This letter

ACTIVITY 10.1 | *Writing a Résumé*

Study the sample résumé in Figure 10–1. Then note, for each heading below, the information that you would be able to include on a résumé if you had to write one now.

Professional objective:

Education:

Honors and awards:

Experience:

Activities:

Interests:

Placement file:

FIGURE 10–1
Sample Résumé

Robert J. Alfred
Johnson Avenue
Corbin, ME 44407
(207) 123-4567

Professional Objective:

To secure a mathematics teaching position in a secondary school that encourages innovation and creativity.

Education:

2005–2006	Course work toward M.S., Mathematics Education, University of Parkersburg, Parkersburg, Tennessee—anticipated completion date June 10, 2006
2004	B.S., Mathematics Education—University of Highpoint, Greenville, North Dakota
Certification: Grades 8–12
Major: Mathematics Education
Minor: Physical Science
GPA: 3.8

Honors and Awards:

Received Maxwell Student Teacher of the Year Award (2004)
Was in top 10 percent of secondary education graduating seniors (2004)

Experience:

Teaching assistant (for tenth-grade class), Parkersburg Secondary School, Parkersburg, Tennessee, 2005
Student teacher, Marks Secondary School, Greenville, North Dakota, 2004
Math tutor for gifted children during the summer, Greenville, North Dakota, (2004)

Activities:

Debate captain
Active member in Student Teacher Association
Volunteer worker for Special Olympics

Interests:

Sports
Computers

Placement File:

Available upon request from:
Office of Career Services, University of Parkersburg, Parkersburg, TN 55519

reminds the interviewer of your visit and strengthens your candidacy. It can be brief, but it should make the following points:

- Express your appreciation for the interview.
- Reemphasize your qualifications, pointing out how they meet the position's requirements.
- Provide supplemental information not given before.
- Restate your appreciation.

You may also want to follow up your interview with a phone call or e-mail message to make sure that all necessary materials have been received and to inquire if further information is needed.

Collecting Letters of Reference

Letters of reference increase an employer's confidence in an applicant's ability. Avoid including references who might be considered biased, such as relatives.

Letters from appropriate persons (i.e., your academic advisor, student-teaching supervisor, or mentoring teacher; professors of courses you have taken) should reflect the writers' knowledge of your academic preparation and career objectives and should be positive statements of support for the position you seek. Be sure you ask permission of each individual you list as a reference. If you want the career services office to keep letters of reference in your file, provide the person writing the reference with any required checklist of pertinent personal characteristics and a stamped envelope preaddressed to the placement office. With an "open file" (nonconfidential), you can read the letters; with a "closed file" (confidential), you are unable to read your letters of reference.

Developing Interviewing Skills

CASE STUDY 10.2

A Fruitless Interview

John had just graduated from a university with a bachelor's degree in elementary education. He wanted to teach at Sanford, an elementary school close to home, and work with fifth-grade students.

John was busy during his last semester, so he didn't investigate ways to apply for a teaching position. He decided to contact Mr. Jenkins, a teacher at Sanford, to ask if he knew of any openings for the coming year. Mr. Jenkins thought there might be an opening in first grade, but he wasn't sure.

One day at a party, John overheard someone discussing the possibility of a job opening in the fourth grade at Brookside, another school in the same system. John wasn't really interested in teaching at Brookside, but he decided to contact the Director of Schools anyway.

Before going for the interview, John decided he would compile some kind of résumé. He took a few minutes to write it, and this was the result:

Name: John Mackay

Age: 24

Sex: Male

College: City University

Degree: B.S. in Education

Experience: I student-taught in the third grade at Cordell Elementary School. They were nice kids, but I like the higher grades, like fifth, better.

On his way to the director's office, John thought, "I've heard that they need male teachers in the elementary school. There weren't many guys in elementary education in my graduating class, so they should be glad to get me.

Maybe they will give me a fifth-grade job at Sanford and move somebody else."

John walked into the Board of Education building and asked to see the director. The secretary told John he would need to make an appointment because the director would be busy with meetings all day. John set an appointment for the next day.

Traffic delays caused John to be late for his appointment, but he did not apologize. Shaking hands with the director, John took a seat and answered questions about his school experience and his interest in the job. John admitted that he was not really very interested in the open position, but would rather teach fifth grade at Sanford. The director said that he could not offer John a job teaching fifth grade at Sanford, but a first-grade position might be available there. John said he didn't think he wanted to teach first graders, and he wasn't really interested in teaching at Brookside. The director said that he would do his best and would let John know if any openings became available.

Before John left, the director asked him for references. John said he did not have a reference list, but he would provide the names of teachers he had worked with who might give him a good recommendation.

As John left the office, he had the feeling that the director did not intend to call him. He shrugged and thought, "I don't need either of those jobs. I can find a better one if I get in touch with the right people."

What suggestions would you make to John about the following?

1. Finding a job
2. Developing a résumé
3. Applying to a school system
4. Getting letters of reference
5. Interviewing skills

This part of the chapter suggests ways to improve on John's interviewing skills.

Before going to an interview, check with the career services office for available resources and books on interviewing. Here are some tips for successful interviews:

- Dress conservatively. Be neat and well groomed.
- Arrive promptly for your appointment.
- Know the name and position of the interviewer.
- Make a good first impression. Look the interviewer in the eye as you give a firm handshake.
- Look alert and interested.
- Use correct grammar and diction.
- Listen carefully to the interviewer's questions and answer thoughtfully and directly.
- Avoid saying "um" or "uh" to fill gaps in conversation, and try not to end sentences with "okay?" or "you know." Sound sure of yourself and confident of your abilities.

Always prepare for an interview beforehand by gathering information about the school and the system.

The best advice for successful interviewing is to be prepared. One way to prepare is to find out about the school's demographics, academic accomplishments, organizational structure, teacher-pupil ratio, benefits and services, and other considerations, such as relationships between school and community. Many schools maintain a website where much of this information can be reviewed.

Another way to prepare is to think through answers to questions you can anticipate, such as those in Activity 10.2. You will have a chance to ask questions also, so think of some you may wish to ask, such as these:

What are the schoolwide discipline policies?

What kinds of professional development opportunities will be offered to help me during my first year?

How are teachers evaluated?

What types of schools and situations are new teachers placed in?

What is the beginning salary, and what are some benefits?

Completing Activity 10.2 will help you prepare for an interview.

Professional Portfolios

You should take a professional portfolio, containing samples of your very best work that is relevant to the job you are seeking, to the interview. It might also include your résumé, transcript, statement of your teaching philosophy, sample lesson and unit plans, overview of a special project you developed, and student assessments.

This book contains additional suggestions for items to include in your portfolio. Be selective, so that you don't overwhelm your interviewer with too much material, and organize your portfolio carefully, perhaps providing a Table of Contents. A three-ring binder lets you tailor the contents to each job description by adding or removing items. Many prospective teachers now include videotapes or CD-ROMs of themselves teaching lessons so that potential employers can evaluate their classroom performance.

An electronic, or digital, portfolio provides another option. It includes essentially the same content, but it offers additional ways for you to display your abilities. Digital or electronic portfolios have the potential for using animation, scanned images that show selected projects, and voice-over explanations of your performance. Web editors, designed to create multimedia materials, and Web browsers are practical programs that you can use to create and display electronic portfolios. You can store and display information on CD-ROM, which makes distribution, copying, and storage easy—providing a clear advantage over bulky paper portfolios. An electronic portfolio also provides an opportunity to demonstrate your technological skills to your prospective employer.

CONTINUED PROFESSIONAL GROWTH

After you actually have a job as an educator, you may be tempted to settle into a routine. It is, after all, easier to use the same lesson plans year after year without bothering to revise and update them. If a plan worked the first time, it ought to be good enough now, right?

Wrong! Every year, you will have students with different instructional needs, and you must adjust instruction if the students are to benefit fully. Educational research is continually revealing more effective strategies or best practices, organizational plans, assessment techniques, and teaching procedures. There will always be changes going on within your discipline that could enhance the effectiveness of your teaching.

Professional Organizations and Publications

Professional organizations for teachers abound—general organizations, encompassing all grade levels and disciplines, and specific organizations, focusing on particular grades or subject areas. These organizations frequently have local, state, regional, and national activities, and your involvement can vary. Activities usually include regular meetings (discussions, speakers, panels), conferences and conventions, and service projects. Members often receive benefits such as reduced rates for conferences and conventions, journals and/or newsletters, and group study opportunities.

A list of some professional organizations available to educators follows. This is not a comprehensive listing, but it gives you an idea of the diverse organizations available to you.

American Association of Physics Teachers, 1 Physics Ellipse, College Park, MD 20740-3842

Association for Childhood Education International, 17904 Georgia Ave., Suite 215, Olney, MD 20832

Association for Educational Communications and Technology, 1025 Vermont Avenue NW, Suite 820, Washington, DC 20005

Council for Exceptional Children, 1920 Association Drive, Reston, VA 20191-1589

International Reading Association, 800 Barksdale Road, PO Box 8139, Newark, DE 19714-8139

Modern Language Association of America, 10 Astor Place, 5th Floor, New York, NY 10003

National Association of Agricultural Educators, 1410 King Street, No. 400, Alexandria, VA 22314

National Association for the Education of Young Children, 1509 16th Street NW, Washington, DC 20036

National Association of Geoscience Teachers, c/o Dr. Robert Christman, Dept. of Geology-9080, Western Washington University, PO Box 5543, Bellingham, WA 98227-5443

National Communication Association, 5105 Blacklick Road, Building E, Annandale, VA 22003

National Council for the Social Studies, 3501 Newark Street NW, Washington, DC 20016

National Council of Teachers of English, 1111 West Kenyon Road, Urbana, IL 61801-1096

National Council of Teachers of Mathematics, 1906 Association Drive, Reston, VA 20191-1593

National Education Association, 1201 16th Street NW, Washington, DC 20036

National Science Teachers Association, 1840 Wilson Boulevard, Arlington, VA 22201-3000

Opportunities for professional growth may be obtained by attending professional conferences at the local, state, regional, and national levels.

ACTIVITY 10.2 | ***Preparing for an Interview***

Think about the following questions that you may be asked during an interview, and write some possible responses. You may want to rehearse your responses with an experienced teacher or supervisor who could help you polish them.

1. Why did you select teaching as a career?

2. What are some effective strategies you would use to manage your classroom?

3. What class organizational pattern do you prefer, and why?

4. How will you take individual differences into account in your classroom?

5. What are some instructional materials that you would like to use in your classroom? Why?

6. What types of student evaluation will you use? Why?

7. How do you plan to remain up-to-date in your field?

8. What is your philosophy of education?

9. Where do you see yourself 10 years from now?

Teachers of English to Speakers of Other Languages, 1600 Cameron Street, Suite 300, Alexandria, VA 22314-2751

Many professional publications can benefit the individual teacher, and quite a few of them are connected with professional organizations. Journal articles cover a wide range of topics, including classroom management, methods, materials, teachers' liability, accountability, curriculum revision, new developments in different disciplines, and many others. Search out articles related to your situations and needs, read them, and grow professionally. Completing Activity 10.3 will help you to identify some organizations that would be most beneficial to you.

Professional Growth Opportunities and Graduate Work

To keep their teachers up-to-date, school systems budget a certain amount of money each year for professional growth opportunities. Based upon each individual teacher's professional growth plan, systems ask teachers to attend a variety of functions to earn a certain number of "points" each school year. You may be able to earn points by attending the meetings and conferences of the professional organizations of your choice; participating in specially planned, relevant professional activities at your school; or working on curriculum development or textbook review committees.

Graduate courses can also help you improve your teaching; in fact, many states require a certain amount of graduate work for renewing teaching certificates or licenses. Certification or licensure in additional areas expands your knowledge and increases your employment opportunities. If you actually enroll in a degree program and steadily take relevant courses, your advanced degree may also lead to a salary increase. *The Graduate School Guide* is a directory of advanced professional degree programs offered by more than 1,000 colleges and universities.

Professional Growth Through National Board Certification

In response to *A Nation at Risk,* the Carnegie Forum on Education and the Economy's Task Force on Teaching as a Profession published the report *A Nation Prepared* (1986). The report provided the foundation for a national certification process with rigorous standards. The National Board for Professional Teaching Standards (NBPTS) was established and the following five core propositions for quality teaching were identified:

1. Teachers are committed to students and their learning.
2. Teachers know the subjects they teach and how to teach those subjects to students.
3. Teachers are responsible for managing and monitoring student learning.
4. Teachers think systematically about their practice and learn from experience.
5. Teachers are members of learning communities.

With the establishment of the NBPTS, educators are provided opportunities for professional growth through a voluntary certification process that identifies those educators who can demonstrate competencies that meet the expectations or standards of the National Board.

FOR YOUR PORTFOLIO

INTASC Standard: 9
Identify some specific ways you plan to continue your professional growth after you graduate.

DISCUSSION QUESTIONS

1. What factors should you consider in developing a résumé?
2. How can you present yourself effectively during an interview?
3. How can you remain current in your field after you complete your preservice training?
4. What contributions can professional organizations make to your growth as a professional?

ACTIVITY 10.3 | **Professional Organizations and Publications**

Research the professional organizations cited earlier in the chapter and others that you have heard about in class or from your mentoring teacher. List up to four organizations that you believe might be good for you to join. Indicate for each one the focus of the organization and its publication or publications.

1. Name:
   Focus:
   Publication(s):

2. Name:
   Focus:
   Publication(s):

3. Name:
   Focus:
   Publication(s):

4. Name:
   Focus:
   Publication(s):

Assessment Instruments

This Appendix contains instruments for the mentoring teacher in the school and the college or university supervisor to use to assess the student teacher's or practicum student's performance.

Overall Assessment

Student _____

Mentoring Teacher _____

College Supervisor _____

Grade Level and/or Subject Area _____

Date _____

KEY TO ABBREVIATIONS:

EE = Exceeds expectations
ME = Meets expectations
NI = Needs improvement
BE = Below expectations

	EE	ME	NI	BE
1. Conducts self in an ethical manner				
2. Handles the stress of teaching appropriately				
3. Has positive relationships with:				
a. Students				
b. Supervisors				
c. Peers				
d. Other school personnel				
e. Parents				
4. Learns from classroom observations				
5. Plans effectively for instruction				
6. Uses a wide range of instructional resources well				
7. Is effective in teaching content				
8. Handles discipline well				
9. Understands how to use various organizational plans				
10. Supervises study effectively				
11. Maintains a positive classroom environment				
12. Motivates students to learn				
13. Adjusts instruction to meet students' needs				
14. Evaluates students' progress well				
15. Assists with extracurricular activities as appropriate				
16. Has a good knowledge base				
17. Has good communication skills				
18. Maintains a professional appearance (appropriate dress, neatness, and cleanliness)				
19. Has a positive attitude toward teaching				
20. Seeks continued professional growth through professional reading, attendance at meetings, and/or conferences with professionals				

Early Progress Check

Student _____

Mentoring Teacher _____

College Supervisor _____

Grade Level and/or Subject Area _____

Date _____

KEY TO ABBREVIATIONS:

EE = Exceeds expectations
ME = Meets expectations
NI = Needs improvement
BE = Below expectations

	EE	ME	NI	BE
1. Shows enthusiasm for student teaching				
2. Is punctual in arriving at school and for each class				
3. Is becoming familiar with the faculty of the school				
4. Has learned students' names				
5. Shows readiness to help in classroom in a variety of ways				
6. Asks questions designed to prepare him or her for teaching				
7. Investigates the instructional resources of the school				
8. Interacts positively with other student teachers				
9. Knows school rules, routines, and disciplinary procedures				
10. Is planning for future participation				

Periodic Progress Check

(File Sequentially for Comparison Purposes)

Student _____

Mentoring Teacher _____

College Supervisor _____

Grade Level and/or Subject Area _____

Date _____

KEY TO ABBREVIATIONS:

EE = Exceeds expectations
ME = Meets expectations
NI = Needs improvement
BE = Below expectations

	EE	ME	NI	BE
1. Plans lessons thoroughly				
2. Has clear objectives for lessons				
3. Ties new material to previous learning				
4. Motivates students to study material				
5. Chooses content wisely				
6. Has good grasp of content				
7. Uses a variety of materials and resources				
8. Uses appropriate materials and resources				
9. Budgets time well				
10. Evaluates students' learning appropriately and accurately				
11. Has enthusiasm for teaching				
12. Relates well to other school personnel				
13. Handles noninstructional activities willingly and effectively				
14. Accepts constructive criticism and learns from it				
15. Shows signs of effective self-evaluation				

Discussion Topics for Conferences between Student Teacher and Mentoring Teacher or Student Teacher and College Supervisor*

Questions for Mentoring Teachers or College Supervisors to Ask

EARLY IN THE EXPERIENCE

1. Have you become familiar with the school's physical layout? If not, how do you plan to accomplish this goal soon?

2. Have you met the other school personnel with whom you will be working? Do you have any questions or concerns about these working relationships?

3. Have you gotten to know the students whom you will be teaching? If not, how can you get to know them better in a short time? Do you have any concerns about dealing with any of the students to whom you have been assigned? If so, what are they?

4. Are you networking with the other student teachers or practicum students in your group to share concerns, problems, and solutions? If not, how could you begin to do this? Do you see the benefits of such networking?

5. Do you understand what is expected of you during your student teaching or practicum experience? If not, what things need to be clarified?

LATER IN THE EXPERIENCE

1. What have you learned from observing your mentoring teacher or other school personnel?

2. Have you been devoting enough time and effort to planning your lessons? What makes you think so?

3. Have problems surfaced during your teaching that you did not know how to handle? What were they? Where did you turn for help? What else might you have done?

4. Have you had any problems with classroom management? What kinds of problems? How might these problems be handled, considering both the structure of the class to which you have been assigned and your status as a student teacher or practicum student (rather than a regular classroom teacher)?

5. Have you been using a variety of instructional resources and teaching approaches in your lessons? What have you used? How could you make use of other strategies and resources to facilitate the learning of your content?

6. What have you learned about teachers' responsibilities that go beyond teaching?

7. Do your students have special needs that must be considered? What kinds? How have you tried to accommodate them?

8. Have you promoted a positive classroom atmosphere? How have you attempted to do this? How have the students responded?

9. Have you been able to evaluate your students' learning effectively? What problems have you had with evaluation? Are there appropriate forms of evaluation that you have not tried? What might you try next?

NEAR THE END OF THE EXPERIENCE

1. Do you feel comfortable performing the duties of a teacher? If not, with which ones are you uncomfortable? What can you do in the time remaining to correct this problem?

2. Have your students been learning from your lessons? If not, have you analyzed your lessons for possible flaws? Have you retaught lessons that were not effective?

* Note: These are just some suggestions that can help to keep a conference focused on important concerns. No conference would be likely to use all of the questions in a category, but all of them might be addressed over time.

3. Have you helped your students to enjoy learning? What are some ways in which you have accomplished this?

4. How have your career goals been affected by your experiences? Are you comfortable with the students and subject matter with which you have been working, or will you seek employment at another level or in another teaching area?

5. Has your philosophy of education been changed by this experience? If so, how? If not, how did the experience reinforce your original position?

Questions for Student Teachers or Practicum Students to Ask

EARLY IN THE EXPERIENCE

1. Am I doing the types of things that will best prepare me for the responsibilities I will have?

2. Are there people who are using different strategies and materials in the school that I could observe?

3. Am I assuming the correct amount of responsibility for this point in the term? If not, what should I be doing?

4. How can I interact with students more effectively?

LATER IN THE EXPERIENCE

1. Do my plans look complete, coherent, and effective? If not, how do they need to be changed?

2. Am I overlooking resources that would enrich my lessons? If so, what are they?

3. Am I being responsive enough to my students? If not, what more should I be doing, or what should I be doing differently?

4. Do my evaluation procedures appear to be appropriate? If not, what should I try?

5. Is my classroom management plan appropriate and effective? If not, what do you suggest?

6. Am I carrying my share of the non-instructional responsibilities? If not, what should I be doing?

NEAR THE END OF THE EXPERIENCE

1. Have I met your expectations in my non-instructional activities? Please explain why or why not.

2. Have my lessons been well planned and delivered, so that you have felt that the students were learning? Please explain why or why not.

3. Have my evaluation procedures been good enough to provide you with the information about the students that you need for reporting purposes? Please explain why or why not.

4. Has my attitude promoted a positive feeling in the classroom? Please explain why you feel that way.

5. Do you believe that I have the qualities to be a successful teacher? Please explain why or why not.

Discussion Topics for Seminars*

1. What different types of students does this school serve? What types of adjustments need to be made for this student body?

2. What things have happened in your classes that have caused stress? How have you handled them? In what other ways might they have been handled?

3. Should teachers be involved with extracurricular activities? Why or why not? What have you learned while working with extracurricular activities in your situation?

4. How have you seen teachers work together for common goals? Can you think of other ways that you could work with peers for common goals?

5. Why is it valuable to observe in the classrooms of a variety of teachers and at different grade levels? What have you learned from such observations?

6. What instructional resources have you used in your lessons besides textbooks? How effective were they? What other resources do you plan to use? Where will you obtain them?

7. What problems have you encountered with time management? How might you avoid these problems in the future?

8. What discipline problems have you encountered? How have you handled them? How effective were your techniques? What else could you have done?

9. In what ways have you organized your classes for instruction? Have you tried whole-class, small-group, and individual organizations? Have you tried cooperative learning? Were some patterns more effective for certain types of lessons than others?

10. What assessment procedures have you used? Did you encounter any problems in using any of them? Which ones were most effective?

11. What motivational techniques have you used in your classes? Which ones have been most effective? What else do you intend to try?

12. What teaching strategies have you used? Have you tried both teacher-directed and student-centered strategies? Do you see a difference in students' involvement when different strategies are used? How will this affect your teaching?

13. What part does homework play in your teaching situation? What kinds of homework are most effective? Why?

14. How does your use of questions affect what students learn? Are you including enough higher-order questions in your lessons?

15. Do some of your students have trouble reading their textbooks with understanding? What can you do to improve their chances of learning the material?

16. Where can you obtain ideas for teaching strategies that will enhance your teaching skills?

* Note: One form of assessment is observation of the responses that student teachers make during discussion of important topics. Here are some discussion topics that may be used in seminars, from which much assessment information can be gleaned. The discussion questions at the end of each of the chapters in the book are also good for this purpose.

Sample Unit and Lesson Plans

Unit Outline

Laura Beaty

Title: Farm

I. Abstract:

    A. *Rationale:*

        In this unit we will be discussing the different animals found on the farm and the food products available in grocery stores that are grown on the farm. It will also include the tools and machinery that farmers use and the buildings found on the farm and introduce the concept of an assembly line. Finally, *The Little Red Hen* will be used in a culminating activity to tie it all together at the end of the week. Each of these areas is equally important when discussing the farm because each makes the children aware of the environment around them.

    B. *Source:*

        This unit is based upon the concepts designated for kindergarten in the Tennessee Comprehensive Curriculum Guide in the area of Social Studies. A source for this unit is *Terrific Topics: Farm*, which is published by Carson-Dellosa Publishing Company, Inc. This valuable resource integrates the area of Language Arts, Math, Science, Music, Arts and Crafts, Social Awareness, and Cooking into the farm theme.

    C. *Duration:*

        The duration of the unit is one hour each day for a week.

    D. *Goals and Related Instructional Objectives:*

        1. TLW (The learner will) recognize the animals that appear on the farm.

            A. TLW name (when webbing) the animals that can be seen on a farm.

            B. TLW classify a food product (e.g., eggs) under the correct animal (e.g., hen).

            C. TLW list (orally) the farm animals that appear in *The Little Red Hen.*

        2. TLW recognize the chores that take place on the farm.

            A. TLW act out the correct chore that goes with each animal.

            B. TLW dramatize the chores that the Little Red Hen is responsible for.

        3. TLW recognize the source of food and the process it goes through before it is bought in the store (reinforcing the idea of the assembly line).

            A. TLW demonstrate the steps used to change cream (milk) into butter.

            B. TLW break down (orally) the steps that the wheat goes through before it becomes bread.

        4. TLW recognize the tools and machinery the farmer uses on the farm.

            A. TLW name (when webbing) the tools and machinery that can be seen on a farm.

            B. TLW dramatize and demonstrate how the Little Red Hen uses her tools.

        5. TLW understand the amount of time and effort that working on a farm involves.

            A. TLW dramatize and demonstrate the amount of time and effort that the Little Red Hen had to commit to when tending to her wheat.

            B. TLW conclude (orally) from this story that working on a farm requires commitment, hard work, determination, and planning ahead.

    E. *Procedures for Introducing the Unit:*

        There will be a farm center set up in the room that will include a folder game, matching games, storytelling cards, books, records, and the milking cow. Posters and bulletin boards will also be set up in the room that show farm scenes.

II. Instructional Considerations:

A. *Target Group:*

There are 24 kindergarten students in the classroom: 11 girls and 13 boys. All of the children are American Caucasians except for one Mexican-American student, one Asian-American student, one African-American student, one Indian student, and one British Caucasian student. There are mixed achievement levels; however, the children are not grouped in kindergarten. There is also one English as a Second Language student who easily understands English.

B. *Instructional Environment:*

This lesson will be taught in the classroom between the hours of one and two o'clock. This time is also second circle time so the children will be in a relaxed environment sitting on the carpet. There is a wide variety of books arranged on the floor available for the children to look at. A video will also be shown that will show baby farm animals as they grow.

C. *Assessment of Required Prior Knowledge/Skills:*

Readiness for the unit will be determined on the first day when we make a class web of things that can be seen on a farm. This will help to determine what knowledge the children already have in relation to the farm and what concepts should be emphasized.

D. *Provision for Individual Differences:*

There will be a wide variety of levels of books available for the children to look at. Also, the farm center is available for the children during center times.

III. Materials and Media:

A. *Books:*

1. Bedford, Annie North. *The Jolly Barnyard.*
2. Brady, Peter. *Tractors.*
3. Capucilli, Alyssa Satin. *Inside a Barn in the Country.*
4. Carle, Eric. *Rooster's Off to See the World.*
5. Carson Dellosa Publishing, Inc. *Terrific Topics: Farm.*
6. Chase, Edith Newlin. *The New Baby Calf.*
7. Dunn, Judy. *The Little Duck.*
8. Fleming, Denise. *Barnyard Banter.*
9. Freund, Rudolf. *The Animals of Farmer Jones.*
10. Gibbons, Gail. *The Milk Makers.*
11. Gross, Ruth Belov. *What's on My Plate?*
12. Hall, Donald. *Ox-Cart Man.*
13. Hansen, Ann Larkin. *All Kinds of Farms.*
14. Hansen, Ann Larkin. *Crops on the Farm.*
15. Hansen, Ann Larkin. *Farm Machinery.*
16. Hansen, Ann Larkin. *Farmers.*
17. Henderson, Kathy. *I Can Be a Farmer.*
18. Hiskey, Iris. *The Little Calf That Couldn't Moo.*
19. Jacobson, Karen. *Farm Animals.*
20. Kent, Jack. *Little Peep.*
21. Kightley, Rosalinda. *The Farmer.*
22. Lindbergh, Reeve. *The Day the Goose Got Loose.*
23. Llewellyn, Claire. *Tractor.*
24. Martin, Bill Jr. and John Archambault. *Barn Dance!*
25. McGirr, Barbara. *Farm Animals.*

26. Miller, Jane. *Seasons on the Farm.*

27. Sears, Nancy. *A Pop-Up Book: Farm Animals.*

28. Shooter, James. *Baby Animals on the Farm.*

29. Wildsmith, Brian and Rebecca. *Wake Up, Wake Up!*

30. *See How They Grow: Farm Animals.* (video)

B. *Center:*

-Pig and sheep puppets   -Baby farm animals match up game
-Farm bingo   -Animal and name match up
-Plastic eggs filled with seeds (musical eggs)   -Milking cow

C. *Other Materials:*

Monday:

-chart paper   -markers   -farm lotto cards
-buttons   -scissors   -pictures of farm animals
-crayons   *-Inside a Barn in the Country*

Tuesday:

-manila paper   -large pictures of animals (e.g., cow, pig, sheep)
-crayons   -scissors   -pictures of food products
-tape   *-What's on My Plate?*

Wednesday:

-paper bags   -cow faces   -crayons
-scissors   -glue   -cardboard cow
-sawhorse   -rubber glove   -staples
-bowl or bucket   -milk   -pictures of farm tools
-"Did You Feed My Cow?" by Ella Jenkins   *-Ox-Cart Man*

Thursday:

-whipping cream   -baby food jars   -popsicle sticks
-crackers   *-The Milk Makers*

Friday:

-masks of each character in *The Little Red Hen*   -props from the book
-plastic egg   *-The Little Red Hen*

IV. Evaluation of Learning:

A. *Formative Evaluation:*

Monday: Most of the formative evaluation was done in the form of oral questioning. We talked about "What is the farm?" and "What are some of the different types of farms?" The children made a web of what can be seen on the farm. We also talked about "What animals wouldn't be found on the farm?" They used deductive reasoning to play a farm animals bingo game. I think more time should have been devoted to the different types of farms.

Tuesday: Most of the formative evaluation was done in the form of oral questioning. We talked about products and what animals they come from. The children looked at picture cards and were asked, "What foods and other products do you see?" After naming the foods they were asked, "What animal do you think this food or clothing product came from?" The children drew a picture of a product and matched it to the cow, pig, or sheep. The children really grasped hold of this concept well, except for the English as a second language student. I think I should have made some more adjustments for him.

Wednesday: Most of the formative evaluation was done in the form of oral questioning. We talked about tools and what the farmer used them for. The children looked at picture cards and were asked, "What tools and machinery do you see?" The children were asked, "What chores are you responsible for?" and we discussed the chores on the farm. The children then experienced one of the farm chores (milking the cow). Overall, I think it went well, although I think my timing was off, and it should have been more fast-paced.

Thursday: Most of the formative evaluation was done in the form of oral questioning. We talked about milk and what happens to it after it is taken from the cow and before we buy it in the store. The children were asked, "What do you think happens to the milk before we buy it?" They were also asked, "How difficult would it be to milk every cow by hand (since they had experienced it)?" "What would they use to help milk the cows faster?" After we had talked about an assembly line and the process the milk goes through, we made butter using whipping cream. I think this activity would have been more effective if the children had worked together at a table (like an assembly line) to make the butter, instead of in pairs.

B.   *Summative Evaluation:*

The Little Red Hen

Laura Beaty

Unit: Farm

Grade: Kindergarten

Goals:

1. TLW recognize the animals that appear on a farm.
2. TLW recognize the chores that take place on a farm.
3. TLW recognize the sources of food and the processes it goes through before it is bought in the store (reinforcing the idea of an assembly line).
4. TLW recognize the tools and machinery the farmer uses on the farm.
5. TLW understand the amount of time and effort that working on a farm involves.

Instructional Objectives:

1. TLW list (orally) the farm animals that appear in the book.
2. TLW dramatize the chores that the Little Red Hen is responsible for.
3. TLW break down (orally) the steps that the wheat goes through before it becomes bread.
4. TLW dramatize and demonstrate how the Little Red Hen uses her tools.
5. TLW conclude (orally) from this story that working on a farm requires commitment, hard work, determination, and planning ahead.

Required Prior Knowledge/Skills:

The students need to understand the basic idea of what things are found on a farm (animals, crops, farm tools, and buildings). They also need to understand that farmers are responsible for caring for each of these areas (demonstrated by their chores).

Instructional Procedures:

SET/INTRODUCTION:

1. Attention getter: Show the children the cover of the book. Ask them to identify the name of the story.
2. Actively involve all students: "Raise your hand and tell me what you think the book is about just from looking at the cover."
3. Communicate the objectives of the lesson to the students: "Today, we will be reading and acting out the story of *The Little Red Hen*."
4. Relate the learning to previous learning: "What did we learn about living on a farm? What do we find on farms? What do farmers do?"
5. Relate the learning to the students' real lives: "We need to know about life on the farm because it affects us every day. The farmers grow the food that we later buy at the store."

INSTRUCTION/BODY:

1. Teaching:
   A. Read *The Little Red Hen* to the class in circle time.
   B. Talk about the different characters that are in the story. Then, talk about whether or not animals really do the things that the characters do. Explain what fact is and what fantasy is.

    C.   Talk about the different tools that the characters use. Are these really things that one could find on a farm?

    D.   Talk about the wheat and the process that it goes through to become a loaf of bread.

2.   Monitor and Adjust: Watch to see that all students understand the different steps that the food goes through before becoming what could be bought in the store.

3.   Supervised Practice: Ask a few children to come up and act out the story using masks and props while the teacher reads the story.

    CLOSURE/CONCLUSION:

1.   Check to see that all students understand by asking the following questions:

"Who were the characters in the story?" Little Red Hen, goose, cat, dog, pig, rabbit, and bear

"Is the story fact or fantasy?" fantasy

"What tools did the Little Red Hen use to grow and harvest the wheat?" shovel, watering can, knife, thresher, and wheelbarrow

"What did the Little Red Hen do to the wheat to make it into bread?" She planted it, cared for it, cut and threshed it, took it to the mill to be ground into flour, and mixed it with other ingredients to bake bread.

2.   Next week, the class will be taking a trip to Hidden Hollow to actually see some of the animals we have learned about this week.

Supplemental Activities:

ENRICHMENT:

Allow the children to play "Chicken, Chicken, Who's Got Your Egg?" Choose one student to be the chicken. Have the student sit with his back to the class with the egg behind him. Tell the students that the person you tap on the shoulder is to quietly sneak up behind the chicken and take the egg, then return to his seat and hide the egg behind him. Encourage all of the students to hide their hands as if they have the egg. Once the students are all ready, the class asks, "Chicken, chicken, who's got your egg?" The chicken then turns around, surveys the class, and guesses who has the egg. He is allowed three guesses. If he does not guess correctly, the student with the egg becomes the next chicken. If he does, he gets another turn.

Resources:

-*The Little Red Hen*

-Masks of each character from the book

-Props similar to those used in the book

-Plastic egg

The Rain Forest

Laura Beaty: One-Week Unit First Grade

Goals and Expectations:

1. TLW understand the importance of the rain forest in terms of plants and animal life and use of products from the rain forest, as well as the need to conserve the remains of the rain forests.
2. TLW use the math concepts of addition and subtraction in the form of word problems to solve and answer questions about life in the rain forest.
3. TLW appreciate and experience literature written about the rain forest, including *The Great Kapok Tree*.
4. TLW utilize library and writing skills to report information and create stories about the rain forest.
5. TLW distinguish the differences between vertebrates and invertebrates, as well as learn the characteristics of the categories of vertebrate creatures.
6. TLW learn the geographical locations of the rain forests in our world.

Instructional Environment:

ROOM DECORATIONS:

The room is decorated like a rain forest. Trees made from netting and butcher paper surround the room. Enlarged drawings and pictures of rain forest animals are on the walls. Tissue paper flowers and butterflies hang from the ceiling. Rain forest music plays in the background.

CENTERS:

A rain forest hut for reading is in one corner of the room. Grass hangs from the roof to cover the opening of the hut. Students may take a rain forest book into the hut and read.

An art, writing, and games center is set up on a table. Various colors of construction paper, pencils, markers, rulers, glue, scissors, yarn, and feathers are provided for students to play with and make rain forest animals. Activities at the center include: word searches, coloring sheets, hidden word finds, and story writing/book making.

This unit is a thematic, interdisciplinary unit. The stories used in class are used to teach the phonics, math, science, and social studies lessons. The whole atmosphere of the class deals with the rain forest.

OTHER PARTS OF THE ENVIRONMENT:

There are two computers in the back of the classroom. A shelf of books, games, and other center items is on the back wall. There is an overhead projector in the front of the room, as well as a dry-erase board.

CULMINATING PERFORMANCE:

Oral reports are presented on the rain forest party day. The rain forest party will consist of snacking on rain forest food items such as fruit, fruit punch, etc. We will play some "rain forest" games, too.

Assessment:

Prior Knowledge
- The learner can read basic readiness words.
- The learner can add/subtract numbers 12 and below.
- The learner can utilize basic handwriting skills.

Culminating Performance Scoring Guide

The oral report will be scored on a rubric, and a numerical grade will be given on the written information.

Student Progress

Student progress will be monitored by informal questioning and basic graphic organizers. Assignments will also be collected to monitor students' progress.

Provisions for Individual Differences:

Special Students: They will have assignments that provide kinesthetic and tactile stimulation. Assignment length and difficulty will also be adjusted for specific students as needs require.

Learning Centers: The learning centers will be a supplement for the talented and gifted students and the other students who finish their classroom work early.

Book Corner: The book corner will be used for extracurricular reading. The book hut is also used to encourage reading.

Resources:

Cooper, D. L. (1994). *Rainforest: Whole language theme unit.* Grand Rapids: Instructional Fair, Inc.

Evans, J., & Moore, J. E. (1990). *Storybook characters.* Monterey, CA: Evan-Moor Corp.

Miller, I., & Agopian, L. (1995). *Rain forest: Extended thematic unit.* Huntington Beach: Teacher Created Materials.

Science Anytime. (Primary Program Units A-D). (1995). New York: Harcourt Brace and Co.

Laura Beaty

Lesson Plan Title: Vertebrate Animals

From Unit: The Rain Forest

Unit Goal or Academic Expectation:

TLW distinguish the differences between vertebrates and invertebrates, as well as learn the characteristics of the categories of vertebrate creatures.

Instructional Objectives:

1. TLW orally identify the difference between vertebrate and invertebrate animals.
2. TLW utilize a graphic organizer, a semantic feature analysis chart, to identify similarities and differences of the different categories of vertebrates and list animals of each category.
3. TLW verbally list differences between cold-blooded animals and warm-blooded animals.
4. TLW identify characteristics of vertebrates in relation to certain animals by coloring the animals that have given features.
5. TLW verbally identify rain forest animals in each of the vertebrate categories.

Required Prior Knowledge/Skills:

1. TLW read key words such as *animals*, *rain forest*, *tree*, *bird*, and *fish*.
2. TLW use graphic organizers to visualize ideas.

Instructional Procedures

SET/INTRODUCTION:

Using the science big book, have the children look at the pictures of unidentified animal coverings and try to guess what type of animal each covering belongs to. Write their guesses under the covering. Use these questions to encourage discussion and activate prior knowledge:

What words tell about the body covering of this animal? What other photographs show a body covering like this one? How are the body coverings alike? In what other ways might the animals be alike?

Where might you find an animal with a body covering like this one? What other animals might you find there?

What are some other animals with a body covering like this? How might these animals be different from animals with other kinds of body coverings?

Then tell the students which animal classification the students belong to.

INSTRUCTION/BODY:

1. Discuss the difference between vertebrate and invertebrate animals. Stress the main idea that invertebrate animals have no spine. Allow students to list animals that are vertebrates and invertebrates.

2. Create a semantic feature analysis chart to compare the different types of vertebrates, mammals, birds, fish, reptiles, and amphibians. Write characteristics at the top of the chart and have children examine a picture of each type of vertebrate to see if the characteristic applies. If it does, put a check in the box—if not, an "x." After each category and characteristics has been examined, have the students orally summarize the characteristics of each type of vertebrate.

3. Discuss the difference between warm-blooded and cold-blooded animals. Have the students list some warm-blooded and cold-blooded animals. Are there certain types of vertebrates that are cold-blooded? Using the characteristics and animal examples, circle, on the board, the type of

vertebrates that are cold-blooded. Relate them to your personal frame of reference by giving the example that people's bodies stay at the same temperature.

4. Connect the idea of vertebrate animals to the rain forest unit by asking students to look around the room and on pictures to name animals from each category of vertebrate that live in the rain forest.

5. Using the animal handout, the students will listen as different features are called out, such as "webbed feet." Then students will color the animal that has webbed feet and draw a line between the characteristic and the vertebrate animal.

CLOSURE/CONCLUSION:

Ask the students to identify orally the types of vertebrates by raising their hands to answer. Then let the students know that tomorrow they will study mammals in the rainforest. Have the students make a list of the rain forest animals.

SUPPLEMENTAL ACTIVITIES:

1. Big Book Making: Children can use inventive spelling to make a monkey or lion big book. They can color their giant lion or monkey and staple a story in the middle.

2. Rain Forest Word Search: Students who finish their work early can begin on the word search. This activity helps them learn to spell names of animals in the rain forest, and recognize unusual words that will be in readings and discussion.

Resources:

Cooper, D. L. (1994). *Rainforest: Whole language theme unit.* Grand Rapids: Instructional Fair, Inc.

Evans, J., & Moore, J. E. (1990). *Storybook characters.* Monterey, CA: Evan-Moor Corp.

Miller, I., & Agopian, L. (1995). *Rain forest: Extended thematic unit.* Huntington Beach: Teacher Created Materials.

Science Anytime. (Primary Program Units A-D). (1995). New York: Harcourt Brace and Co.

Signature of Mentoring Teacher: _____

Date: _____

Math Unit Overview

Janet Wheeler

I. Unit topic: Graphs and ordered pairs—Fourth grade

II. Instructional Objectives:

A. Given a bar graph, the learners will answer questions about the graph with few errors.

B. Given a pictograph, the learners will answer questions about the graph with few errors.

C. Given a line graph, the learners will answer questions about the graph with few errors.

D. Given a grid, the learners will locate points and ordered pairs with few errors.

E. Given a card with information, the learners will construct the correct graph or grid with few errors.

III. Required Prior Knowledge and Skills:

A. Prior skills: The student should be able to add, subtract, and compare two like groups of numbers.

B. Teaching strategies: I will use the inductive method of teaching. I will give examples, then let the students draw their own conclusions. I also will use the guided discovery approach if I think the students need more structured help.

C. Materials and media:

Monday: unifix blocks, paper, and chalkboard

Tuesday: bar graph quiz, poster board, squirt guns, pins, and paper

Wednesday: pictograph quiz, poster board, and paper

Thursday: line graph quiz, poster board, and paper

Friday: ordered pairs quiz, graph paper, note cards with information, paper, and rulers

THURSDAY'S LESSON PLAN

(Excerpted from the entire unit plan as a sample)

IV. Instructional Procedures:

A. Set:

1. Have students think of an object in the classroom.

2. Ask students to describe the location of the object using two clues. (Let several students do this orally and let a student guess what the object is.)

3. Say: "Over the last few class meetings we have been studying graphs. Today we will be discussing grids, which are drawn on graph paper, and how to plot points on them. Grids are often used with maps."

B. Instruction:

1. Say: "I want you to look around the room and see if you find something that looks similar to a grid. A grid is one large rectangle or square shape with smaller square shapes inside it. I will draw one on the board for you. Point to something in the room that looks like a grid." Ask several people what they are pointing at.

2. Say: "I have made a grid on this poster board. As you notice, the grid is numbered on the left side and across the bottom. I have three letters on the grid with dots beside them."

3. Say: "Look at the letter J. Who can tell me how we would locate this letter?" (Wait for responses.)

4. Say: "The dots on the grid are called points. Notice how the zero is in the corner of the grid, then the next number on each side is 1."

5. Ask: "Who can tell me how to find the B? The W?" (Wait for responses.)

6. Ask: "If I had the numbers (6, 4), where would the point go? (9, 6)? (1, 3)?" (Wait for responses.)

7. Say: "The two numbers I have just put on the board are called an ordered pair. Thinking about the examples that we have just done, in what direction do we go for the first number in the ordered pair?" (to the right) "The second number?" (up)

8. Let several students come to the board and plot points. Then have them tell the ordered pairs for those points.

C. Closure:

Ask the following questions:

1. "What is the name of the graph we are working with today?" (grid)

2. "What are the dots called on the grid?" (points)

3. "What are the two numbers called?" (ordered pair)

4. "In what directions do we move on the grid?" (right, then up) Then tell the students:

5. "In our next class meeting, we will be constructing graphs and grids."

V. Evaluation:

Monday: Assign pages 138–139 of text. (Pages cover bar graphs.)

Tuesday: Give quiz over bar graphs; assign pages 140–141 on pictographs.

Wednesday: Give pictograph quiz; assign pages 144–145 on line graphs.

Thursday: Give line graph quiz; assign pages 146–147 on ordered pairs.

Friday: Give ordered pairs quiz; review for test; quiz will be a grid with points on poster board. Ask class 10 questions about grid. (Example: "What letter is located at (6, 8)? What is the ordered pair for point J?")

Evaluate the students throughout the unit by checking homework and giving daily quizzes. In some of the daily lessons require them to make graphs or answer questions about a graph done in class. Collect this work with the homework.

Final evaluation (test):

Questions 1–32 count 3 points each. Question 33 (constructing a bar graph) counts 4 points: 1 point for the title, 1 point for correct form, 1 point for correct numbers, and 1 point for correct labeling. There is a 5-point bonus—if the student writes 4 questions about the graph, then he/she receives all points. Each counts 1 point. Students receive 1 point for trying.

Science Lesson Plan

Elementary Science,* Energy in a Nutshell—
Using a Peanut to Illustrate Forms of Energy

Catherine Messengill

Scientific processes: Observing, describing, measuring (mass and temperature), questioning, collecting, recording and analyzing data, drawing conclusions, labeling diagrams.

Rural issues and technology: Farm products are renewable resources that we are looking to now and in the future as fuel sources. Using a peanut as fuel demonstrates the science processes that can be used to discover new technologies.

Elementary science: Grades 4–6, Physical Science. Related Tennessee Science Curriculum Guide Objectives: 454N1, 551D4, 554N2, 651D1, 651C4, 654N3.

Materials: Balance or scale for weighing equal amounts of peanut and peanut shell, empty soup can, metal coat hanger, paper clip, matches, thermometer, Styrofoam cup, raw peanuts in the shell (roasted and salted in shell will work also).

Vocabulary: Temperature, thermometer, heat energy, light energy, potential energy.

Instructional Procedures (Directions for Teachers)

SET:

Show students a peanut in its shell, and ask them if it has energy stored in it. Tell students that to-day we will experiment to see if we can prove that a peanut has stored (potential) energy.

LESSON:

If all students agree that the peanut has energy (they will usually say that it does because you can eat it and get energy), discuss the following questions before the experiment. If some questions cannot be answered by students, write the questions on the board, and say they will be answered by our experiment.

How could we measure the potential energy in a peanut? (Hint: How do we measure the potential energy in a stick of wood?)

When we burn a peanut, the potential energy is changed to what form(s) of energy? (heat energy and light energy)

When we eat a peanut, the potential energy is changed to what form of energy? (chemical energy)

Which do you think has more potential energy, a peanut or peanut shells? (Some students will say a peanut because it weighs more; some will say the shells because they burn faster.)

How can we make sure we are burning the same amount of peanut and peanut shells? (We can weigh them.)

What instrument do we use to measure heat energy?

How are we going to contain the heat energy given off by the burning peanut in order to measure it? (Listen to students' suggestions; then explain that we can use the burning peanut and shells to heat water and then measure the rise in temperature of the water.)

*"Energy in a Nutshell: Using a Peanut to Illustrate Forms of Energy," from *SPRITES*. Sponsored by TTU/TVA Environmental/ Energy/Science Education Center, and TTU Rural Education Research and Service Consortium. Developed by Catherine Messengill, 1987.

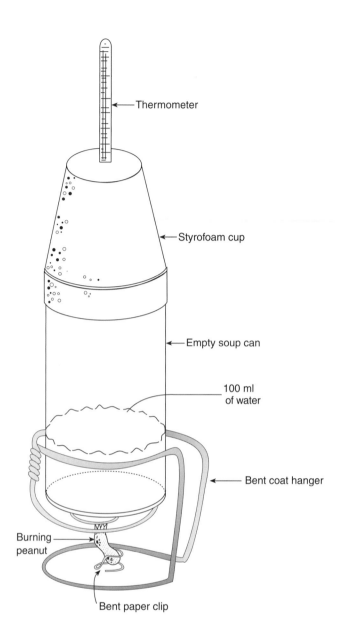

- Thermometer
- Styrofoam cup
- Empty soup can
- 100 ml of water
- Bent coat hanger
- Burning peanut
- Bent paper clip

THE EXPERIMENT:

Show students the homemade apparatus that will be used, and have them draw and label it in their science notebooks.

Have students make a chart like the following to record the data.

Fuel	Temperature of Cold Water	Temperature After Burning	Difference in Temperature
Peanut			
Peanut shells			

PERFORM EXPERIMENT:

1. Weigh equal amounts of peanut and peanut shells, and attach paper clip stands to each.
2. Put 100 ml of cold water in can; record temperature in chart.
3. Burn peanut underneath. (You may also want to record time it takes to burn peanut.)
4. Take temperature of water, and record it.
5. Repeat with fresh water and peanut *shells*.

CLOSURE:

Which had more potential energy, the peanut or the peanut shell?

Why?

Which burned faster?

What if we compared peanut oil and fuel oil? Could you design an experiment to do this?

Are peanuts a renewable or nonrenewable resource?

Where did the peanut get its stored energy in the first place, and why is it there? (from the sun; stored for the young plant to get started)

What is gasohol? What agricultural products is this fuel made from?

RELATED ACTIVITIES:

Language arts: Who was George Washington Carver? Did he make a fuel from peanuts?

Math: Weigh your peanuts on a gram scale. Can you figure out how many peanuts are in a pound of peanut butter? (one pound = 454 grams)

Social studies/geography: Which state produces the most gasohol?

PLAN BOOK ENTRY FOR ENERGY LESSON:

Objective: To demonstrate forms of energy.

Materials: Balance scale, empty soup can, metal coat hanger, paper clip, matches, thermometer, Styrofoam cup, peanuts

Procedures: Do experiment on energy with peanut. (See Science Curriculum Guide, p. 97)

Assignment: Learn about George Washington Carver.

Unit Title: There's an Owl in the Shower

Emily Habegger Parten

Duration: Two weeks   **Target Group:** Sixth grade

Goals or Academic Expectations:

1. TLW understand the importance of conserving the existing wildlife and forests, as well as the effects that destroying the environment has on the ecosystems and human prosperity.
2. TLW learn about the author—Jean Craighead George—and understand why she writes stories about nature, as well as the processes writers go through as they create stories.
3. TLW spell key words from the novel correctly (20 words).
4. TLW understand key vocabulary words from the story by defining them using context clues and dictionary skills.
5. TLW monitor self-reading by answering a daily journal question.
6. TLW try different reading techniques in order to monitor understanding (Say Something, Partner Reading, Silent Reading, Listening).

Instructional Environment:

Each student will have his or her own book to read during class. Asking questions will be encouraged. The room will also be set up daily according to the type of reading for the day. For example, students will be allowed to sit in bean bags and on the floor for partner reading and individual reading. The focus will be on enjoying reading the book.

The students will also create their own owls and bring them to class. These owls will be posted around the room and in the halls to decorate according to the theme.

Culminating Performance:

The culminating performance will be a game of "Owl-Pardy." This game will imitate *Jeopardy*, but all of the students will participate. Going clockwise around the room, students will choose a category on their game sheet. The categories will cover vocabulary, characters, spelling, and environmental inferences. The instructor will ask a selected question and give all of the students time to respond. Then the student who chose the question will be given a chance to answer. At the end of the game, all of the game boards will be collected.

Assessment:

Prior Knowledge:

- The learner can read at a fourth-grade level.
- The learner can use a dictionary.
- The learner can utilize handwriting skills.

Culminating Performance Scoring Guide:

Scores will be based on the number of correct answers. Students will be graded on a curve in relation to the "norm" of each class.

Student Progress:

Student progress will be monitored by informal questioning and answers to owl journal questions. Assignments will also be collected to show proof of work. A spelling test and vocabulary test will also be given (see test sheets).

Provisions for Individual Differences:

Special Students: They will have adjusted assignments to fit their learning abilities. Assignment length and difficulty will be adjusted as needs require.

Resources:

George, Jean Craighead. *There's an Owl in the Shower.*

Questions and Answers: jean@jeancraigheadgeorge.com

Lesson Plan Title: Introduction to the Novel

Emily Habegger Parten

From Unit Title: *There's an Owl in the Shower*

Unit Goal or Academic Expectation:
1. TLW learn about the author and understand why she writes stories about nature.
2. TLW self-monitor reading by answering a daily journal question.

Instructional Objectives:
1. TLW orally read the spelling words and learn correct pronunciation.
2. TLW make predictions about the story and write them down.
3. TLW create an owl journal by cutting and stapling.
4. TLW use listening skills to understand the instructor reading the first chapter of the book and demonstrate this understanding by answering questions.
5. TLW silently read the book and self-monitor understanding by responding to a journal question and backing up their answers with proof from the book.
6. TLW create background knowledge about the author by connecting the novel to previous work and learning new things about her experiences and writing style.

Required Prior Knowledge/Skills:
- The learner can read at a fourth-grade level.
- The learner knows that an owl is an animal.
- The learner can utilize handwriting and cutting skills.
- The learner can use phonetics to sound out unknown words.

Instructional Procedures:
SET/INTRODUCTION:

Play owl sounds from a tape recorder. Have the students guess what kind of animal is making the noises. Then introduce some different kinds of owls and show students photographs of different kinds of owls. Then name the kinds of owls found in surrounding areas (connecting to personal frame of reference). Then pass out a copy of the book to each student.

INSTRUCTION/BODY:

Introduce the author by drawing notice to her name. Ask the students to name other books the author has written and the topics of those books.

Have students look at the cover of the book and the title. Write their predictions about the story on the board. Then read the first chapter of the book orally to them. They can follow along or listen. Model self-monitoring by asking questions throughout the oral reading and by using context clues to figure out unknown words.

Allow students to make their owl journals before they begin silent reading. Provide an owl pattern and sheets of paper for each student. Then students can cut out the owl and staple the sheets to his belly (see example).

Pass out the vocabulary sheets and spelling words. Have the students pronounce the spelling words in order to become familiar with them. Then ask students to volunteer meanings for the spelling words. Explain how the vocabulary chart works and assign a due date for the chart.

Allow students to find comfortable reading spots and begin silent reading. Assign Chapters 2–3.

CLOSURE/CONCLUSION:

Ask questions about the in-class reading: "Why did Borden's dad lose his job? Why does Borden want to shoot a spotted owl? Why does cutting cause mountainsides to erode? How does cutting down the forest affect the owls?" Then have students answer the journal question put on the board: "Whose side are you on? The cutters' or the owls'? Why?"

SUPPLEMENTAL ACTIVITIES:

Owl Project: Allow students to construct an owl from any type of available materials. Then have students name the owl and present it to the class. The students should research the type of owl being made and their creation should reflect that owl type.

Resources:

George, Jean Craighead. *There's an Owl in the Shower.*

Owl Sounds Tape. Personal recording.

Questions and Answers: jean@jeancraigheadgeorge.com

Signature of Mentoring Teacher: _____

Date: _____

Stress and Exercise Unit Introduction

LEVEL: Seventh and Eighth Grade

Cindy McCloud

Goal:

The learners will become familiar with stress and how exercise can minimize neurological and biological stress.

Objectives:

1. Given a diagram of the circulatory system, the learners will label the appropriate parts with 100% accuracy.
2. Given an essay test, the learners will explain how exercise can relieve stress on the heart with 100% accuracy.
3. Given a multiple choice test, the learners will identify appropriate symptoms of stress with 100% accuracy.

Required Prior Knowledge:

Basic health awareness

Set:

Say: "When I say the word *stress*, you may think about weight stress on a house's foundation, stress on a heart due to excess fat, or excess mental stress due to the test you will be taking tomorrow."

Demonstrate stress by popping a balloon. Explain that this puts a small amount of stress on your nerves and might even have made your heart jump.

Say: "Today we are going to discuss the inner workings of your heart and how aerobic activity helps reduce mental and physical stress."

Instruction:

Ask students to define *stress*.

Briefly discuss how the circulatory system works.

Ask: "What type of exercise is best for the heart?" (Answer: aerobic exercise such as dancing, biking, walking, or running.)

Ask: "Why is this the most effective type of exercise in strengthening the heart? What does psychological stress mean? How can exercise help reduce depression?"

Be ready to explain that anxiety before a test or depression can be a form of stress and that exercise can help reduce depression by enhancing self-esteem, increasing wellness and vigor, promoting clear thinking, enhancing quality of life, causing a person to have more energy and vitality, taking care of extra energy that could be applied to worry. In other words, you sleep better and feel better!

Say: "Stress, like fat, is a necessity in our lives. Too much or too little can be detrimental. Exercise plays an important role in managing stress. Exercise helps keep stress manageable."

Have students name situations involving stress and write these on the board. Ask students how each situation can benefit from exercise.

Say: "Exercise can also be harmful, if overexertion occurs. What do I mean by this? How often is it reasonable to exercise? What are some ways to avoid overexertion?"

Be ready to explain that 30 minutes a day is a reasonable amount of exercise and that warming up, stretching, and cooling down can help to avoid overexertion.

Perform a classroom experiment: Hand out a chart that is set up for a specific number of days students should keep track of their exercise schedule. Have them fill it out for these days. They can personally see if they sleep better, feel better, and handle levels of stress better after exercising. This applied activity gives them the chance to see exercise benefits for themselves.

Closure:

For review, provide the class with a trivia game, asking them questions reviewing the heart, stress, and management of stress through exercise.

Say: "In the next lesson, we will discuss your charts and certain warm-up techniques for exercise."

Materials and Media:

Exercise schedule

Four articles from the journal *Quest*

One article from the magazine *The Physician and Sports Medicine*

Lesson Plan on Stress

Goal:

The learners will gain knowledge concerning the different aspects of stress.

Objectives:

1. The learners will recognize different life causes of stress and categorize them under physical and mental stress.

2. The learners will work in pairs to list different areas of stress in their lives and work with partners in deciding the best methods to deal with their stress.

3. The learners will participate in a relaxation technique.

Instruction:

1. Pop balloon. Collect reactions from class and write them down on the board.

2. Pop second balloon. Ask: "Was your body more prepared for the second pop? Why or why not?"

3. Say: "Sometimes stress can be predicted, and other times we have absolutely no idea what's about to take place. Today we will decide together some ways you can reduce stress, and by the end of the lesson, you should have enough information to help you deal with expected and unexpected stress." Pop third balloon.

4. Write the words *physical* and *mental* on the board. Ask, "What do these two words have to do with stress? Are the two categories related? Can some of these reactions go under both *mental* and *physical*? Why?"

5. Have students form pairs. Tell the students: "Come up with a list of things that are causing stress in your own life. Exchange papers. On your partner's paper and/or orally, state some ways that would help reduce stress."

6. Say: "Pages 210–211 in the Gardner text discuss some mental, physical, and spiritual ways that you can deal with stress. For this week's journal entry, choose one of your greatest causes of stress and tell how you will deal with it in a positive way."

7. Demonstrate the "guided imagery" technique for relaxation.

Unit Outline

Name: Kimberly Williams
Subject: Biology
Grade(s): 9–12
Text: Biology

Unit Title: The Six Kingdoms
Unit Rationale: To study the diversity of life, biologists use a classification system to name organisms and group them in a logical manner.
Duration: 7 days
Curriculum Sources: Gateways

    5.1 Establish criteria for designing a system of classification and compare historically relevant systems of classification used in biology.

    5.3 Integrate a comparative study of plant and animal anatomical structures so as to recognize relationships among organisms related to structural components, symmetry, metamorphosis, and alternation of generations.

Textbook: Ch 18, 22, 26, 30
Supplementary Materials: Internet access for WebQuest.
Web Sources:
www.kidport.com/RefLib/Science/Animals/Animals.htsm
plantphys.info/principles/taxonomy.html
www.sirinet.net/~jgjohnso/classification.html
www.msnucleus.org/membership/html/k-6/lc/organ/5/lco5_6d.html
www.conservation.state.mo.us

Unit Time Line:				
Day	**Topic**	**Text**	**Performance Expectations**	**Resources**
Day 1	Finding order in diversity. **Lab** Make a "Tree of Life" poster with the six kingdoms.	Chapter 18 Sections 1 and 3 pp. 446–461	5.1 Establish criteria for designing a system of classification and compare historically relevant systems of classification used in biology.	www.msnucleus.org/members/hip/html/k-6/lc/organ/5/lco5_6d.html
Day 2	Vertebrates vs. Invertebrates. **Complex task:** Draw concept map of vertebrate and invertebrate properties.	Chapters 26 and 30 pp. 656 and 766	5.3 Integrate a comparative study of plant and animal anatomical structures so as to recognize relationships among organisms related to structural components, symmetry, metamorphosis, and alternation of generations.	Textbook
Day 3	Basic structure of an Angiosperm. **Complex task:** Dissect a flower (Buttercup).	Chapter 22 Section 5 pp. 569–570	5.3 Integrate a comparative study of plant and animal anatomical structures so as to recognize relationships among organisms related to structural components, symmetry, metamorphosis, and alternation of generations.	Textbook

Day	Topic	Text	Performance Expectations	Resources
Day 4	Mushroom WebQuest. **Lab** Use computer lab for WebQuest.	Computer Lab	5.3 Integrate a comparative study of plant and animal anatomical structures so as to recognize relationships among organisms related to structural components, symmetry, metamorphosis, and alternation of generations.	www.conservation. state.mo.us
Day 5	Structure and function of Protist. **Complex task:** Draw structures of each protist (flagella, cilia, pseudopods).	Chapter 20 Section 1 P. 495	5.3 Integrate a comparative study of plant and animal anatomical structures so as to recognize relationships among organisms related to structural components, symmetry, metamorphosis, and alternation of generations.	Get pond water sample/ Use flex cam and microscope to view protist on television.
Day 6	Eubacteria vs. Archaebacteria. **Lab** Collect bacteria from familiar areas in school and grow in Petri dish to see bacteria colonies.	Chapter 19 Section 1 P. 471	5.3 Integrate a comparative study of plant and animal anatomical structures so as to recognize relationships among organisms related to structural components, symmetry, metamorphosis, and alternation of generations.	Textbook
Day 7	View bacteria colonies. Unit test.		5.1 Establish criteria for designing a system of classification and compare historically relevant systems of classification used in biology. 5.3 Integrate a comparative study of plant and animal anatomical structures so as to recognize relationships among organisms related to structural components, symmetry, metamorphosis, and alternation of generations.	

Unit Evaluation:
   Assessment of Prerequested Knowledge

Complex Task:
   Education Edge Job Clusters
   SCANS Skills
   Intelligence

Unit Test

Lesson I—American History

Chapter 12—"The Civil War 1861–1865"
The Battles of Chattanooga and Chickamauga

Tezra Volkmar

Goal:

The learners will understand the important themes, aspects, trends, and conflicts related to the battles of Chattanooga and Chickamauga during the Civil War.

Objectives:

1. Given a list of vocabulary words, the learners will define major aspects of this lesson and will be able to analyze meanings of and relationships among words. For example, they will identify the regional and geographic relationships and proximity of Chattanooga and Chickamauga. They will also clarify relationships among words by use of semantic mapping (such as *missing in action* and *casualties*).

2. Given a blank United States map, the learners will identify (in the following order) Tennessee, by outlining the state with a pen; Chattanooga, Tennessee, by placing a *C* on it; Georgia, by outlining the state with a pen; and the battle site of Chickamauga, by marking it with an *X*.

3. After watching a videotape of the Civil War monuments of Chattanooga and of Chickamauga battlefields while listening to Johnny Horton's "Johnny Reb," Dwight Yoakam's "I Sang Dixie," and Vince Gill's "Go Rest High on the Mountain," the learners will analyze their opinions on these two battles and their opinions on the Confederacy by completing a semantic differential data sheet.

4. After completing the semantic differential, the learners will analyze and be ready to participate in a class discussion on the topic.

5. After completing the reading on the "Cost of Chickamauga," the learners will answer a series of questions that will prepare them for a class discussion on the topic.

Prerequisite Knowledge:

The students must have prior knowledge of European colonization of America and American history (including the Civil War) up to the fall of 1863. In addition, students should have a general concept of the social, economic, and cultural differences and conflicts existing between the United States' northern and southern regions prior to the war.

Materials:

Vocabulary list, blank United States map, a reading on "The Cost of Chickamauga," questions to coincide with the reading on "The Cost of Chickamauga," videotape of the battlefields of Chattanooga and Chickamauga with Johnny Horton's "Johnny Reb," Dwight Yoakam's "I Sang Dixie," and Vince Gill's "Go Rest High on the Mountain," and the semantic differential data sheet

Procedures:

1. I will begin the lesson by asking the students a variety of questions that will lead into the discussion about the Civil War, especially the battles of Chattanooga and Chickamauga.

2. I will then inform the students that they are going to learn about the battles of Chattanooga and Chickamauga and how these battles affected the outcome of the Civil War by helping to seal the fate of the South.

3. First, I will hand out the vocabulary list and discuss the words and definitions with the students by asking a different student each time to define the next term in his/her own words. I will also put the terms on the overhead projector. When needed for clarity, I will add important points to each term.

Then, I will ask the students to circle two words they feel are related (for example, *casualties* and *missing in action* or *mass graves* and *national cemeteries*). I will then ask a student to come to the overhead to show the class what he/she did and why.

I will then ask each student to draw a line on the left side of the paper to a word that is related to the two he/she just circled. Then, I will call on someone to come to the overhead to demonstrate to the class what he/she just did on his/her paper and to explain to the class why. (For example, a student may draw a line between *tragedy* and *mass graves*.)

I will continue this process of connection, drawing lines to words, circling words, and so forth until all the relationships among the words have been indicated.

4. Next, I will hand out a blank United States map. I will then ask the students to outline the state of Tennessee with their pens. Then I will ask for a volunteer or call on someone to come up to the overhead and demonstrate for the class what he/she did on his/her paper. I will then ask the class members to raise their hands if they had the same answer.

I will then ask the students to place a *C* on where they think Chattanooga, Tennessee, is. Then I will ask for a volunteer or call on someone to come to the overhead to demonstrate for the class what he/she did on his/her paper. I will then ask the class members to raise their hands if they had the same answer.

I will then ask the students to outline the state of Georgia with their pens. Then I will ask for a volunteer or call on someone to come up to the overhead to demonstrate for the class what he/she did on his/her paper. I will then ask the class members to raise their hands if they had the same answer.

At this point, I will hand out a modern-day map of the National Military Park at Chickamauga in Georgia; however, I will not tell the students the battlefield is in Georgia. The map is a limited one and only shows Chickamauga battlefield and the immediate surrounding area (not including Chattanooga). From the information that they have, I will ask the students to put an *X* in the location where they think Chickamauga battlefield is. I will then ask for a volunteer or call on someone to come up to the overhead and demonstrate for the class what he/she did on his/her paper. I will then ask the class members to raise their hands if they had the same answer.

5. At this point, I will ask the students to put down their pens and watch, without taking any notes, the video of the battlefields of Chattanooga and Chickamauga while listening to Johnny Horton's "Johnny Reb," Dwight Yoakam's "I Sang Dixie," and Vince Gill's "Go Rest High on the Mountain."

After the video presentation is over, I will then instruct the students to respond to their semantic differentials. I will tell the students to consider their responses carefully and to support their answers with proof from the video and their previous knowledge of the topic. I will then instruct the students to put their pens down and look up when they are finished.

I will then call on eight people or ask for volunteers and have each one come to the overhead individually and demonstrate his/her answers for the class. I will then ask the students to explain their responses to the class. The class will discuss these answers and the support for the answers from the video and music.

6. Next, I will hand out the reading and questions on "The Cost of Chickamauga," which the students had previously seen on the videotape. I will instruct them to read silently and to complete the questions at the end of the reading. I will tell them they need to read the material carefully for detail because there will be a class discussion on the subject.

After the reading, I will show a videotape of Pvt. Ingraham's grave. I will turn the volume down. I will then ask the students if it is possible to determine his age. (No, there is not enough information.) I will then ask the students to write down his death date. I will then instruct the students to turn to the map on page 323 in their book *The United States and Its People*. This is a map of the battles of Chattanooga and Chickamauga. I will call on a student to tell me the date on the map. The date on the map is September 19, 1863, which signifies the first day of battle. I will then return to the videotape and have one of the students state that Pvt. John Ingraham was killed on September 19, 1863, the first day of battle. I will then return the videotape to the memorial plaque where this is stated. The class will also discuss the importance of the fact that on the tombstone it says Ingraham was a volunteer.

I will then call on a different student to answer each of the questions. I will then write the students' responses on the overhead projector. The class will discuss in detail each answer and supporting details from the reading and other sources.

7. Before concluding the lesson, I will ask, "Why was a little Tennessee railroad town like Chattanooga an important target for the North?" (It opened up the South, especially Georgia, to the North, and the following spring Sherman burned a path through Georgia.)

8. I will ask a series of review questions about the information that the class just covered in the lesson. I will also inform the class that the next lesson will continue to cover the battles of Chattanooga and Chickamauga.

Sample WebQuests

Home | Teacher

WebQuest: The Truth ... and Nothing But the TRUTH!
Evaluating Persuasive Reading

Developed by Pam Petty
http://www.pampetty.com

Middle School ● Language Arts ● Reading

  Student Page

 Introduction

Who is helping you do your thinking? If something is written in print, it has to be true, right? Not so fast ... when people want us to think the way THEY think, they use persuasive "tricks" known as "propaganda techniques" to try and influence our thinking. Are you clever enough to read some persuasive texts and decide what is fact and what is fiction? This project allows you to take real on-line texts and decide for yourself just WHO is trying to persuade you to BELIEVE just WHAT!

For the purposes of this WebQuest, persuasive reading will be defined as: "a type of writing intended to convince the reader to adopt a particular opinion or to perform a certain action. Effective persuasion appeals to both the intellect and emotions."

(http://www.usd435.k12.ks.us/Ed_Center/Communications_Curriculum/
All%20Grades/definitions_reading_forms.htm)

The Task

You and your team have been asked by the Secretary of Education in Washington, DC, to serve as a panel of experts and solve some problems affecting schools all over our country. There are many persuasive documents written on each of the following topics, each expressing strong ideas either pro or con. As a team you will select a topic from one of the following:

- Corporal punishment
- School prayer
- School violence
- Gender issues
- School vouchers

In order to make decisions about your topic, your team will *read* 4 persuasive texts. Each text you read will attempt to sway your opinion to make you believe what the author believes. It is your job to *analyze* the persuasive texts, *synthesize* the information, *write* a personal narrative in response to the text, and help your team put together a *multimedia presentation* using PowerPoint software. The presentation will summarize the 4 texts you read, identify strategies the authors used to sway the reader, and share with others the factual information you found in your readings.

The Process

1. In your group (determined by your teacher), select one of the topics listed above. As a group, make a web of all the things you know about the topic you have selected. Use the Internet or print materials to define any of the concepts you do not clearly understand before you begin the assigned readings.

2. Locate your topic below and start investigating each of the on-line resources listed there. As a group, select 4 texts to use in this project. If the text presents basic information without any persuasive strategies, skip it and keep reading other texts.

    Make your selections from the listings below:

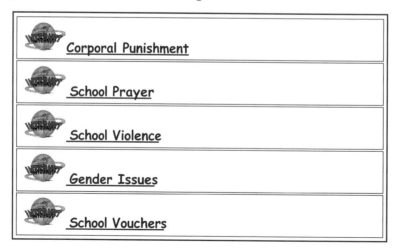

3. Use this **DATA RESPONSE FORMAT** to carefully analyze each text as you read it. Compare your findings with those of others in your group. Combine your lists of propaganda techniques found in each persuasive text.

4. After you have read all the selections and decided which 4 your group will use for this project, complete this **DATA RESPONSE FORMAT**. Use this information as an outline for your presentation.

5. Write a one-paragraph narrative that summarizes your "answer" to the problem posed by your topic. Your writing should include what you agree with and disagree with based on the readings you just performed.

6. Share your narrative with others in your group (your teacher may allow you to "pass" on this if you so desire).

7. Work together as a team to prepare a PowerPoint presentation that:

- Summarizes each of the four persuasive texts
- Points out the various types of techniques used in each text to sway the reader
- Incorporates each group member's "decision" based on their interpretation of the readings (this offers some sort of conclusion your topic)

8. Present your findings to the class.

 Evaluation

Each student will receive two grades for this project, a group grade and an individual grade. A **rubric** for evaluating the final projects will be used by students and by the teacher.

Conclusion

After successfully completing this project, you will be in full control of what you believe ... no longer will anyone be able to pull one over on you! You MUST believe me when I tell you this because 4 out of 5 dentists say it is so ... EVERYONE who is anyone has known this for years and years ... and if you DON'T believe me, then I guess you are just an 'ole silly-head!

Did you solve all the world's problems? Brainstorm some other topics that are important in your life or at your school. Find some information sources (on-line or print materials) and find out what other people are trying to get you to believe. Use your newly acquired skills to determine the techniques the authors use to persuade you to see their point of view ... then use your OWN head to decide what YOU believe. Be ready to express your opinion ... maybe write to an author to share your views on a particular topic ... make YOUR case and PERSUADE them to your way of thinking!

 Back to Homepage

Home | Student

WebQuest: The Truth ... and Nothing But the TRUTH!
Evaluating Persuasive Reading

Developed by Pam Petty
http://www.pampetty.com

Middle School ● Language Arts ● Reading

  Teacher Page

Introduction

In the "information age" in which we live it is imperative to be able to discern fact from fiction in what we read. We must be equipped with the skills to read persuasive texts and sift out kernels of truth that provide the basis for our decision making. Many times clever propaganda techniques are used in persuasive texts that lead us to make decisions that are not fully based in reality. This WebQuest provides learners with opportunities to critically read some texts that present different views on controversial topics.

For the purposes of this WebQuest, "persuasive reading" will be defined as: "a type of writing intended to convince the reader to adopt a particular opinion or to perform a certain action. Effective persuasion appeals to both the intellect and emotions."(http://www.usd435.k12.ks.us/Ed_Center/Communications_Curriculum/All%20Grades/definitions_reading_forms.htm)

This lesson was developed by Pam Petty, Division of Literacy, Western Kentucky University, Bowling Green, Kentucky. This WebQuest represents an example of how real-world applications can be made using technology and the Internet.

Content Area and Grade Level

This WebQuest is appropriate for middle school learners. The unit focuses on language arts and reading instruction. Integration with social studies would be possible.

Curriculum Standards (Kentucky)

The Kentucky Department of Education provides the following criteria for reading comprehension at Grade 7:

Persuasive Reading includes whole texts and excerpts from materials such as magazines and newspaper articles, brochures, letters, proposals, speeches, editorials, electronic texts, essays, opinion columns, and advertisements.

RD-M-3.0.11

Distinguish between informative and persuasive passages.

RD-M-3.0.12

Identify an author's opinion about a subject.

RD-M-3.0.13

Apply knowledge of organizational patterns (e.g., cause and effect, comparison, contrast, sequence) to understand a passage.

RD-M-3.0.14

Distinguish between fact and opinion.

RD-M-3.0.15

Identify the argument and supporting evidence.

RD-M-3.0.16

Identify commonly used persuasive techniques (e.g., expert opinion, statistics, testimonial, bandwagon).

RD-M-3.0.17

The Kentucky Department of Education provides the following criteria for reading comprehension at Grades 8 — 10

Persuasive Reading includes whole texts and excerpts from materials such as magazines and newspaper articles, brochures, letters, proposals, speeches, editorials, electronic texts, essays, opinion columns, and advertisements.

RD-H-3.0.8

Identify purposes of persuasion.

RD-H-3.0.9

Identify an author's position based on evidence in a passage.

RD-H-3.0.10

Recognize the appropriateness of an argument for an intended audience.

RD-H-3.0.11

Accept or reject an argument, giving supporting evidence from the passage.

RD-H-3.0.12

Compare and contrast differing points of view in two or more passages.

RD-H-3.0.13

Identify a variety of persuasive and propaganda techniques and explain how each is used.

RD-H-3.0.14

Analyze and evaluate the use of persuasion within a passage.

Implementation Overview

This unit is designed to take 5-8 continuous classroom periods. This unit can be extended by examining other current event topics of interest to students. Students will work in groups of 3 or 4 (dependent upon computer access and physical classroom structure). Students will decide on their own how to divide the various tasks required to complete the project. Students will need time to collect data from web sites, respond to the data response formats, create multimedia presentations, and write personal narratives in response to the reading.

Resources Needed

- Links to Internet sites relating to the following topics:

Corporal Punishment

Short of the Goal

Swat Leads to Discrimination Complaint Against Professor

A Blow to the Spirit

The State of Paddling

A Philosophy of Discipline

The High School Cane: A Eulogy

Paddling is Archaic and Ineffective, and Local Schools that use it should Stop

A Case Against Corporal Punishment

The Case for Corporal Punishment

Letter to President Clinton: Civil Rights of School Children

School Prayer

Nailing Down the Flap over School Prayer

Bible Believers Should Oppose School Prayer

A Case Against School Prayer

School Prayer: The Wrong Hill to Die On

Constitutional Amendment on School Prayer or Moment of Silence

Public School Prayer Creates Violence

"Religious Freedom" or Hypocrisy?

Pro School Prayer Position

Anti School Prayer Position

The Case Against School Prayer

School Violence
Staying Safe from Gun Violence
Thinking about Violence in Our Schools
Facts about Violence in Youth and in Schools
Gangs and School Violence
An Overview of Strategies to Reduce School Violence
Looking for Trouble
Study: Bullying Rampant in U.S. Middle Schools
School Lessons: Deflect Bullies, Prevent Violence
Drills, New Security Measure mark Return to School
School Efforts to Ensure Safety and Promote Discipline
Suicide Rage and School Killings vs. Something of Value

Gender Issues
The Absurdity of Feminism
Gender Equity in Education
The War Against Boys
Adults need to do Homework to end School "Gender Wars"
Girls Flag Football among School Gender Equity Plan
Gender Inequity in Education
Teacher Education and Gender Equity
An Equation for Equity
Gender Equity Issues in the Classroom Today
Empowering Women in Sports

School Vouchers
Vouchers: Betraying Public Education
School Vouchers: For All or for None?
Hot Topics: School Vouchers
Who's Vouching for Vouchers?
Do we need Tuition Vouchers or School Choice?
Choice
Vouchers and Educational Freedom: A Debate
False Choices: Vouchers, Public Schools, and Our Children's Futures
Education Vouchers: America Can't Afford to Wait
A Case Against Vouchers

- Computers with Internet access
- Presentation Software (PowerPoint, etc)
- On-Line Teacher Resources
  Kentucky Department of Education: Core Content for Reading Assessment
  Analyzing a Journal Article/Essay
  Propaganda Technique

Data Response Format: Analysis of Text
Data Response Format: Synthesis of Persuasive Readings

- Optional Resources and Lesson Plans for preparing students for this Quest or for extending the learning:

Seventh Grade Block (propaganda techniques)

Advertising Gimmicks: Teaching Critical Thinking

Ad Attack!

Magazine Ads and You, the Teenager

Entry Level Skills and Knowledge

Prior to beginning this unit, learners should have some experience in identifying propaganda techniques. They should know how to navigate through web sites to find specific information. Learners should have experience working in cooperative groups. Previous hands-on experience with presentation software (PowerPoint) or simultaneous training for using presentation software is required.

Evaluation

A <u>RUBRIC</u> will be used to allow students to self-assess and for the teacher assessment. The final product of this WebQuest is a multimedia presentation depicting factual information found by each group on the selected topic. Individual student scores will be based on participation in the group project and on independent writing samples in response to the persuasive readings.

Conclusion

This unit is an interdisciplinary (language arts, reading, social studies) constructionist approach to learning. Students participate in group work, experience navigating the web, learn to read critically and synthesize information, create multimedia presentations, and write narrative responses to persuasive readings. This WebQuest could easily be adjusted for older or younger students, and teachers can adapt the activities to their students' individual needs.

 Back to Homepage

Data Response Format: Analysis of Text

Name: _____

Members of Group: _____

Topic: _____

1. Title of Reading: _____

2. Written by: _____

3. What do you know about the author? _____

4. Does the title give you any hints as to what the author thinks about the topic (positively or negatively)? _____

5. Is this text providing BASIC information or is the author trying to make you think his or her way?

_____

(if 5 = BASIC, finish reading the article and move on to the next one ... you do not need to complete the remainder of this form)

6. Make a list of all the FACTUAL information in this text.

7. Make a list of all the information in this text that is merely the OPINION of the author.

8. What argument is the author trying to make? _____

_____

9. What evidence does the author provide to support his or her argument? _____

_____

_____

_____

10. List examples of any of the following types of propaganda techniques:
NOTE: Check out these resources for examples and definitions of these and other propaganda techniques:

<u>Propaganda Techniques</u>

<u>Definition of Propaganda Techniques</u>

<u>Propaganda Technique</u>

expert opinion: _____

_____

statistics: _____

_____

testimonial: _____

_____

bandwagon: _____

_____

other: _____

_____

11. How effective was the author in convincing you of his or her case? _____

_____

 Back to Student Page

Persuasive Reading Rubric

Your Name: _____ **Group Topic :** _____

Group Members: _____

Persuasive Reading Rubric	Possible Points	Self-Assessment	Teacher Assessment
Participated in group activity	10		
Work showed understanding of evaluating persuasive reading	10		
Synthesis of factual information found in multiple on-line resources (data response formats)	10		
Creativity and quality of presentation	10		
Completion of all WebQuest activities by due dates	10		
Total Possible Points	**50**		

Rate each category according to the following scale: 9-10 = excellent, 7-8 = very good, 5-6 = good, 3-4 = satisfactory, 1-2 = poor, and 0 = unsatisfactory.

 Back to Student Page

Home   Student   Teacher

Teacher Page
Overview
of
WebQuest

● **Introduction**

This WebQuest features Ian Falconer's Caldecott honor book **Olivia** (2000). Trade books offer teachers and parents many opportunities to improve reading comprehension skills. Falconer's references to famous works of art and music provide additional learning opportunities.

The primary purpose of using quality children's literature in the classroom is to instill a love of reading. As with any book, <u>Olivia</u> should be first read for pleasure before embarking on activities based on the book. Students should be allowed opportunities to ask questions, make comments, and simply enjoy this delightful story.

The Tasks provided for students in this WebQuest facilitate reading comprehension skills. Students will be asked to interpret passages from the story, to describe the characters and the problems and solutions of the story. Students will be performing tasks that help them link their real lives with Olivia's. Family interactions in the story will be discussed. Also, discussion of art and music allusions in the book will be encouraged.

● **Content areas**
This multidisciplinary WebQuest includes the following content areas: reading, art, music, social studies. It is directed toward early elementary. First and possibly second grade students will require extra assistance performing the tasks in this WebQuest.

● **Objectives (Kentucky Curriculum Standards):**

Reading

RD-E-1.0.6
Explain the meaning of a passage taken from texts appropriate for elementary school students.
RD-E-1.0.8
Describe characters, plot, setting, and problem/solution of a passage.
RD-E-1.0.9
Explain a character's actions based on a passage.
RD-E-1.0.10
Connect literature to students' lives and real world issues.

Art

AH-E-4.2.35 Recognize that artists choose to express themselves in different styles and subject matters. (2.23, 2.24, 2.25, 2.26)
AH-E-4.2.36 Styles: realistic, abstract, non-objective

Music

AH-E-1.2.32 Identify and discuss various styles of music (blues, spirituals, popular, rock, rap, country, game songs, folk songs, work songs, lullabies, marches, patriotic, bluegrass). (2.24, 2.25, 2.26)

Social Studies

SS-E-2.3.1
Various human needs are met through interaction in and among social groups (e.g., family, schools, teams, and clubs).

● **Implementation Overview**

Students will work in groups of 3 or 4 (dependent upon computer access and physical classroom structure). Students will decide on their own how to divide the various tasks required to complete the project, although teachers may find it better to assign tasks based on each child's needs to be successful. Students will need time to collect data from web sites, respond to the data response formats, and to prepare presentations for their classmates. This unit can be extended by examining other topics of interest to students using Olivia as a springboard.

Young students (grades 1, 2) will need extra support in doing this WebQuest. Teachers will need to prepare students for following the format of a WebQuest and for working together cooperatively. A nice modeling technique might be to take one of the options on the student page and do it together as a whole group activity.

> Many of the lessons include activity pages that need to be printed out. I would recommend printing these out ahead of time, and making enough copies for your students. You will find a list of the pages in the student evaluation section.

● **Special Resources Needed:**

- Computers with Internet access
- Multiple copies of <u>Olivia</u> (preferred - one copy per group)
- Presentation Software (PowerPoint, etc.)
- On-Line Teacher Resources

 Author Information on Ian Falconer: <u>http://www.sfopera.com/bios/bios_a-f/ifalconer.htm</u>

 Jackson Pollock's Autumn Rhythm # 30: <u>http://www.metmuseum.org/collections/view1.asp?dep=21&item=57%2E92</u>

NOTE: This site includes artist information. Teachers should read and share highlights with students.

Art ideas for painting like Jackson Pollock:
<u>http://pbskids.org/arthur/parentsteachers/activities/acts/active_art.html</u>

 Metropolitan Museum of Art: <u>http://www.metmuseum.org/home.asp</u>
NOTE: Search "Robert Pollock" to see many of his other works of art.

 Edgar Degas' life and art:
<u>http://www.metmuseum.org/explore/Degas/html/index.html</u>
Note: Click <u>HERE</u> to order *The Dance Class* poster by Edgar Degas.

Note: Click <u>HERE</u> to order *Ballet Rehearsal on the Set* by Edgar Degas (pictured in the book ($9.00).

 Edgar Degas - major site for information and artwork photos:
<u>http://artcyclopedia.com/artists/degas_edgar.html</u>

 Maria Callas - click <u>HERE</u> to order her CD: **Maria Callas The Legend.**
Click <u>HERE</u> to order her CD: Maria Callas: The Voice of the Century.

● **Entry Level Skills and Knowledge**
Students will need to be able to read and write; however there are alternative materials built into this WebQuest that allow for ability levels. For very young students, an adult will need to be assigned to each group to facilitate reading and writing.

● Evaluation

A <u>RUBRIC</u> will be used to allow students to self-assess and for the teacher assessment. Teachers may also want to use the <u>Scoring Guide</u> specifically designed to evaluate student performance in group work associated with doing a WebQuest. The final product of this WebQuest is group presentation sharing information found by each group on the selected topic. Individual student scores will be based on participation in the group project and on independent writing samples.

Student Handouts for each Task:

Task 1: <u>Venn Diagram</u>
Task 2: <u>Graphics</u>
Task 3: <u>Art Contest</u>
Task 4: <u>Good Idea/Bad Idea</u>

● Conclusion

This unit is an interdisciplinary (reading, art, music, social studies) constructionist approach to learning. Students participate in group work, experience navigating the web, learn to read critically and synthesize information, create presentations, and write to communicate. This WebQuest could easily be adjusted for older students, and teachers can adapt the activities to students' individual needs.

Credits

Many thanks to the following resources:

Detroit Institute of Arts Visual Resources Art Image Database [http://www.diamondial.org/home.html]: famous artwork used in Task 3.

The Artchive (click on the Mona Lisa to view art and read about artists) [http://www.artchive.com/]

Falconer Photo (smiling): **http://www.sfopera.com/bios/bios_a-f/ifalconer.htm**

Falconer Photo: Book jacket. Falconer, I. (2000). . New York: Atheneum. *Olivia*

 Back to Olivia WebQuest Homepage

Student Page

OLIVIA

WebQuest

Ian Falconer, author of **Olivia**, has another story about Olivia coming out in October 2001 (<u>Olivia Saves the Circus</u>). But he is already thinking of writing and illustrating another story about Olivia. He has had dozens of adults and editors give him advice about what they liked and didn't like about his first book, but Mr. Falconer really wants to hear what KIDS thinks about this book. The author is really trying to get kids to think about their own lives as they read Olivia's adventures. He also wants to know if the illustrations he draws get your attention. Click on Mr. Falconer's photo below if you accept this challenge:

There is work to be done! Now that you have read or heard the book, *Olivia*, your job is to perform the tasks listed below. When you read a book, do you notice how your life is like the character's lives? Do you notice how your life is different? Do you pay attention to the pictures in books and see how they tell part of the story just like the words do? Do you know how to look at art and decide if you like it or not? Why don't all people like the same kinds of art and music? We all have to make decisions about the way we act. Does Olivia make the same decisions as you would make? Once you have completed all the tasks, you should send Mr. Falconer a summary of your findings so that he can know what to include in his next book.

<u>Task 1</u>	<u>Task 2</u>	<u>Task 3</u>	<u>Task 4</u>

Rules:

You will be working with 3 other students in a group. In group work, everyone works! Each student will perform a different role in each group:

Person 1: Reader - it is this person's job to read to the group.

Person 2: Materials Manager - it is this person's job to make sure the group has the materials (paper, pencils, printouts, etc.) necessary to perform the task.

Person 3: Scribe - it is this person's job to make any notes or fill out any forms as the group dictates.

Person 4: Reporter - it is this person's job to report the group's progress/ findings to the teacher/class.

See a word you don't know? Check <u>HERE</u> for an on-line dictionary.

 Getting Ready to Go:

To learn more about this book and the author your teacher will share with you information from the following website:

<u>http://www.kidsreads.com/authors/au-falconer-ian.asp</u>

Task 1: Olivia's Life and My Life

Sometimes when we read books we see things that remind us of our own lives. We understand stories better when we can relate to the characters' lives. This task will help you decide how your life is like Olivia's life and how it is different.

Print out one <u>Venn Diagram</u> for each person in the group.

1. The Reader should read the story again to all group members.

2. The Materials Manager should provide the Venn Diagram and a pencil to each group member.

3. Each person should fill out the Venn Diagram according to their own life and to Olivia's life. Things they have in COMMON should go in the space where the circles overlap. (Example: Olivia has a cat. If you have a dog, you would write that in the GREEN circle. If you have a cat, you would write that in the space where the green and the blue circle overlap.)

4. The Scribe should compare all four Venn Diagrams and decide who has the most in common with Olivia. The Scribe should share this information with the group.

5. The Reporter should be ready to share findings with teacher or classmates.

Extra: Click <u>HERE</u> to read another story. Draw your own Venn Diagram to compare and contrast your life with the characters in the story.

<u>top</u>

TASK 2: Busy, Busy Olivia

Part of understanding a story is making sure you understand the pictures and the names of things in the story. This task will help you make connections between the story and real life.

Print out the <u>graphics sheet</u> you will need for this task.

Steps:

1. The Reader should read the story again to all group members.

2. The Materials Manager should provide the graphics sheet and the pencil and paper to the Scribe.

3. The group should look at the graphics sheet and point out any items on the sheet that were shown or mentioned in the story.

4. The Scribe should **circle** the items that **were in the story** and put an on **"X"** the items **not in the story**.

5. The Reporter should be ready to share findings with teacher or classmates. The Reporter should click <u>HERE</u> to find the answer guide for this task ... AFTER the Scribe has marked the graphics sheet.

<u>top</u>

Task 3: Olivia, the Artist

Print out the "<u>Art Contest</u>" form you will need for this task.

Not everyone likes the same types of art or music. In the book, Olivia has a favorite piece of art and she sees a piece of art she does not really understand. Your task is to look at some famous artwork, decide which ones you like, which ones you don't like, and give reasons for why you do or do not like them.

  Famous Pieces of Art:

1. <u>Autumn Rhythm Number 30 - Jackson Pollock</u>
2. <u>Persistence of Memory</u>
3. <u>The Beeches</u>
4. <u>Lake George</u>
5. <u>The Dance Class - Edgar Degas</u>

6. <u>Celia Thaxter's Garden, Isles of Shoals, Maine</u>
7. <u>The Repast of the Lion</u>
8. <u>The Grand Canal, Venice</u>
9. <u>Still Life with Apples and a Pot of Primroses</u>
10. <u>Garden at Sainte-Adresse</u>

1. The Reader should assist all students in the group by reading the name of the artwork from the screen so that other group members can locate it on the Art Contest page.

2. The Materials Manager should make sure that each group member has a copy of the "Art Contest" form.

3. Each person should look at the art work on-line and fill out the Art Contest form indicating which pieces of art they like (and why) and which pieces they do not like (and why).

4. The Scribe should compare each students' completed Art Contest form and tally the results. The Scribe should share with the group which pieces of art were voted "best" and "worst."

5. The Reporter should be ready to share findings with teacher or classmates.

6. What do you know about the artist? Search HERE to find out about the artist. (You will see the artists' names on the left side of the screen.) What kind of artwork did he or she use?

7. Each student should draw/paint an original piece of artwork that has the same "features" of the one you voted best. "Features" might include using the same art techniques as the famous artist (watercolor, pen and ink, etc.), drawing a picture of the same type subjects (example: draw your own flowers, etc.), or using the same colors. If you are interested in painting like Jackson Pollock, click here: http://pbskids.org/arthur/parentsteachers/activities/acts/active art.html and follow the directions!

NOTE: Your teacher may have you listen to music by Maria Callas and compare that to other musical performances or other types of music.

top
Olivia: Making Good Choices

In every story the characters have to make choices. Some of them are good choices, and some of them are not so good. In this task you will look at some of the choices Olivia made and decide if they are good choices or bad choices, and brainstorm ideas of how else she might have handled the situation.

Print out the "Good Idea/Bad Idea" form each student in your group will need for this task.

1. The Reader will read aloud from the handout each choice that Olivia made in the story allowing discussion by the group on each one.

2. The Materials Manager should print out or distribute one "Good Idea/Bad Idea" handout.

3. Each group should discuss the decisions Olivia made as the Reader reads aloud from the handout.

4. The Scribe should mark whether the choice was a "good idea" or a "bad idea" based on what the group decides. The Scribe should then write down the BEST reasons given by the group for why the choices were good or bad.

5. The Reporter should make a list of all the ideas that group members have of how Olivia might have made better choices. The Reporter should be ready to share these ideas with the teacher or other classmates.

NOTE: The Eloise books (see list below) show Eloise making choices also. Read your favorite Eloise book, make a list of all the decisions she makes, and discuss these with your group. Make a list of "better" choices that Eloise could make.

top

Evaluation

Did you do a good job on all these tasks? How do you know? Take a few minutes and fill out the Self-Evaluation Rubric for this WebQuest. Mark your answers honestly and really judge your own work. ☺

You and your classmates have had some experiences with this book and have had some time to think about what you liked and what might be better in the next book. Take a few minutes to put together a class "report" or summary of your findings and send those to Ian Falconer, c/o Antheneum Books for Young Readers, Simon and Schuster Children's Publishing Division, 1230 Avenue of the Americas, New York, NY 10020. You never know, he MIGHT just write you back!

Conclusion

If you enjoyed reading about Olivia and her active life, you might also like to read books about Eloise:

- *Kay Thompson's Eloise in Paris (Eloise Series)* by Kay Thompson, Hilary Knight (Illustrator)
- *Kay Thompson's Eloise at Christmastime* by Kay Thompson, Hilary Knight (Illustrator)
- *Eloise's Guide to Life : How to Eat, Dress, Travel, Behave and Stay Six Forever!* by Kay Thompson, Hilary Knight (Illustrator)
- *Kay Thompson's Eloise in Moscow* by Kay Thompson, Hilary Knight (Illustrator)

As you read the books about Eloise, draw your own Venn Diagrams to show how you are like her and how you are different. Make lists of things that she does that you think are cool and about adventures you would like to see her have in the future. Talk about the decisions she makes and how she might make better ones. The number one rule is: **Read for FUN FIRST,** then continue to enjoy the book as you explore the characters and the story!

top

 Back to Olivia WebQuest Homepage!

Contact the author of this site: Pam Petty

Selected References

AAEE 2000 job search handbook for educators. (2000). Columbus, OH: American Association for Employment in Education.

Albert, L. (1996). *Cooperative discipline.* Circle Pines, MN: American Guidance Service, Inc.

Allain, V., & Pettus, A. (1998). *Teaching diverse students: Preparing with cases.* Bloomington, IN: Phi Delta Kappa.

Allen, C. (2001). *The multigenre research paper: Voice, passion, and discovery in grades 4–6.* Portsmouth, NH: Heinemann.

Allen, D. (1994, November/ December). Teaching with technology: Literature and software. *Teaching K–8, 25,* 20–23.

Allen, D. (1995, January). Teaching with technology: Creative problem solving. *Teaching K–8, 25,* 18, 22–25.

Allen, D. (1996, February). Teaching with technology: Break the language barrier. *Teaching K–8, 26,* 16–18.

Allen, J. S. (1996, February). Potato barrels, animal traps, birth control, and unicorns: Re-visioning teaching and learning in English classes. *English Journal, 85,* 38–42.

American Association for the Advancement of Science. (1993). *Project 2061: Benchmarks for science literacy.* Washington, DC: Author.

Anderson-Inman, L. (1998, February). Electronic journals in technology and literacy: Professional development online. *Journal of Adolescent & Adult Literacy, 41,* 400–405.

Artesani, A. J. (2001). *Understanding the purpose of challenging behavior.* Upper Saddle River, NJ: Merrill/Prentice Hall.

Ban, J. (1994). A lesson plan approach for dealing with school discipline. *The Clearing House, 67,*(5), 257–260.

Basden, J. D. (2001, November). Authentic tasks as the basis for multimedia design curriculum. *T.H.E. Journal, 29,* 16–21.

Beane, J. A. (1995, April). Curriculum integration and the disciplines of knowledge. *Phi Delta Kappan, 76,* 616–622.

Bennett, W. J. (1986). *What works: Research about teaching and learning.* Washington, DC: United States Department of Education.

Berg, J. (2003). *Improving the quality of teaching through national board certification: Theory and practice.* Norwood, MA: Christopher-Gordon.

Bertrand, J., & Stice, C. (Eds.). (1995). *Empowering children at risk of school failure: A better way.* Norwood, MA: Christopher-Gordon.

Berwick, B. (1994, April). Kids behind the camera: Education for the video age. *Educational Leadership, 51,* 52–54.

Betts, F. (1994, April). On the birth of the communication age: A conversation with David Thornburg. *Educational Leadership, 51,* 20–23.

Beyer, B. K. (1995). *Critical thinking.* Bloomington, IN: Phi Delta Kappa Educational Foundation.

Beyond 'effective teaching.' (1992, April). *Educational Leadership, 49* (Series of articles).

Bigelow, B. (1997). On the road to cultural bias: A critique of *The Oregon Trail* CD-ROM. *Language Arts, 74,* 84–93.

Bodine, R., & Crawford, D. (1998). *The handbook of conflict resolution education.* San Francisco, CA: National Institute for Dispute Resolution.

Bolles, R. N. (1997). *The 1997 what color is your parachute? A practical manual for job-hunters and career changers* (Rev. ed.). New York: Ten Speed.

Bomer, R. (1998, September). Transactional heat and light: More explicit literacy learning. *Language Arts, 76,* 11–18.

Bone, A., & Busekist, S. (1996, February). Toward a whole partnership. *English Journal, 85,* 35–37.

Brophy, J. (1992, April). Probing the subtleties of subject-matter teaching. *Educational Leadership, 49,* 4–8.

Brunner, C. (1996, May/June). Judging student multimedia. *Electronic Learning, 15,* 14–15.

Brush, A., & Brewster, J. (2004, January/February). Take your students to great museums online. *Instructor, 113,* 30–35.

Buchleitner, W. (1999, May/June). Teaching with technology: Exploring nature on the Web. *Early Childhood Today, 13,* 14–15.

Bullock, A., & Hawk, P. (2005). *Developing a teaching portfolio: A guide for preservice and practicing teachers.* Upper Saddle River, NJ: Merrill/Prentice Hall.

Bussert-Webb, R. (1999, April). To test or to teach: Reflections from a holistic teacher-researcher in South Texas. *Journal of Adolescent & Adult Literacy, 42,* 582–585.

Cable in the Classroom Fact Sheet. (1999, March). *Cable in the Classroom, 9,* 2.

Cambron-McCabe, N., McCarthy, M., & Thomas, S. (2004). *Public school law: Teachers' and students' rights.* Boston, MA: Pearson Education, Inc.

Campbell, D., Cignetti, P., Melenyzer, B., Nettles, D., & Wyman, R. (2001). *How to develop a professional portfolio: A manual for teaching.* Boston. MA: Allyn & Bacon.

Canning, C. (1991, March). What teachers say about reflection. *Educational Leadership, 48,* 18–21.

Canter, L. (1986). *Assertive discipline, Phase I* (Video recording). Santa Monica, CA: Canter and Associates.

Canter, M. (1987). *A model for effective discipline.* Bloomington, IN: Phi Delta Kappa Educational Foundation.

Carico, K., & Logan, D. (2004, March). A generation in cyberspace: Engaging readers through online discussions. *Language Arts, 81,* 293–302.

Chapman, C., & King, R. (2003). *Differentiated instructional strategies for reading in the content areas.* Thousand Oaks, CA: Corwin Press.

Charbonneau, M. P., & Reider, B. E. (1995). *The integrated elementary classroom.* Boston: Allyn & Bacon.

Charles, C. M. (1989). *Building classroom discipline* (3rd ed.). New York: Longman.

Charles, C. M. (2002). *Essential elements of effective discipline.* Boston, MA: Allyn & Bacon.

Choate, J., & Rakes, T. (1998). *Inclusive instruction for struggling readers.* Bloomington, IN: Phi Delta Kappa.

Cipaai, E. (2002). *Positive behavioral supports.* Upper Saddle River, NJ: Merrill/Prentice Hall.

Clark, R. W., & Wasley, P. (1999, April). Renewing schools and smarter kids: Promises for democracy. *Phi Delta Kappan, 90,* 590–596.

Coelho, E. (1994). *Learning together in the multicultural classroom.* Markham, Ontario: Pippin.

Coffey, J. (1996, May/June). Go west, young explorers! In Just for educators: Your own web guide. *Electronic Learning, 15,* 6.

Coiro, J. (2003, February). Reading comprehension on the Internet: Expanding our understanding of reading comprehension to

encompass new literacies. *The Reading Teacher, 56,* 458–464.

Commeyras, M. (1999, February). How interested are literacy educators in gender issues? Survey results from the United States. *Journal of Adolescent & Adult Literacy, 42,* 352–362.

Connors, E. T. (1979). *Student discipline and the law.* Bloomington, IN: Phi Delta Kappa.

Cooperative learning. (1989, December/1990, January). *Educational Leadership, 47* (Entire issue).

Cox, C., & Batstone, P. (1997). *Crossroads: Literature and language in culturally diverse classrooms.* Upper Saddle River, NJ: Merrill/Prentice Hall.

Cramer, G., & Hurst, B. (2000). *How to find a teaching job.* Upper Saddle River, NJ: Merrill/Prentice Hall.

Cunningham, P., & Allington, R. (1994). *Classrooms that work.* New York: HarperCollins.

Cunningham, P., & Allington, R. (1999). *Classrooms that work* (2nd ed.). New York: Longman.

Dill, V. S. (1998). *A peaceable school.* Bloomington, IN: Phi Delta Kappa.

Diller, D. (1999, May). Opening the dialogue: Using culture as a tool in teaching young African American children. *The Reading Teacher, 52,* 820–828.

Dodge, B. (1997). Some thoughts about WebQuests. Retrieved from *http://edweb.sdsuedu/ courses/edtec596/ about_WebQuests.html.*

Dodge, B. J. (2004). The WebQuest design process. Retrieved from *http://webquest.sdsu.edu/ designsteps/index.html.*

Doherty, C., & Mayer, D. (2003, April). E-mail as a "contact zone" for teacher-student relationships. *Journal of Adolescent & Adult Literacy, 46,* 592–600.

Dudley-Marling, C. (1997, Spring). "I'm not from Pakistan": Multicultural literature and the problem of representation. *The New Advocate, 10,* 123–134.

Dugger, W. E., Jr. (2001, March). Standards for technological literacy. *Phi Delta Kappan, 82,* 513–523.

Dunn, K., & Dunn, R. (1987, March). Dispelling outmoded beliefs about

student learning. *Educational Leadership, 44,* 55–62.

A DVD primer. (1999). *T.H.E. Journal, 26*(6), 23.

El-Hindi, A. E. (1998, May). Beyond classroom boundaries: Constructivist teaching with the Internet. *The Reading Teacher, 51,* 694–699.

Ellis, S., & Whalen, W. (1990). *Cooperative learning: Getting started.* New York: Scholastic.

Farr, R., & Tone, B. (1994). *Portfolio and performance assessment.* Fort Worth, TX: Harcourt Brace.

Fogarty, R. (1998, May). The intelligence-friendly classroom. *Phi Delta Kappan, 79,* 655–657.

Forbes, L. S. (2004, October). Using Web-based bookmarks in K–8 settings: Linking the Internet to instruction. *The Reading Teacher, 58,* 148–153.

Foster-Harrison, E., & Adams-Bullock, A. (1998). *Creating an inviting classroom environment.* Bloomington, IN: Phi Delta Kappa.

Frank, M. (1994). *Using writing portfolios to enhance instruction and assessment.* Nashville, TN: Incentive.

Fredericksen, E. (2000, March). Muted colors: Gender and classroom silence. *Language Arts, 77,* 301–308.

French, M., & Andretti, A. (1995). *Attention deficit and reading instruction.* Bloomington, IN: Phi Delta Kappa.

Garcia, E. (1994). *Understanding and meeting the challenge of student cultural diversity.* Boston: Houghton Mifflin.

Garcia, E. (2002). *Student cultural diversity.* Boston: Houghton Mifflin.

Gardner, H. (1983). *Frames of mind: The theory of multiple intelligences.* New York: Basic Books.

Glazer, S. M. (1994, August/ September). How you can use tests and portfolios, too. *Teaching K–8, 25,* 152, 154.

Goldman, S. R. (1997). Learning from text: Reflections on the past and suggestions for the future. *Discourse Processes, 23,* 357–398.

Goodlad, J. (1994). What schools are for (2nd ed.). Bloomington, IN: Phi Delta Kappa.

Grabe, M., & Grabe, C. (2000). *Integrating technology for meaningful learning.* Boston: Houghton Mifflin.

Grant, C. A., & Cooper, J. M. (Ed.). (2003). *An educator's guide to diversity in the classroom.* Boston: Houghton Mifflin.

Greenlaw, M. J., Shepperson, G. M., & Nistler, R. J. (1992, March). A literature approach to teaching about the Middle Ages. *Language Arts, 69,* 200–204.

Greever, E. A. (2000, March). William's doll revisited. *Language Arts, 77,* 324–330.

Guild, P. (1994, May). The culture/learning style connection. *Educational Leadership, 51,* 16–21.

Hadaway, N. L., & Mundy, J. (1999, March). Children's informational picture books visit a secondary ESL classroom. *Journal of Adolescent & Adult Literacy, 42,* 464–475.

Hancock, V., & Betts, F. (1994, April). From the lagging to the leading edge. *Educational Leadership, 51,* 24–29.

Harp, B. (Ed.). (1994). *Assessment and evaluation for student centered learning* (2nd ed.). Norwood, MA: Christopher-Gordon.

Harvey, S. (1998). *Nonfiction matters: Reading, writing, and research in grades 3–8.* York, ME: Stenhouse.

Head, S. (2000). Portfolios go electronic. In *2000 job search handbook for educators.* Columbus, OH: American Association for Employment in Education.

Heide, A., & Henderson, D. (1994). *The technological classroom.* Toronto, Ontario, Canada: Trifolium.

Heinich, R., Molenda, M., Russell, J. D., & Smaldino, S. E. (1999). *Instructional media and technologies for learning.* Upper Saddle River, NJ: Merrill/Prentice Hall.

Hennessey, G. S. (2003, September). CyberHunt and activities: Extreme planet earth. *Instructor, 113,* 62–65.

Henson, K. (2004). *Constructivist teaching strategies for diverse middle-level classrooms.* Boston, MA: Pearson.

Hibbing, A. N., & Rankin-Erickson, J. L. (2003, May). A picture is worth a thousand words: Using visual images to improve comprehension for middle school struggling readers. *The Reading Teacher, 56,* 758–770.

Hicks, B., Montequin, L., & Hicks, J. (2000, January). Learning about our community: From the underground railroad to school lunch. *Primary Voices K–6, 8,* 26–33.

Hobbs, G. J. (1992, March/April). The legality of reducing student grades as a disciplinary measure. *The Clearing House, 65,* 204–205.

Holland, H. (1996, May/June). Way past word processing. *Electronic Learning, 15,* 22–26.

Horne, A., Draper, K., & Sayger, T. (1994). Teaching children with behavior problems takes understanding, tools, and courage. *Comtemporary Education, 65*(3), 122–127.

Horney, J. (2003, August). CyberHunt activities: Classroom inventions. *Instructor, 113,* 58–59.

Howes, E. V., Hamilton, G., & Zaskoda, D. (2003, March). Linking science and literature through technology: Thinking about interdisciplinary inquiry in middle school. *Journal of Adolescent & Adult Literacy, 46,* 484–504.

Hurst, B., & Reding, G. (2000). *Professionalism in teaching.* Upper Saddle River, NJ: Merrill/Prentice Hall.

Inclusion. (1995, December). Themed issue. *Phi Delta Kappan, 77.*

The Inclusive School. (1994, December/1995, January). Themed issue. *Educational Leadership, 52.*

The instructional power of an electronic encyclopedia. (1996, April). *Curriculum Administrator, 30,* 28–29.

Interstate New Teacher Assessment & Support Consortium. (1992). *A Program of Council of Chief State School Officers.* Washington DC.

Interview to win. (1996). *Planning job choices: 1996,* 54–60.

Jackson, J. F. (1999, December). What are the real risk factors for African American children? *Phi Delta Kappan, 81,* 308–312.

Jensen, R. A., & Kiley, T. J. (2000). *Teaching, leading, and learning.* Boston: Houghton Mifflin.

Johnson, D., Johnson, R., Stevahn, L., & Hodne, P. (1997, October). The three C's of safe schools. *Educational Leadership, 55,* 8–13.

Karten, T. (2005). *Inclusion strategies that work! Research-based methods for the classroom.* Thousand Oaks, CA: Corwin Press.

Kellough, R. D. (2001). *Surviving your first year of teaching: Guidelines for success.* Upper Saddle River, NJ: Merrill/Prentice Hall.

Kerr, A., Makuluni, A., & Nieves, M. (2000, January). The research process: Parents, kids, and teachers as ethnographers. *Primary Voices K–6, 8,* 14–23.

Kilbane, C., & Milman, N. (2005). *The digital teaching portfolio workbook: Understanding the digital teaching portfolio process.* Boston, MA: Pearson Education, Inc.

Kirby, E., & Kirby, S. (1994). Classroom discipline with attention deficit hyperactivity disorder children. *Contemporary Education, 65*(3), 142–144.

Knowles, J. G., & Cole, A., with Presswood, C. (1994). *Through preservice teachers' eyes.* Upper Saddle River, NJ: Merrill/Prentice Hall.

Kohn, A. (1993). Choices for children: Why and how to let students decide. *Phi Delta Kappan, 75*(1), 8–20.

Kohn, A. (1994, December). *The risks of rewards.* Urbana, IL: ERIC DIGEST (EDO-PS-94-14).

Kohn, A. (1996a). *Beyond discipline: From compliance to community.* Alexandria, VA: Association for Supervision and Curriculum Development.

Kohn, A. (1996b, September). What to look for in a classroom. *Educational Leadership, 54*(1), 54–55.

Koskinen, P. S., Blum, I. H., Bisson, S. A., Phillips, S. M., Creamer, T. S., & Kelley, T. B. (1999, February). Shared reading, books, and audiotapes: Supporting diverse students in school and at home. *The Reading Teacher, 52,* 430–444.

Labbo, L. D. (2004, April). Author's computer chair. *The Reading Teacher, 57,* 688–691.

Landrum, J. (2001, November). Selecting intermediate novels that feature characters with disabilities. *The Reading Teacher, 55.*

Lapp, D., Flood, J., & Fisher, D. (1999, April). Intermediality: How the use of multiple media enhances learning. *The Reading Teacher, 52,* 776–780.

Leu, D. J., Jr. (2002, February). Internet workshop: Making time for literacy. *The Reading Teacher, 55,* 466–472.

Leu, D. J., Jr., & Leu, D. D. (2000). *Teaching with the Internet: Lessons from the classroom.* Norwood, MA: Christopher-Gordon.

Levy, J. (1996). *Graduate school in your plans? Planning job choices: 1996, 39,* 85–88.

Lindblad, A. (1994, May-June). You can avoid the traps of cooperative learning. *Clearing House, 67,* 291–293.

Lindroth, L. (2003, April). Technology in your classroom: Hot websites. *Teaching K–8, 33,* 16.

Lipson, M. Y., Valencia, S. W., Wixon, K. K., & Peters, C. W. (1993, April). Integration and thematic teaching: Integration to improve teaching and learning. *Language Arts, 70,* 252–263.

Love, K. (2002, February). Mapping online discussion in senior English. *Journal of Adolescent & Adult Literacy, 45,* 382–396.

Lyons, N. (1999, May). How portfolios can shape emerging practice. *Educational Leadership, 56,* 63–65.

Maddux, C. D., Johnson, D. L., & Willis, J. W. (2001). *Educational Computing: Learning with Tomorrow's Technologies.* Boston: Allyn & Bacon.

Manning, M. L., & Lucking, R. (1993, September/October). Cooperative learning and multicultural classrooms. *Clearing House, 67,* 12–15.

March, T. (2000). Working the Web for education: The 3 R's of WebQuests: Let's keep them real, rich, and relevant. Retrieved from *www.infotoday.com/ MMSchools/ nov00/march.htm.*

Maring, G. H. (2002). Video conferencing. Presentation at International Reading Association Convention, San Francisco, California.

Marshall, M. (1998). *Fostering social responsibility.* Bloomington, IN: Phi Delta Kappa.

Martin, L. M. (2003, May). Web reading: Linking text and technology. *The Reading Teacher, 56,* 735–737.

Martinez-Roldan, C. M., & Lopez-Robertson, J. M. (1999, December/2000, January). Initiating literature circles in a first-grade bilingual classroom. *The Reading Teacher, 53,* 270–281.

Mather, M. A. (1996). Exploring the Internet safely: What schools can do. *Technology and Learning, 17*(1), 38–40, 42.

May, A. (1996). The professional performance portfolio. In *The job search handbook for teachers* (30th ed.). Evanston, IL: ASCUS.

May, S. W. (2003, March). Integrating technology into a reading program. *T.H.E. Journal, 30,* 34–38.

McCarthy, R. (1994, May/June). Assessing the whole student. *Instructor Special Supplement,* 18.

McCaslin, N. (1990). *Creative drama in the classroom* (5th ed.). White Plains, NY: Longman.

McDaniel, T. (1994). A back-to-basics approach to classroom discipline. *The Clearing House, 67*(5), 254–256.

McGillian, J. K. (1996, May/June). Cyber patrol: How can we make sure our young techies stay safe? *Creative Classroom, 10,* 69.

McGrath, B. (1998, April). Partners in learning: Twelve ways technology changes the teacher-student relationship. *T.H.E. Journal, 25,* 58–61.

McMurtry, K. (2001, November). E-cheating: Combating a 21st century challenge. *T.H.E. Journal, 29,* 36–41.

Medley, A. (1991). Sweaty palms: The neglected art of being interviewed (Rev. ed.). New York: Ten Speed.

Melton, L., & Pickett, W. (1997). *Using multiple intelligences in middle school reading.* Bloomington, IN: Phi Delta Kappa.

Melton, L., Pickett, W., & Sherer, G. (1999). *Improving K–8 reading using multiple intelligences.* Bloomington, IN: Phi Delta Kappa.

Menkart, D. (1999, April). Deepening the meaning of heritage months. *Educational Leadership, 56,* 19–21.

Meyerson, M., & Kulesza, D. (2002). *Strategies for struggling readers: Step by step.* Upper Saddle River, NJ: Merrill/Prentice Hall.

Miller, H. (1998, April). Teaching and learning about cultural diversity: Victims, heroes, and just plain folks. *The Reading Teacher, 51,* 602–604.

Miller, R. C., & Endo, H. (2004, June). Understanding and meeting the needs of ESL students. *Phi Delta Kappan, 85.*

Miller, W. C. (1979). *Dealing with stress: A challenge for educators.* Bloomington, IN: Phi Delta Kappa Educational Foundation.

Morrell, E. (2002, September). Toward a critical pedagogy of popular culture: Literacy development among urban youth. *Journal of Adolescent & Adult Literacy, 46,* 72–77.

Moss, J. F. (1990). *Focus units in literature: A handbook for elementary school teachers.* Katonah, NY: Richard Owen.

Mossberg, W. (1998, November 12). Personal technology: Search engines can cut time you waste on the Web. Personal technology from the *Wall Street Journal.* Online at *http://ptech.wsj.com/archive/ ptech–19981112.html.*

Moulton, M. R. (1999, April). The multigenre papers: Increasing interest, motivation, and functionality in research. *Journal of Adolescent & Adult Literacy, 42,* 528–539.

Nassman, B. (2000). *Teacher-tested classroom management strategies.* Upper Saddle River, NJ: Merrill/Prentice Hall.

National Council for the Social Studies. (1994). *Expectations of excellence: Curriculum standards for social studies.* Washington, DC: Author.

National Council of Teachers of English/International Reading Association. (1996). *Standards for the English language arts.* Urbana, IL: Author.

National Council of Teachers of Mathematics. (1998). *Principles and standards for school mathematics: Discussion draft.* Reston, VA: Author.

National Research Council. (1998). *National science education standards.* Washington, DC: National Academy Press.

Newkirk, T. (2000, March). Misreading masculinity: Speculations on the great gender gap in writing. *Language Arts, 77,* 294–300.

Nicholson-Nelson, K. (1998). *Developing students' multiple intelligences.* New York: Scholastic.

Notebook. (1999, May). *Cable in the classroom, 9,* 3.

Novelli, J. (1994, February). Putting (real) life into learning with technology. *Instructor Middle Years,* 30–36.

Novelli, J. (1996, May/June). Switched-on books. *Instructor, 105,* 55, 80.

Ogle, D. M. (1986, February). K-W-L: A teaching model that develops active reading of expository text. *The Reading Teacher, 39,* 564–570.

Ogle, D. M. (1989). The know, want to know, learn strategy. In D. Muth (Ed.), *Children's comprehension of text: Research into practice.* Newark, DE: International Reading Association.

O'Neil, J. (1994, August). Making assessment meaningful. *ASCD Update, 36,* 1, 4–5.

Orlich, D. C., Harder, R. J., Callahan, R. C., Treviasan, M. S., & Brown, A. H. (2004). *Teaching strategies: A guide to effective instruction.* Boston: Houghton Mifflin.

Panaritis, P. (1995, April). Beyond brainstorming: Planning a successful interdisciplinary program. *Phi Delta Kappan, 76,* 623–628.

Parks, S. (1999, April). Reducing the effects of racism in schools. *Educational Leadership, 56,* 14–18.

Peters, T., Schubeck, K., & Hopkins, K. (1995, April). A thematic approach: Theory and practice at the Aleknagik School. *Phi Delta Kappan, 76,* 633–636.

Patterson, N. (2003, September). Sharing the power: Links to comprehension strategies online. *Voices from the Middle, 11,* 66–67.

Peterson, K. M. (2004, January/February). CyberHunt activities: Ben Franklin. *Instructor, 113,* 62–64.

Phillips, M. (1996, May/June). Beyond the "best CDs" list. *Electronic Learning, 15,* 16.

Pike, K., Compain, R., & Mumper, J. (1994). *Connections: An integrated approach to literacy.* New York: HarperCollins.

Product watch: Math and science tools. (2004, April). *T.H.E. Journal, 31,* 34–38.

Raphael, T., & Au, K. (Eds.). (1998). *Literature-based instruction: Reshaping the curriculum.* Norwood, MA: Christopher-Gordon.

Rekrut, M. D. (1999, April). Using the Internet in classroom instruction: A primer for teachers. *Journal of Adolescent & Adult Literacy, 42,* 546–557.

Research/Center for children and technology: Teaching visual literacy. (1994, November/December). *Electronic Learning, 14,* 16–17.

Responding to hate at school. (1999, Fall). *Teaching Tolerance, 16,* 54–56.

Riel, M., & Fulton, K. (2001, March). The role of technology in supporting learning communities. *Phi Delta Kappan, 82,* 518–523.

Robinson, F. P. (1961). *Effective study.* New York: Harper and Row.

Rock, H. M., & Cummings, A. (1994, April). Can videodiscs improve student outcomes? *Educational Leadership, 51,* 46–50.

Roe, B. D. (2000). Using technology for content area literacy. In S. B. Wepner, W. J. Valmont, & R. Thurlow (Eds.), *Linking literacy and technology: A guide for K–8 classrooms.* Newark, DE: International Reading Association.

Roe, B. D., & Smith, S. H. (1997). University/Public Schools Keypals Project: A collaborative effort for electronic literature conversations. In *Rethinking teaching and learning through technology.* Murfreesboro, TN: Proceedings of the Mid-South Instructional Technology Conference.

Roe, B. D., & Smith, S. H. (2005). *Teaching reading in today's middle schools.* Boston: Houghton Mifflin.

Roe, B. D., Smith, S. H., & Burns, P. C. (2005). *Teaching reading in today's elementary schools.* Boston, Ma: Houghton Mifflin.

Roe, B. D, Stoodt-Hill, B. D., & Burns, P. C. (2004). *Secondary school literacy instruction: The content areas.* Boston: Houghton Mifflin.

Rogers, B. (1998). *"You know the fair rule" and much more.* Melbourne, Australia: ACER.

Romano, T. (1995). *Writing with passion: Life stories, multiple genres.* Portsmouth, NH: Boynton/Cook.

Ross, E. P. (1994). *Using children's literature across the curriculum.* Bloomington, IN: Phi Delta Kappa Educational Foundation.

Ross, E. P. (1998). *Pathways to thinking.* Norwood, MA: Christopher-Gordon.

Rothstein-Fisch, C., Greenfield, P., & Trumbull, E. (1999, April). Bridging cultures with classroom strategies. *Educational Leadership, 56,* 64–67.

Routman, R. (1991). *Invitations.* Portsmouth, NH: Heinemann.

Roy, P., & Hoch, J. (1994, March). Cooperative learning: A principal's perspective. *Principal, 73,* 27–29.

Rubinstein, G. (1999). *Reluctant disciplinarian.* Fort Collins, CO: Cottonwood Press.

Sayeski, K., & Cooper, J. M. (Ed.). (2003). *An educator's guide to inclusion.* Boston: Houghton Mifflin.

Scarlett, W. G. & Associates. (1998). *Trouble in the classroom.* San Francisco, CA: Jossey Bass.

Schaerer, J. (1996). Wave of the future: Televideo interviewing. In *The job search handbook for educators* (30th ed.). Evanston, IL: ASCUS.

Scharrer, E. (2002, December/2003, January). Making a case for media literacy in the curriculum: Outcomes and assessment. *Journal of Adolescent & Adult Literacy, 46,* 354–358.

Scherer, M. (1994, April). Review: Electronic fieldtrips. *Educational Leadership, 51,* 38.

Schifter, D. (1996, March). A constructivist perspective on teaching and learning mathematics. *Phi Delta Kappan, 77,* 492–499.

Schon, I. (1999, October). Enticing Spanish-speaking adolescents: Recent books in Spanish for every taste. *Journal of Adolescent & Adult Literacy, 43,* 126–132.

Schrock, K. (2003, August). Web sitings: Lesson plan sites. *Instructor, 113,* 66.

Schrock, K. (2003, September). Web sitings: Link up to literature. *Instructor, 113,* 73.

Schrock, K. (2004, January/February). Websitings: Get clicked into the arts. *Instructor, 113,* 76–77.

Sefton-Green, J. (2001, May). Computers, creativity, and the curriculum: The challenge for schools, literacy, and learning. *Journal of Adolescent & Adult Literacy, 44,* 726–728.

Selye, H. (1974). *Stress without distress.* Philadelphia: Lippincott.

Sharp, V. (1996). *Computer education for teachers.* Madison, WI: Brown and Benchmark.

Sherbet, S. (2000). Portfolios for the educator's job search. In *2000 job search handbook for educators* (pp. 22–23). Columbus, OH: American Association for Employment in Education.

Short, K., & Burke, C. (1991). *Creating curriculum.* Portsmouth, NH: Heinemann.

Singham, M. (1998, September). The canary in the mine: The achievement gap between black and white students. *Phi Delta Kappan, 80,* 9–15.

Slavin, R. E. (1990). *Cooperative learning: Theory, research, and practice.* Upper Saddle River, NJ: Merrill/Prentice Hall.

Slavin, R. E. (1991, February). Synthesis of research on cooperative learning. *Educational Leadership, 48,* 72–82.

Smith, F. (1998). *The book of learning and forgetting.* New York: Teachers College Press.

Smith, M. M. (1996, May/June). The creative edge. *Electronic Learning, 15,* 47–54, 68.

Smolin, L. I., & Lawless, K. A. (2003, March). Becoming literate in the technological age: New responsibilities and tools for teachers. *The Reading Teacher, 56,* 570–577.

Solvie, P. A. (2004, February). The digital whiteboard: A tool in early literacy instruction. *The Reading Teacher, 57,* 484–487.

Sourcebook. (1999, May). *Cable in the Classroom, 9,* 17.

Spires, H. A., & Estes, T. H. (2002). Reading in Web-based learning environments. In C. C. Block & M. Pressley (Eds.), *Comprehension instruction: Research-based best practices* (pp. 115–125). New York: Guilford.

St. Clair, J., & Schwetz, L. R. (2003, April). *Between the Lions* as a classroom tool. *The Reading Teacher, 56,* 656–659.

Sturtevant, E., & Linek, W. (Eds.). (1994). *Pathways for literacy: Sixteenth Yearbook of the College Reading Association.* Pittsburg, Kansas: College Reading Association.

Sullivan, J. (1998, September). The electronic journal: Combining literacy and technology. *The Reading Teacher, 52,* 90–92.

Teclehaimanot, B., & Lamb, A. (2004, March/April). Reading, technology, and inquiry-based learning through literature-rich WebQuests. *Reading Online, 7*(4). Available: *www. readingonline.org/articles/ art_index.asp?HREF= teclehaimanot/index.html.*

Thomas, S. B. (Ed.). (1994). *The yearbook of educational law.* Topeka, KS: National Organization on Legal Problems of Education.

Thompson, G. (1994b). *Teaching through themes.* New York: Scholastic.

Thompson, G. (1994a). Discipline and the high school teacher. *The Clearing House, 67*(5), 261–265.

Thompson, G. (1998). *Discipline survival kit for the secondary teacher.* San Francisco, CA: John Wiley & Sons, Inc.

Tompkins, G. E. (1998). *50 literacy strategies step by step.* Upper Saddle River, NJ: Merrill/Prentice Hall.

Turnbull, R., & Cilley, M. (1999). *Explanations and implications of the 1997 amendments to IDEA.* Upper Saddle River, NJ: Merrill/Prentice Hall.

Valencia, S., Hiebert, E., & Afflerbach, P. (Eds.). (1994). *Authentic reading assessment: Practices and possibilities.* Newark, DE: International Reading Association.

Wade, S. E., & Moje, E. B. (2000). The role of text in classroom learning. In M. L. Kamil, P. B. Mosenthal, P. D. Pearson, & R. Barr (Eds.), *Handbook of reading research, volume III.* Mahwah, NJ: Lawrence Erlbaum.

Walker-Dalhouse, D. (1992, February). Using African-American literature to increase ethnic understanding. *The Reading Teacher, 45,* 416–422.

Wang, M., Haertel, G., & Walberg, H. (1998). *Building educational resilience.* Bloomington, IN: Phi Delta Kappa.

Wasicsko, M. M., & Ross, S. (1994). How to create discipline problems. *The Clearing House, 67*(5), 248–251.

Wentz, P., & Yarling, J. (1994). *Student teaching casebook for supervising teachers and teaching interns.* Upper Saddle River, NJ: Merrill/Prentice Hall.

Wiedmer, T. L. (1998, April). Digital portfolios. *Phi Delta Kappan, 79,* 586–589.

Wildstrom, S. H. (1999, February 8). Search engines with smarts. *Business Week,* 22.

Williams, B. T. (2003, April). What they see is what we get: Television and middle school writers. *Journal of Adolescent & Adult Literacy, 46,* 546–554.

Willis, W. (1998). Software: Focus on videotapes. *T.H.E. Journal, 25*(6), 24–25.

Wolfgang, C. (1995). *Solving discipline problems* (3rd ed.). Boston: Allyn & Bacon.

Wong, H., & Wong, R. (1998). *The first days of school.* Mountain View, CA: Harry K. Wong Publications, Inc.

Wooten, D. A. (2004a, Spring). A time of discovery. *Curriculum Connections, 1,* 30–49.

Wooten, D. A. (2004b, Spring). Go west, young readers. *Curriculum Connections, 1,* 14–29.

Wormeli, R. (2001). *Meet me in the middle.* Portland MA: Stenhouse, Pub.

Woterson, M. (2001). *Partners against hate: Program activity guide: Helping children resist bias and hate.* Washington, DC: Antidefamation League.

Write the résumé employers want to see. (1996). *Planning job choices: 1996, 39,* 33–38.

Zahorik, J. A. (1995). *Constructivist teaching.* Bloomington, IN: Phi Delta Kappa Educational Foundation.

Index